T0322023

The Performer

The Performer

Art, Life, Politics

RICHARD SENNETT

ALLEN LANE
an imprint of
PENGUIN BOOKS

ALLEN LANE

UK | USA | Canada | Ireland | Australia
India | New Zealand | South Africa

Allen Lane is part of the Penguin Random House group of companies
whose addresses can be found at global.penguinrandomhouse.com

First published 2024
001

Set in 12/14.75pt Dante MT Std
Typeset by Jouve (UK), Milton Keynes
Printed and bound in Great Britain by Clays Ltd, Elcograf S.p.A.

The authorized representative in the EEA is Penguin Random House Ireland,
Morrison Chambers, 32 Nassau Street, Dublin D02 YH68

A CIP catalogue record for this book is available from the British Library

ISBN: 978–0–241–63764–7

www.greenpenguin.co.uk

For QQ

Contents

Contents

Preface: On Stage

The author sets out his wares

One Art

'All the world's a stage,' Shakespeare has the 'melancholy Jaques' declare in *As You Like It*. It's not an original thought. The idea of life as theatre can be traced back to antiquity, to the Roman poet Juvenal declaring 'all Greece is a stage and all Greeks are actors,' and forward to the American sociologist Erving Goffman, who believed that 'social life is a mosaic of performances.' But the thought conceals more than it reveals.

When I started to write this essay on society and the performing arts, a cluster of demagogues had come to dominate the public realm. Donald Trump in America and Boris Johnson in Britain are skilled performers. Malign performances of their sort draw on the same materials of expression, though, as other kinds of expression. Blocking, lighting and costuming are non-verbal devices used in all kinds of performances, as are the pacing of words and sounds, the expressive movement of arms and feet.

Physically, performance constitutes an art – an impure art. We certainly shouldn't try to straighten its crooked timber by tethering performances to the right social values. That was Rousseau's idea in his tract on the theatre in the mid eighteenth-century *Letter to D'Alembert*, and it's what authoritarian regimes have always done. Purity in the name of virtue is inherently repressive. We should want to understand art in all its impure fullness. But equally we should want to make art that is ethical without succumbing to repression. An ancient god suggests how this might happen.

Janus Presides

When someone is called 'Janus-faced' it usually means that they are dishonest; the face presented to the world is not who the person really is. The Romans thought differently about Janus. He was a god of transitions, of passages, of possibilities. The first day of January is named after him because it marks crossing a threshold of time. In ancient times Janus-faced plaques were set over the lintels of doorways and gates to mark movement from the street to the inner spaces of houses.

Every Roman rite opened with a prayer to Janus, people hoping that the future would turn out well. But he was not a reassuring god. As a god of transitions and transformations, he inaugurated the journey in time and space but left the destination open. Thus, early Christian theologians thought that Janus, unlike Jesus, was a cruel god, because he refused to answer people's prayers, to tell them how things would work out. All Janus would do is call attention to the new page in the calendar, to the lintel over the door. But this indeterminacy has its good side.

Performing art made in the good spirit of Janus focuses on process rather than a finished and fixed product. Over time performances mutate because there is no one fixed interpretation; the good artist is always looking for ways to refresh a work, to move it forward, to do it differently. Equally, an open performance asks spectators to participate in the journey of expression rather than passively watch performers travel. They should participate as critics, as judges. If Janussian art is open, it is not formless. As experience accumulates, the artist learns the particular points when expression can be changed and how.

I do not imagine that practising art openly, under the sign of Janus, will dissolve the power of manipulative, malign performances; malign expression is too emotionally compelling. But art-making can push back, by offering a model for freedom: one in which the claims of truth, of correctness, no longer rule, and expression becomes instead an exploration.

An Infamous Phrase

I've never believed the famous declaration that 'the past is a foreign country'. What would it have been like to be an African warrior captured, enslaved and shipped to America in the seventeenth century? Of course, we can't understand all the particulars of his experience, but to deny that we can relate to him as a fellow human being is absurd; in turn, we are not so special that he wouldn't be able to make sense of us. In the same vein, it's sheer arrogance to believe that Plato, Machiavelli or Kant have nothing relevant to tell us because they lived, poor things, before modernity.

In all my writing, I've tried to look for the bonds between people that stretch across time as well as space. The differences which do exist may reveal possibilities of living or of expression that have decayed or been throttled by power. The past critiques the present.

This Book

From which comes the story told in these pages. Book One considers the unsettling, ambiguous, dangerous powers of performed expression. Book Two examines where performances take place, and more specifically the gradual separation of stages from streets. Book Three focuses on how, at a crucial moment in history, the performer stepped forward as a distinctive person. Book Four looks at the spectator, who today plays a benighted role. Book Five explores how the gloom might be lessened, somewhat, by more dignified ways of performing. Book Six imagines how performing might lift up both politics and everyday life.

Me

I come at performing from a particular personal vantage point, as a performer. In my youth I trained to become a professional musician, playing mostly classical chamber music; then I worked as a sound artist for experimental dance groups. A hand injury and surgery that went wrong put an end to the cello, and I lost heart at making sound art. So I made a big switch, finding a niche as a writer on society, particularly on labour in cities and on the design of public spaces. In making a new life for myself, though, I didn't put the old one entirely out of mind.

Twice I tried to explore the relations of art and society, sociologically – first in *The Fall of Public Man*, in 1977, and then in *The Conscience of the Eye*, written fourteen years later. Whatever their academic virtues, these books were not written from the vantage point of the artist. As a player, the one thing I have always known is that the great danger is to reduce performing art to a simple manifestation, a representation, of society. The ethical problems of performing lie deeper, inside the art.

'Performing' covers a huge swathe of different sorts of performances. I wish my experiences in making art were broader; outside Western classical music, I am a musical innocent. But I've tried to put this shortcoming to good use by exploring how high art might speak to everyday life. For biographical reasons which will also become clear, I've little experience of acting – another limitation I've tried to counter by focusing on the bodily aspects of theatre which are shared with us, musicians and dancers who don't speak on stage.

If I live long enough, I'll write three essays on the presence of art inside society: this one on performing, another on narrating and a third on picturing. In my view, these three run the gamut of expression in human beings; they constitute our expressive DNA. They are of course distinctive: reading a story is not like watching it dramatized on stage, nor seeing it as a film. Still, the ethical connection is stronger than the medium: all three can harm as well as inspire.

I should explain the phrase in the paragraph above, 'if I live long enough'. I am nearly eighty; the Grim Reaper could visit me any time, so I'm writing the three essays as self-standing texts and hoping for the best.

Remembering and Thinking

The advice given to young authors is usually to write about what you know. This is bad advice. When young, you should stretch your imagination. But for the elderly writer the advice is good; now it's urgent to make sense of how you have lived. Remembering, however, can be a danger. In a café, sitting silently with a forbidden cigarette in hand – pleasure at eighty is rightly more important to you than health – you easily become lost in your musings. These memories may well be boring or irrelevant to others. You need to ask if, how and why anything which happened to you might matter to people whose lives differ from your own. You need to discipline remembering.

Presence of the City

There is a particular affinity between art and the city. 'The arts result from overcrowding,' the critic William Empson once declared, meaning that dense places stimulate people, who, comparing and competing, see new ways of making things. These creative stimulations don't come if the 'creatives' are isolated, or confined to a village or to a campus of like-minded people.

Ville and *cité* are French terms for two aspects of urban life. The *ville* is the physical place on the map, its buildings and spaces; the *cité* consists of the behaviours and beliefs of the people who inhabit the physical environment. The two don't fit neatly together. For instance, different cultures inhabit the same housing types differently. By contrast, a good design can challenge the taken-for-granted ways people live. Cities don't work like well-oiled machines in large part because there's friction between *ville* and *cité*.

As applied to performing art, the stage is a physical building, the street a physical alignment of spaces around it. The material *ville* of performing consists also of costumes, masks and make-up, painted scenery, the lighting of theatres, the technology of recording studios. The *cité* of art, by contrast consists of the meanings of a text, the efforts of the performer to interpret it, and the needs, desires and values which an audience brings to the performance. Again there is tension between art's *ville* and its *cité*, between its materiality and its meanings. This tension shapes the experience of a performance, creating its edginess and complexity.

Without Whom

I should straight away confess that I haven't tried to slot this book into the burgeoning academic field of 'performance studies'; I've wanted to think things out for myself. Undoubtedly as a result I've done the academic equivalent of reinventing the wheel. Still, I hope to engage my reader, who also is probably no academic specialist.

I owe a particular debt to the late Patrick O'Connor, whose passion for music halls, faded South American divas and the *chanteuse* Josephine Baker opened up pleasures unaccounted by the Juilliard School of Music. To the musicians Richard and Marcia Goode I owe decades of discussing, with equal passion, cooking and the Meaning of Art. I am grateful to Ian Bostridge, who has set me an example of how to write informally and evocatively about music. Most of all, I want to thank the pianist and poet Alfred Brendel, my friend of fifty years.

Two people opened me up to performances outside my comfort zone. In the 1970s Robert Gottlieb dragged me to the New York City Ballet, at the time the greatest dance troupe in the world, which he knew and I didn't. John Guare similarly took me to plays I was at the time too snobbish and narrow-minded to attend on my own.

This volume joins books on performing by musician-friends who write: George Lewis, Georgina Born and Alex Ross. I am also indebted to the insights of people I don't know, particularly the sociologist Jeffrey Alexander, the musicologist Richard Taruskin and the philosopher Judith Butler.

I've learned from chats with several younger friends: John Bingham-Hall and Gascia Ouzounian, my partners in the Theatrum Mundi project; the dancer Adesola Akinleye, who has given me the courage to perform again, if badly; Daniel Jütte, who is so learned and so careful a reader. In this parade of youth, and most personally important to me, is Andrew Barratt, who has read this essay, suspiciously, word by word, and who has focused me on what's happening rather than what happened.

Finally, I want to thank my demanding though kindly editor Stuart Proffitt and my agent-cum-psychiatric nurse Cullen Stanley. Emily Villareal and Niki Puskas were devoted researchers. The copy-editor Bela Cunha has improved what came to her as a messy and ill-organized text.

This book was supported by a grant from the Leverhulme Foundation.

Introduction: Art and Life in the Summer of 1963

*I am too young to understand three tensions
between art and life*

I. Art in the Service of Power

My father's cousin Sylvia and I are at the Thalia movie theatre in New York in early summer 1963. She is doubly an exile: as an adolescent, first from Odessa to Munich during Stalin's purges in 1936, then from Munich to New York during Hitler's purges in 1938. Now in middle age Sylvia has made a career for herself as a puppeteer in New York, occasionally serving as a substitute Ollie (a dragon) on the TV show *Kukla, Fran and Ollie*; more usually she performs at Punch and Judy shows in schools where her still thick foreign accent evidently passes muster with the kids.

The Thalia was an art-house theatre specializing in foreign films of little commercial value. In the 1960s small venues like this cropped up all over the city in neighbourhoods where artists, foreigners and university students congregated; 95th and Broadway put the Thalia squarely in that polyglot community on Manhattan's Upper West Side. The Thalia was in the basement of a building which housed a more popular theatre above; it was an odd space, shaped like a ship tipped up by a wave, the seats lower than the screen. Since it often threaded together films by a director, dedicated patrons spent hours there, so that the ship of art, poorly ventilated, smelled strongly of sweat.

At Sylvia's request we attended a retrospective of films by Leni Riefenstahl, which she watched intently but silently. Though voluble when she had a hand inside a puppet and let loose, having fun, off stage Sylvia was given to short, Delphic statements if she spoke at all – perhaps due to her garbled English, or because of her memories.

Riefenstahl's film *Triumph of the Will*, which celebrates Hitler's visit to Nuremberg in 1934, connects art and life wordlessly. Its soundtrack is organized brilliantly. In the film's opening, we hear aeroplane noise while seeing sky; the Führer is hidden in the clouds, but the noise tells us he is there, about to descend from the clouds to the city. The mixed rustle of street sounds signals the usual urban jumble of activities and peoples below; the Nazi Horst Wessel Song is heard but muffled by the whirr of the plane's propellers. Then silence. Soon his motorcade appears; he is coming. Now there is organized shouting, 'Heil Hitler!' Riefenstahl shoots the parade in slow time, as a gradual unfolding. When the Führer ascends to the podium stage, everything speeds up; his speech is a sudden explosion, revving up and arousing.

By such means, theatre of a non-verbal kind makes his charisma come alive. Indeed, the weakest moments in *Triumph of the Will* occur when Hitler actually speaks, spewing out clichés the public knew by then practically by heart. Riefenstahl compensates by focusing on his facial expressions, arm gestures, his movements around the podium. She makes the demagogue's hold over the people physical and visceral.

There's nothing crude about this wordless power. The film makes, for instance, cunning use of Wagner's *Die Meistersinger*. The composer created in Beckmesser an archetypically scheming Jewish figure. In Act II, Scene 6, Beckmesser's power is tested and then defeated, in some of the most knotted, tense music Wagner ever composed. What follows, the 'Awaken Chorus' at the opening of Act III, is by contrast peaceful, many of the unresolved harmonic gestures suddenly smoothed out. *Triumph of the Will* appropriates the 'Awaken Chorus' to accompany shots of Nuremberg peacefully awakening the morning after Hitler's visit. A sublime moment in opera marks Hitler's power over a city – compelling even to me, a Jew.

We stay for the next film in the festival, *Olympiad*, which is about the Berlin Olympics in 1936, and which I have just viewed again, even more struck by her art. Here Riefenstahl shows champion swimmers 'diving into cleanliness', as Rupert Brooke wrote innocently of swimming some years before. Repeated again and again, cheering and silence mixed in each repetition (there are cuts of this film in which at each leap off the board the sound goes dead, as though we are holding our breath), the divers' nakedness becomes a symbol of the idealized blond Aryan body.

Naked bodies have done political work ever since ancient times, representing virtuous strength. Nakedness in the Nazi context symbolized a pure body, as in the heroic torsos of the Nazi sculptor Arno Breker. The logic of racial contempt follows from this image of the bodily Aryan ideal. The supposedly Jewish body is composed of sagging flesh and hairy skin. But Breker statues are trash, and indeed most political art is just cliché, the message delivered like a sledgehammer blow. Crudeness makes the message accessible. Whereas Riefenstahl's art is anything but crude; high art is put in service to the Nazi state.

Wordless, high art, of course, does not explain the politics. The filmmaker exploited damages and confusions in its audiences whose roots lay elsewhere: the loss of a prior war, the great inflation of the 1920s, endemic state corruption . . . But the theatre then transformed these events so that fascism cast a spell over the public in a way that was hard to challenge, because it transcended words. The traumas morphed into experiences which didn't admit discussion.

Sylvia never lost the fear that she should have a bag packed, just in case she had to leave at a moment's notice. Still, in the Thalia she was contemplating a fellow performer's power; leaning forward towards the screen, she was mesmerized by Riefenstahl. I should have discussed this malign enchantment with Sylvia, but didn't. When we are young, we instinctively avoid subjects we can't understand, and it's not a time of life which wants to know about indelible, irremediable loss

I was instead absorbed in a personal problem which I thought, quite mistakenly, to be different.

II. The Dignity of Art

I went to New York in 1963 in order to firm up my music-making. I'd enrolled in the University of Chicago two years before on a scholarship; I'd thought to use the university as a kind of hotel with lectures served after breakfast, but academic work was far more demanding than my seventeen-year-old self had imagined – particularly at the University of Chicago, then a bastion of intellectual rigour. Also I was beginning to get concerts with a quartet of slightly older musicians, and found it difficult to fit these trips into my class schedule. Frank Miller, my mentor at the Chicago Symphony, suggested I go to New York and there devote myself full time to music at the Juilliard.

The conservatory then sat at the western edge of Harlem. Autobody shops, parking lots and warehouses lined the streets, which were usually void of people. Yet the Juilliard building, a massive fortress of brick and stonework, walled in musicians and dancers as though danger lurked just outside. Music conservatories at that time were indeed well named. They operated like hothouses whose gardener-maestros nurtured, pruned and weeded young musical plants. Very few people of colour, and not many women, then studied at Juilliard. And in no way was the conservatory 'counter-cultural'; I doubt very much if our teachers could identify the smell of pot, which in any event didn't waft through the halls. Just as the conservatory embodied cultural orthodoxy, so did we: self-disciplined kids practising four to six hours a day, mostly obedient to the gardeners.

This isolation lessened for a moment in the late spring of 1963 when a civil rights demo marching down Broadway lured people out of the building to watch and listen. The protesters had hired the services of a New Orleans blues band, but though many Juilliard students were sympathetic to the politics, it would have been physically impossible for cellists, harpists or tympani players to join the marching musicians. Few musicians inside the fortress knew the tunes, nor did correct phrasing of the opening bars of the Schubert Cello Quintet seem to offer insight into the struggle for racial justice.

Politics apart, Juilliard's hothouse atmosphere prompted the fear among a fair number of students that classical music, to switch metaphors, was a museum art in which the performer functions like a conservator, renewing and refreshing Schubert in performance – as the paintings in a museum are cleaned and restored. In part our fear of being irrelevant to our own time reflected the shift in the weight given in the 1960s to popular art at the expense of classical art; Bob Dylan was an infinitely more exciting musician than the academic, now justly forgotten composer Easley Blackwood. We worried about being aesthetes – but our teachers had quite another experience of being cut off.

The majority of musicians studying at Juilliard or at the Mannes School of Music lived in huge apartments on the Upper West Side vacated by families who had fled to the suburbs. These buildings were and are particularly attractive to musicians because their thick concrete floors and solid plaster walls make it possible to practise late at night without too much protest from neighbours. Many of our teachers also lived in such apartments. Their dwellings were likely to be furnished with an ashtray from a café in Munich from which the Nazis had expelled the teacher, or a treasured early edition of the poems of Novalis which the refugee had managed to pack into her luggage.

Sylvia's father, after fleeing Europe, wound up in Chicago, where every night he relived his torture sessions instead of sleeping. Whereas the exiled musicians, if distraught, were not destroyed; art kept them going. Art practised for its own sake is an unfashionable idea in classrooms today. It suggests, evidently, aesthetes and connoisseurs savouring rare drawings in panelled libraries. This snootiness comes, in the language of the cultural studies classroom itself, from a 'privileged position'. Belief in art for its own sake instead kept our persecuted teachers sane. This meant preserving not just music made by Jewish composers such as Mendelssohn and

Mahler, but the broad spectrum of humanistic expression in writing, painting and theatre suppressed by the Nazi regime. 'Conservatory' meant to the exiles 'conserve', and for them the word 'aesthete' named the faith in art which gave them strength.

As I was to learn that year, art practised for its own sake sustained artists in Harlem for whom 'exile' was a social rather than a political displacement.

In the ferment of the civil rights struggle, Juilliard made a gesture to the neighbourhood: it opened up one of its rehearsal studios for community use. Musicians in Harlem responded because the rehearsal room contained a good drum set, which is an expensive and surprisingly delicate piece of kit. A bit of coffee-pot fraterniz-ation ensued. It turned out that those who marched were ambivalent about playing New Orleans tunes to draw in the crowds. 'Sambo music', they said, thinking of easy-listening New Orleans jazz as something commercialized and colonized for white tourists. The artistic passion of the marching musicians was 'second-stage bebop', a complex, innovative music.

You can hear what this music sounds like in an album recorded by Ornette Coleman in 1960 called *Free Jazz: A Collective Improvis-ation*. There is a double quartet of instruments, sorted stereophonically so that they play against each other as well as together; the rhythms are complex combinations like 5/8 pulsing at different speeds in the two quartets. The melodic material is sparser than the first-stage bebop baroque of Charlie Parker, who worked a generation before Coleman; harmonic dissonances are now written out, even though this is billed as 'free jazz', to make sure that leading tones (the notes that might seem to be taking you to a resolving harmony) are left hanging. *Free Jazz* lasts a long time, but has no beginnings, middles, and closures; it's pure process.[1]

A few friends and I went to hear practitioners of free jazz in a club on 125th Street. The musicians were not in Coleman's class, but they were really good, and not on another planet from pieces engaging us such as Pierre Boulez's *Le Marteau sans maître*. What was surprising was their relation to the Harlem community.

Big jazz clubs along 125th Street, like the Apollo, catered to tourists, especially French tourists, who were thrilled to travel – in buses, not on foot – from downtown to *le ghetto* uptown; the music in these places was of *le hot jazz* sort, easy-listening big-band swing recorded and distributed for international consumption. The musicians we heard played in a dingy room sparsely filled with customers. They performed along one wall, the cleared space serving in place of a raised stage. To be sure, the music was difficult, but it didn't make much of an impression one way or another on the customers, who were locals rather than French tourists. Treating the place as a social club, they chatted, smoked and drank, the art functioning just as background.

At the time I didn't make any sort of connection between the post-bebop musicians and our Mitteleuropean teachers. I now see the jazz musicians experienced a cut-off between art and society both unlike and yet not unlike the classical players.

Unlike because, in contrast to the exiled teachers, the post-bebop players suffered from indifference rather than persecution. The jazz musicians were willing to play 'Sambo music' for the sake of the cause, but their own art didn't mean much to the community. The quartet had all been born in Harlem – their parents having migrated earlier from the Deep South – and knew its every nook and cranny, as only kids growing up in a place do. As artists, however, they were suffering from a kind of internal exile. The club's owners dismissed them for not playing 'accessible' music.

The lifeline to Juilliard vanished shortly thereafter, as our conservatory abandoned Harlem, becoming part of the art factory which is the Lincoln Center for the Performing Arts three miles downtown. Still, the musicians persisted, as I discovered when I ran into the bass player several years later at Patelson's, a sheet-music store behind Carnegie Hall that functioned as a public square for all New York musicians until it was torn down to make way for luxury condominiums. Like the singer Alberta Hunter, Carl now worked in a hospital. She spent decades as a nurse, he as a porter; like her, he continued to make music in the hours after work.

It's all too easy to romanticize the neglected genius. Neither the exiles nor the internal exiles would have been happy to think of themselves simply as victims; instead, Carl and Alberta Hunter led quiet lives, as did most of our teachers, who were not stars but persisted because they derived a sense of self-worth and meaning from practising art. The question which has lingered in my mind is what specifically sustained them, because performing artists need audiences and especially live audience contact. We cannot work in isolation, as a writer might be able to do.

This inner sustenance has become particularly puzzling because the cultural scene has ever less room for aesthetes like Carl. Over the last fifty years, 'little concerts' have gradually faded in New York. Audiences want to know who is playing rather than what's being played; if they don't recognize the name, they don't go. The economics of performing fuse with a cult of personality more general in society, embodied by Facebook and other forms of self-advertising online. In contrast, all I saw then was that Carl, like my Juilliard teachers, had somehow been sustained by performing – even if that art was not wanted.

III. Divided Paths

By the autumn of 1963 I was making forays downtown to the flourishing dance and experimental music scene located at the Judson Memorial Church in Washington Square in the middle of Greenwich Village. The Judson choreographers wanted to dance to urban sounds. In the autumn I was asked to fill in for three months for a pregnant member of the group in the recording of these sounds; we taped wailing sirens, honking traffic jams, rain, the humming of an electricity generating station. Uptown I had been a quite arrogant hot-shot; downtown I took orders from the choreographers, spending most of the three months splicing and gluing together the tapes.

Evoking this effort does not make demands on the cursed

fragility of my memory, since the downtown scene has now passed from the obscurity in which we then dwelt to an iconic, curated and archived status, celebrated in official venues such as the Museum of Modern Art in New York. But though the museum has packaged it as an emblem of the avant-garde, something has been lost: our frequent frustration in trying to bridge high art and everyday life.

Washington Square had the right urban bones for bohemian myth. Young people playing guitars lounged around its central circular fountain; the drunk and the drug-addicted slept on benches on the north, shady side of the ten-acre park; elderly people kept to the exposed benches on the west side where they gossiped from dawn to dusk. The scene constituted a standing invitation to tourists, one which was accepted – the French again, perhaps arriving in the very same buses that had driven them to *le hot jazz* on 125th Street.

On the south side stood Judson Church, an architectural copy of the small-town churches from which most of its Italian parishioners originally came, but this one was not Catholic. Indeed, in 1957, when Howard Moody, a leading voice in the civil rights movement, was made its pastor, the place became essentially nondenominational. Judson's engagement with the arts began five years later, when Al Carmines joined Moody; a fearsomely educated priest, Carmines was also a composer and a lyricist. From 1962 to 1964 the Judson Dance Theater rehearsed in Judson's robing and youth fellowship rooms, performed in the basement of the church, and occasionally spilled outside to co-opt the space around the fountain in Washington Square.

The choreographers targeted the elderly park-bench dwellers more than the guitar-strumming kids or the drug addicts in the square: white and old, the Italians and Poles were visibly working class, and therefore 'The People'. Moody, a popular figure with them, assured the community that our effort was 'of service' to the church. He was helped by the fact that we were visibly hard at work and didn't make a point of looking arty, in contrast to the kids in the park who dressed the part of Liberated Youth in tie-dye shirts and see-through blouses. Carmines urged the dancers to understand themselves as political actors: you are dancing in the same place where Howard Moody organizes protests against racial injustice. It's all one and the same project.

High art and everyday life were, however, disconnected in two ways, one physical, the other spiritual. The dancers did seek to make a physical link by incorporating untutored natural movements like walking or tripping into dancing. Yvonne Rainer, in teaching the elderly, used step sequences which could be mastered in a short time. Rainer loathed that sort of Broadway theatre in which the star mesmerizes an adoring, submissive audience. Provoked by Yvonne, Trisha Brown sought to make what she called 'democratic dance'. She worked out a technique in which the moving body follows the path of least resistance in jumping (no astounding difficult leaps), turning slowly rather than twirling rapidly, or falling for real rather than sinking down gracefully.

The impulse to mix high art and everyday movement was not unique to the Judson dancers, or to dance. In music, the mix of high with everyday stretches back to the very origins of the art. The political inflection of this connection is a modern one. For instance, Béla Bartók collected, recorded and incorporated into his own compositions folk music from Hungary and Romania. In 1904 he wrote to his wife: 'Another completely different factor makes contemporary [twentieth-century] music realistic: that, half consciously, half intentionally, it searches for impressions from that great reality of folk art, which encompasses everything.'[2] This 'realism' in sound served as a political rebuke: how ordinary people sound is, as he put it elsewhere, a 'healthy' sound, rebukes the decadent, self-writhing, bourgeois music he thought emanated from Vienna.

The Judson dancers showed the difficulty of making the politically inflected connection between high and popular work. Trisha Brown, while the proponent of 'democratic dance', believing that even the old people in the park could execute its movements, nonetheless made the connection impossible. Using the city as a stage, she placed dancers on top of separate tenement buildings, where they performed with one another by sending something like bodily smoke signals across the roofs: when I bend forward, you arch back-ward. These dance moves were nothing like the ways repairmen puttered or tenants exercised up there. The dances sometimes occurred at the roof-edge, which only a skilled dancer could man-age without suffering catastrophically from vertigo. So too, Brown's initial effort to craft moves anyone could make morphed into exper-iments which disoriented even the professionally trained body. For instance, she fitted dancers with harnesses so that they could go up walls to dance, their legs free of gravity but deprived of the security of placement on solid ground. Rather than expressing everyday movement, this experiment explored how far it could be subverted. Her problem of relating to the public lay in the very adventurous-ness of her art. It still lies there.

An event in 2020 made me think again about the knotted-up rel-ation of inclusive art and artistic innovation. I had the privilege of serving on a jury which awarded the Kenyan writer Ngũgĩ wa Thiong'o a prize for his lifetime of work.* In 1977 he started a theatre to break down the barriers between performer and public, to 'de-mystify the stage' through plays written in Kikuyu, making a more direct connection to the Kenyan public than works written in English. As the script of *Ngaahika Ndeenda* was translated to me, the translator explained that some words or phrases were radical depar-tures in Kikuyu, and must have been hard to follow. Ngũgĩ's art has since become increasingly experimental, and so ever more challen-ging to the public. Yet he was then and remains now a socially committed artist; he has not given up on including his public.

Thinking back on my time at Judson, what now seems admirable was the dancers' unwillingness to forgo risk for the sake of inclu-sion, to refuse sacrificing difficulty for the sake of 'accessibility' – that repressive, arts-bureaucrat, media-friendly version of art and every-day life. The Judson dancers, like Carl or Alberta Hunter, had the courage to practise art for art's sake. I'd say that in the end such

* The Premio Catalunya, awarded annually by the government of Catalonia, in Spain.

integrity honours an audience more than does 'accessibility', which is really a cognomen for condescension – 'they wouldn't get it.' Rather than something gone wrong, tension between art and the everyday makes the experience ultimately more challenging, deeper, for both the maker and the audience. We should thus want to keep the difficulty open, rather than close it down by favouring easily consumable, 'friendly' art.

In retrospect, Judson offered me a first glimpse of a kindred tension more spiritual than sociological. Art was made in the Judson basement. Upstairs in the chapel, baptisms welcomed new life, marriage vows were exchanged, the dead were commemorated. Walking up walls seemed unrelated to these rituals. Rituals are seldom events which people make up out of whole cloth. Whereas in art the originality of the artist matters, in ritual originality is not the point. So how are these two domains of performance related? Twenty years later, the question became urgent in a a great crisis for gay men of my generation.

BOOK ONE

Troubling Performances

Acting and Ritual Stand Side by Side, Uneasily

Performances in the face of death

I. On an AIDS Ward

In the early 1980s, St Vincent's Hospital in Greenwich Village contained one of the few large AIDS wards in the city. Many hospitals did not equip themselves to treat this disease, at least in large numbers; if they had to take in a patient, he was most often put in isolation. St Vincent's, by contrast, had an open ward for AIDS patients in which family, lovers, and friends could come and go freely without using a special door or donning surgical gloves as was required in some other places. This was all the more surprising because St Vincent's was a Catholic hospital, and the Catholic Church hierarchy in New York treated homosexuality as a venial, verging on a mortal, sin. Even so, the sisters on the AIDS ward chatted easily with their patients while washing them, cajoling the men to eat even though little food would stay down, gossiping with visitors who kept useless all-night vigils. I knew the place only too well, because many friends went to St Vincent's to die.

Charles was my overly organized assistant during the day who directed and acted in plays at night. At St Vincent's, where he lodged midway through his fatal journey, he was invited to direct a reading of Shakespeare's *As You Like It* with fellow patients on the ward, as he had previously staged an all-male version of this play in a theatre near the Judson Memorial Church on Washington Square.

The patients, mostly youngish, had chosen their play well, since the script can be realized by gender crossings which are pleasurable rather than in-your-face – pleasures which Virginia Woolf understood in writing *Orlando*, her riff on Shakespeare's play. *As You Like It* begins in a dark place, a kingdom in which a usurper menaces its rightful leader. Escaping persecution, the Duke, his family and entourage flee to the magical Forest of Arden, where, after various astounding happenings, the defeat of a lioness sets in train events which put everything to rights.

It is perfectly true that in Elizabethan times all plays were performed by males, with boy actors playing the parts of women; nothing transgressive then about that. In the 1980s, though, it was provocative to see on stage grown men, often moustachioed, in dresses, embracing one another. It was particularly odd to watch men playing women within the confines of a Catholic hospital. In the ward, the players were costumed in hospital gowns, their make-up consisting of a flesh-coloured cream which disguised the reddish-brown lesions of Kaposi's sarcoma on necks, faces and hands. The results on the whole were convincing, pleasing the actors, releasing them from dwelling on the cancerous sores on their bodies. In bed or sitting in chairs – few had the strength to stand for long or move about – the patient/actors read out their lines, often smiling to themselves as they went along.

His own lungs weakened by the disease, so speaking in a half-voice, Charles performed the role of the melancholy Jaques in hospital, as he had previously on stage. He suffered a fit of coughing in the midst of Jaques' famous speech beginning 'All the world's a stage / And all the men and women merely players'. When the coughing stopped, he then repeated the entire speech, as though responding to an enthusiastic audience. He spoke lightly, ironically, as if amused by the words.

How prissy I had been two decades before, when I worried about being left out of life, my generation of men threatened by a disease no one could do anything about. In retrospect, there seems something heroic about the actors refusing – if only for two hours – to be patients, submissive to their fate. Don't pity us, don't pray for our souls – at least, not yet! We have escaped to the Forest of Arden.

The grieving friends and family, however, did not enter into the spirit of things; we remained stony-faced. Nor was it clear what the priests come to administer spiritual balm made of this transvestite performance, especially of the ward sisters who seemed to enjoy it. The priests wanted to offer prayers of consolation, ritual words and gestures which might have connected us close to those soon to die. But the actors were having none of it – and pushed away the priests', and our, pity. The divide between making art and observing a sacred ritual which appeared a generation before in the Judson church had taken a mortal twist.

The not-so-sub subtext of the very conservative Catholic Diocese of New York in the 1980s was that dying gay men had to seek forgiveness in order that they and their relatives, friends and even lovers could be bound together as one. Forgiveness of sin was what Charles, and I think the others, baulked at. He didn't consider his homosexuality a sin nor his illness a divine punishment. Catholicism that is more generous, larger in spirit, can frame the same bedside rituals as relieving life's pains; the performers in drag *As You Like It* sought a final pleasure. They acted.

I should say that Charles was not at ease. Just as the friends and families watching *As You Like It* needed a frame for the end of life, so did Charles as he sank closer to death. His attitude towards the priests on their daily visits seemed to soften. He no longer smiled sardonically at them, he acknowledged them, but still waved them away when they began to pray for him. Rather than the defiant act of performing, at the end he showed courage – the courage to die alone, without consolation.

II. A Ritual of Consolation

Ritual is a Performance

Anthropologists and others have debated endlessly the meanings of ritual. The anthropologist Victor Turner once provided a definition which, though dry, is as good as any:

A ritual is a stereotyped sequence of activities involving gestures, words, and objects, performed in a sequestered place, and designed to influence preternatural entities or forces on behalf of the actors' goals and interests . . . Rituals tend to be organized in a cycle of performances (annual, biennial, quinquennial, and so on) . . . Rituals of consolation infuse emotion into this life-less 'stereotyped sequences of activities' . . .[1]

Human beings have staged rituals since the dawn of organized social life, predating by several thousand years the appearance of written language. At its origins, a ritual was a non-verbal performance. Now, as then, the physical rite consists of collective action, rather than individual expression. To work as collective expression, rituals need fairly strict rules that orient one celebrant to the others and can be passed from one generation to the next. These rules indicate where bodies should move in relation to each other, and what gestures the ritual celebrants should make; rules for when to speak, when to keep silent. Like any performance, ritual also sets standards for how to act well. The strictness of ritual is less forgiving than more mundane activities such as casting a pot: you can cook a good meal in a goodish if not perfectly shaped piece of pottery. Get movement, speech or setting wrong in any detail in prayer and the gods may not end a plague or send rain.

In principle there might seem to be no difficulty about connecting art and ritual as performances: think of any mass composed from Bach to Bernstein. Renaissance composers such as Josquin des Prez crossed back and forth between sacred and secular art by using the same melodies for both masses and profane *chansons*. In jazz, the crossing back and forth appears, for instance, in the late-career performances of Duke Ellington. He turned big-band music composed for him by Billie Strayhorn into religious celebrations. But as he told a music critic in 1965, his 'spiritual concerts' did not aim to follow old ways of experiencing faith; they were meant to make faith new and alive, rather than observe and pass on a tradition. The cliché which evokes 'the dead hand of tradition' seems on the contrary to describe ritual. In wanting to make faith fresh and original, the artist in Ellington is speaking.

Yet performing a prayer you've said a hundred times is not inherently stale; on the contrary, it becomes a living presence for you when you say it. Which is a puzzle. How can non-verbal rituals which are strict in form, and which can be passed on largely intact from generation to generation, still feel fresh, as though you are performing them for the first time?

Kaddish

I've come to think about ritual's living presence in the rituals of consolation in Judaism, my own faith. More specifically, I've since wondered what difference it would make if *As You Like It* had been performed in a Jewish hospital. At the time, this would have been unlikely, because Jewish-run hospitals did not open their doors to dying gay men en masse, as Catholic St Vincent's did. Even so, the focus would have shifted, since our rituals surrounding death are not judgemental, so perhaps Charles would not have pushed away a rabbi.

The timing of consolation is also different in Judaism: consolation occurs after death. The Mourners' Kaddish is a prayer which anchors funerals, recited at the graveside, then repeated within the home for eleven months after the death of a parent, thirty days for the death of a partner or a child. Despite death, the mourner affirms faith in God. In theological terms it is a 'doxology', shaped in the thirteenth century so that Kaddish could be said by everyday mourners as well as by learned rabbis. Grief and justice intermingle in saying Kaddish, because unnatural, involuntary death – genocide or sporadic pogroms – has haunted Jewish history. The Kaddish affirms that those who are killed, as well as those who die naturally, will not be forgotten by others.[2]

Over the thousands of years that Judaism has existed, the correct words and gestures of Kaddish have changed, and they vary somewhat in the different branches of Judaism. But whatever the rules are at a given moment, they have to be performed precisely and correctly in order to channel raw feelings of loss. Saying Kaddish right, like good acting, doesn't depend on the moral standing of the celebrant; the dead who are memorialized could be equally saints or sinners.

Five Rules of Consolation

Rituals like Kaddish depart from theatrical performances in at least five ways.

First of all, rituals are strict in time. When someone dies, you say Kaddish, specified exactly to the day. Kaddish cannot be compressed or expanded; it is not elastic in time. Whereas *As You Like It* can be put on any time. Rituals may draw on myths but myths are not fixed in time in the same way. The Greek word *muthos* means a story which may be recounted in different ways to different people at different times and places; the exterior circumstances are not fixed. Nor is myth's narrative fixed in time. The length that a war lasted, or a love, can be embroidered or altered by a storyteller to hold the interest of the listeners, who already know the rough outlines of the myth.[3]

Ritual's strictness in time signals something basic about creativity itself. The Greek word for 'making' is *poein*, which can be translated as creating something where before there was nothing (the modern word 'poetry' descends from this ancient root). For the performer, *poein* involves riffings and improvisations in gesture and movement. Because the basic outlines of a plot or score are known and set, these alterations draw attention to the performer's own creative presence, to their 'agency' in cultural studies lingo. Whereas in a ritual like saying Kaddish, were you to add riffs and embroideries, you would distract from the power of the ritual itself. Your 'agency' is not the point of you saying Kaddish.

Just as being strict in time, the Kaddish is numerically strict. A minyan consisting basically of ten adult Jews is required to say Kaddish in public. Traditional Judaism is highly sexist by modern lights; only males over the age of thirteen can constitute a minyan; less rigid forms of Judaism now allow women in making up the ten. You might say this is a riff, an embroidery – conservatives in fact make that claim, arguing that it is sacrilege to change the rite. But, in my experience, the admission of women little affects the ritual, since what matters more is the size of the group. The minyan specifies the numbers which constitute a visible community – if these are not right, God will not hear the prayer.

In contrast, you can perform *Hamlet* to ten, a hundred or a thousand spectators. And size is flexible on stage; in a play you can cut out minor characters; in an opera, the size of the chorus can accordion from small to large. To be sure, as in Judaism so in most other religions people can pray alone and silently – but Kaddish is not a meditation. It is a communal performance which precisely, numerically defines 'community'.

If strictly controlled in time and number, Kaddish is portable in space. Migrants are often called 'citizens of nowhere', which has a particular resonance for Jews, who have been displaced persons for thousands of years. A Jewish Iraqi refugee could say Kaddish in a Turkish camp, or perhaps could have found consolation in Brexit Britain.

Portability is shaded differently in ritual and theatre. The Jewish immigrant transports a sacred text whose integrity does not depend on the place where it is performed, whereas the theatrical script may be altered to accommodate the circumstances in which it is performed. Site-specific art like Trisha Brown's dancers on the roofs of lower Manhattan's tall buildings, for instance, has to be pretty radically rethought when the site changes to Marseilles' lower, flatter buildings.

Rituals are embodied. The Kaddish is a written text which has to be said out loud, not just read. In its performance, the congregants sit or stand up at different points; if standing, the reciter will bow at various points of the service. For the last, the Oseh Shalom, the speakers will take three steps backwards, bow to the left, then to the right; these gestures signal leave-taking. Classical Roman ideas of rhetoric imagined that an action such as bowing was a kind of physical colour added to the verbal meaning; the gesture is, as Cicero put it, 'illustrative'. But the bow, signalling that you are leaving, is more than that. It aims to make you feel the consoling message viscerally: you are exiting grief, life calls you.[4]

The bows in Oseh Shalom tell you nothing about the person doing the bowing, nothing about who they are, whereas the same bows in the theatre characterize the actor. In *Hamlet*, for instance, a low, prolonged bow made by Hamlet when his mother, Gertrude, first comes on stage could be a way to signal his bitter feelings.

Finally, most performers have to work to rid themselves of self-consciousness and embarrassment at being exposed on stage, whereas whatever embarrassment people might feel at the beginning of a prayer disappears once they are actually praying. This is, I recognize, a debatable distinction. Some theologians assert that unconscious surrender to the word doesn't happen automatically; you have to prepare – otherwise the prayers will feel alien and you will not say them unselfconsciously. In Judaism, this is why Torah study is said to be all-important. The Torah contains many voices, many points of view; even more varied and contradictory are the commentaries on Torah spanning thousands of years. It is the discipline of study, navigating these complexities, which gradually strengthens the believer's commitment, making the declaration 'I believe' entail no inner catch, no shadow of doubt.

There is another way to frame the unselfconscious aspect of ritual. Surrender of self is easier in religious ritual because the palette of emotion is more varied in art than in ritual. There is more room for irony. In the performance of *As You Like It* in St Vincent's Hospital, the rum setting, the pleasure the actors took in covering up their Kaposi's sarcomas with stage glop, Charles's self-aware delivery, were a big part of the expressive punch – but lost on us, who wanted simply consolation. It's not a question of ritual being inferior to art – rather that its passions are more focused, more channelled.

In sum, this quintet of structures – strictness in time and in number, portability, impersonal embodiment, lack of selfconsciousness – give ritual its power to console.

III. Art That Does Not Console

Could the consoling work of Kaddish be done by art? This was not an abstract question in the 1980s. Many of the men who succumbed to AIDS were estranged from their Jewish families, so their friends and lovers were often obliged to invent ceremonies to honour them.

Allen Ginsberg took on the challenge of transforming the ritual of Kaddish into a work of art in a poem of 1960, 'Kaddish', which mourns his mother, Naomi Ginsberg. She had suffered from schizophrenia for years and finally died in a mental hospital in 1956. Ginsberg's 'Kaddish' relives her suffering, painful stanza by painful stanza, and Ginsberg's helplessness in the face of her madness. Though the poem bears the name of the ritual, it contains none of the ritual's words. Ginsberg dwells in unrelieved grief: there is 'no more to say and nothing to weep for'. The poem invokes loss without consolation, a difference which distinguishes the poem from the ritual.[5]

After finishing 'Kaddish', Ginsberg thought that his poem might be acted as a theatre piece, one which recovered some of the force of the old faith. First he wrote a screenplay, which another writer, Robert Kalfin, then turned into a stage play. Art and life intermingled thanks to the use of videos of Naomi Ginsberg, the videos serving as testimonials that there was a real Naomi. Both Ginsberg and Kalfin hoped that, acted on stage, 'Kaddish' would come closer to feeling like a ritual.[6]

For me, while the poem is Ginsberg's greatest – deeper than his hippie epic 'Howl' – this and later staged versions of 'Kaddish' don't work, in part because the actors' bodies don't do much. The fourth power of ritual is weak. The actors playing Allen and Naomi do scream and sob, but their flailing arms and hair-pulling are pretty standard tropes, adding little imaginatively to the words of the text. The videos underline this insufficiency because they are offered as evidence of suffering, but the projections backfire, as though they were shown to make the action on stage more believable. On stage, the raw shouting and flailing don't evolve over the course of the drama; there are the same gestures at the end as at the beginning. No transformation, therefore no release from grief.[7]

Ginsberg's play poses a question about the audience: how involved should it be in the passions on the stage? The essence of doxologies like the ritual of Kaddish is that any one can perform them, not just rabbis. By analogy, one version in art performance is that audiences are so deeply engrossed that the spectators feel as though they are themselves on stage. Ginsberg wanted to arouse that deep identification; a play, he said, is not an object like a printed poem, it is a shared communal event. This doxology-like involvement was carried a step further by the theatre director Richard Schechner. His performance piece *Dionysus in '69* derived from Euripides' *Bacchae*, an ancient play filled with highly sexed, wild moments of abandon. Schechner used these outbursts to invite the audience in a disused factory to strip off, join in and let their emotions out.

Schechner was anything but mindless about this invitation. His actors had to be well trained in techniques both to break down audience resistance and then to guide the spectators in acting out rage. Participation, Schechner would later write, should not be 'gratuitous'. But, still, this work tried to engage the audience in out-of-control emotions, as did Ginsberg's videos of his mother having psychotic episodes. The impulse is to destroy spectator distance.[8]

Contrast this with the performances staged by Joseph Beuys in the piece called *How to Explain Pictures to a Dead Hare*. Here, as first performed in a commercial gallery in 1965, the artist appeared behind glass in a window, swathed in honey, holding a dead hare in his arms, whom he strokes while whispering comments about the drawings scattered around the gallery. The audience is challenged to figure out what is going on, but the artist kept his distance. Even with the gallery handout explaining that the piece was 'about' Beuys's experience of near-death in the Second World War, 'about' doesn't explain why Beuys coated himself with honey and whispered to the dead rabbit. There was no way to identify, to join in; Beuys made engaging but not participatory art.

I used to believe that music is the most participatory performing art, because it transcends representation and identification. Like Beuys's gallery piece, the listener is engaged by the musical thing in itself without being able to explain in verbal language what it means. Thus it seemed to me evident why so much music does the work of consolation; it speaks directly. But sometimes it doesn't. The reasons have to do with the relation of creation to ritualization within the music itself.

A concrete example of this difficulty appeared in Leonard Bernstein's Symphony No. 3, which he named the 'Kaddish' symphony. This work, created in 1963, was dedicated to President John F. Kennedy, shot to death that autumn, though the composer had started it before that fatal event as a memorial to his own father, with whom he had a complicated, guilt-filled relationship. (We are talking about Jews.) Bernstein was unhappy with the work when he premièred it in New York with the New York Philharmonic, and he would revise it in 1977.[9]

He was unhappy with good reason. The Kaddish symphony is sometimes compared to Mahler's symphonies in its use of vast forces – a big chorus, a huge orchestra, an actor-speaker – but its problems were more akin to those of Mahler's contemporary Anton Bruckner. The Kaddish symphony's musical gestures were overblown; it climaxed again and again with diminishing power. The music sobbed, flailed, screamed, but, as in Ginsberg's 'Kaddish' on stage, it lacked the power to transform suffering.

In rewriting this piece, Bernstein strengthened a musical gesture which created a greater feeling of ritual. Complex, clotted twelve-tone textures now gave way to simple, straightforward diatonic moments. For instance, in the final scherzo we are released from a knot of tones to the calm of a G flat set of chords on the word 'believe'. The passage from twelve-tone to mono-tonic binds together Bernstein's huge forces, which interact ever more; the singers create a knot, then the orchestra unties it, with the speaker mediating between them.

The revision creates a ritual inside the music, but it will never become like the sacred music performed by amateur choirs all over the world; it is too demanding technically. All twelve-tone music is wickedly hard to play if you are not a professional, but in sacred performance the problem of doxology can't be ducked. The ritual Kaddish allows anyone to perform; the composed 'Kaddish' can be enacted only by a few. To put this outside the European context, but within the orbit of AIDS, we might think of Gibson Kente's *The Call*.

This is a theatre piece he wrote for the townships in Johannesburg, South Africa, ravaged by AIDS during the 1990s. Though Kente's play made some use of local amateur actors, the main role demanded a range of gestures and movements, tones of voice and different dictions, representing conflicting states of feeling, which an amateur would find challenging. Kente, a fine actor, played the lead part himself. After he died a year later of the disease, others tried to take his place, but they have found *The Call* almost impossible to revive.[10]

In sum, rather than create a false binary, as though acting and ritualizing have nothing to do with each other, it would be better to think of the two forms of performance standing side by side, uneasily. There is a connection in that they share many of the same expressive materials: body gestures, blocking in a scene and movements around it. But they stand together uneasily, because they are looking in different directions. Ritual looks to a practice which does not vary from place to place, whose organization of words and movements changes slowly, whose timing is strict, a performance which anyone who is in mourning can give. Whereas acting is elastic in time, adaptable to place, puts demands on the skill of the performer, and is focused on their persona. The sum of acting's parts can be transgressive, whereas a ritual such as Kaddish aims at reintegration into the community.

On the AIDS ward, there was nothing to choose between these two; at least I could feel sympathetically to both Charles and the priests. In the performance of *As You Like It* there was a creative defiance of death, in the ritual offered by the priests lay a reassuring acceptance of death. Both these ways of facing death lodged uneasily within me – and I suspect, though our circumstances may well differ, they stand side by side uneasily within you.

2

The Moral Ambiguity of Performing

How play-acting loses its innocence

I. Innocent Play-acting

When you were five you were quite willing to credit that toads talk. When you were seventy you smiled indulgently at this childish illusion – but then reading *The Wind in the Willows* aloud to your grandson you adopted a distinctive voice for Toad and contrived Toad-ish gestures to reinforce the words. Gradually you began to believe in the Toad you were acting out.

Performances of Mr Toad follow separate channels for ritual and acting. Woe to you if you embroider on the Toad story because you've read it a hundred times. Whether in his comfy bedroom or away in the family's mosquito-infested holiday home, your grandson wants you to become Toad, as a pleasure on which he can rely. His interest as a listener is in the fixity of performance, its ritual character.

But the matter is different if your grandson performs Mr Toad himself, especially if he does so with the book closed. He takes pleasure in making things up, improvising and embroidering. The child psychologist Anna Freud believes that in listening to a story the child wants to hear reality confirmed as solid and reliable, whereas in acting the child takes ownership of that reality by playing with its terms, fashioning a persona. The divide between art and ritual thus appears early in the developmental process.

In the back of my country garden lived a toad, which my grandson watched intently every time he came to visit. Toad-study at first led him just to mimic the way a toad moves its legs, but then he worked out the structure hidden beneath the surface – not that he could prove it biologically; rather, his imagination went to work. Mr Toad morphed into a bird, the webbed legs becoming wings. He was learning that just as a living thing can take different forms so an actor can perform different parts – the same grandson able to play Mr Toad, Bird Man and an Angel at different moments in a school pageant.

Playing with Toys

Learning to act different roles is coupled in early life with playing with toys. So argued the historian Johan Huizinga in a classic study of play, *Homo Ludens*. If Mr Toad were a stuffed animal, the child could hold conversations with him, perhaps gesturing with the toy toad's flipper so that Mr Toad could make a point. Huizinga thought that it didn't matter what the toy toad was made of or how big it was, because the child's imagination transformed the object into a living presence.

Later psychologists were not happy with Huizinga's assertion; for them the material toy matters. The most prominent of the post-Huizinga toy psychologists was Jean Piaget, who explored the role objects play in the transition from symbolic to analytic thought, a developmental process spanning the years from two to twelve. Toys like stuffed toads start off merely as graspable, punchable things; in a further stage, the toys themselves need to be deconstructible, taken apart. Only when the stuffed toad is in shreds will the child begin to ponder its structure. The toy then needs to be reassemblable, not perhaps just as it was, but held together by tape or loose stitching. The object will then, in the child's mind, come back to life. This is a lesson in metamorphosis. The lesson applies to performance: from one character, another character can be made.[1]

In the studies of D. W. Winnicott, toys were taken to be 'transitional objects' which gradually led the child beyond his or her own bodily sensations. Winnicott's frame differed somewhat from Piaget's, because he believed experience of the transitional object was sensuous as well as cognitive. Winnicott therefore emphasized the materials of which toys are made as well as their inner architecture.

Both Piaget and Winnicott figured in my grandson's play: sometimes he studied the toad's flipper without touching it, at other times he stroked the velvet surface of the toy toad, as though it were a pet.

All three writers believed that playing with toys is important developmentally, because, as Winnicott put it, 'the abstractions of politics and economics and philosophy and culture . . . [are] derivative of play.' In particular, the adult's ability to play different roles is grounded in juvenile experience. This is not quite so welcome a process as it might seem. Though children can be physically rough on their toys, the process of learning through them how to play different parts is innocent; the child does not know that he or she is learning an expressive power which eventually can do harm to others, and to him or herself.[2]

To see how play-acting in adult life can become ethically ambiguous, I'd ask the reader to make a big leap backwards in time and place. This ambiguous ability to play-act shaped the life and thoughts of Machiavelli, the greatest political thinker of the Renaissance.

II. Machiavelli Masked and Robed

Masked

Machiavelli's great essay *The Prince* argues that a ruler must be an actor in order to survive. The Prince has to pursue policies, such as raising taxes or forming alliances, which his subjects would resist if he presented them openly. If he is to be free to act rationally behind the scenes, he must appear unpredictably before the curtain, his sudden shifts diverting his subjects from his policies, throwing them off balance. One week he seems furious, in order to inspire fear among his subjects; the next he praises them as would a loving father. What will the Prince do or say next? The people can't predict. The Prince keeps his subjects riveted by a persona which, because it is shape-shifting, never becomes stale. Still, he needs to keep his own head clear, not be swept away by disturbances he inspires in others.

Machiavelli's Prince draws on the early-developed capacity to play more than one part. But something new has appeared in this role-playing adult: the Prince doesn't wholly surrender to his performance. It is a mask. For this reason, demagogues like Donald Trump are not best described as Machiavellian; the Prince swaps masks at will, whereas Trump believes his own fantasies and is deeply invested in a single role.

Multiple-masking derived from Machiavelli's own experience as a senior diplomat, involved in negotiations in which Florence was either betraying or being betrayed by other city-states. In many of these negotiations he was front-of-house, rather than a shadowy backstage intriguer. Somewhat surprisingly, *The Prince* doesn't really analyse the techniques of deceiving well, of lying convincingly, in public. The text instead names historical examples of princes who were good at seeming other than who they really were. Machiavelli's interest in the theatre, however, was deep. He was the author of plays such as *Mandragola*, which anatomized how to get away with infidelity in domestic life. We can only infer that he might have thought deceiving a husband or wife deploys the same skills as those which can gull the public.

Machiavelli's near contemporaries translated the Prince's public persona into concrete staging, as in the details of how a throne of state should be decorated and where it should be placed; how a ruler should mount a throne and descend from it. Setting the political stage was no longer chained to precedent; the Prince's handlers could manipulate the setting – a political reflection of Victor Turner's belief that, in the Renaissance, culture shifted from ritual to theatre. Indeed, we might think these manipulations are just like the obsession today with the acting and stagecraft of politicians. Consultants now are paid a fortune to coach the politician on how to stride into a rally as though joyfully and how to leave it quickly, seemingly regretfully. But whereas Machiavelli was hiding serious purposes behind these theatrics, practising what might be called virtuous manipulation, now they have become the very substance of politics.

Role Distance

Machiavelli was not a good sociologist – which, I realize, may be a compliment rather than a criticism. He did not probe a grave consequence of wearing a mask in public, which is that it can rebound on the wearer. If always feeling on stage, a person can become depressed, feeling that there is no 'real me' apart from their roles. The performer needs to strike some distance from their roles, not for Machiavellian reasons of hiding a project which cannot be exposed to the light of day – rather, to be relieved of the pressures of performing for others. This stepping back is what sociology calls 'role distance'.

The writings of the sociologist Erving Goffman explored role-playing in a modern institution seemingly far from the power-plays in a Renaissance court. In *Asylums*, Goffman's 1961 account of patients in mental hospitals, doctors and nurses expected the patients to behave according to their diagnoses. Patients were often saner than they appeared but had to behave crazily in order to get along with the medical staff. Goffman is a Machiavellian, though the Machiavellian mask is worn by the powerless rather than the powerful. Still, the mask does the same work of hiding strategy and cunning.

Role distance has a philosophical pedigree, deriving from a text written in 1955 by the philosopher J. L. Austin, *How to Do Things with Words*. Austin coined the term 'performative' to describe how words work. The sentence 'I do' has no inherent meaning; it can intend 'yes, I do want another glass of wine' or 'yes, I do want to marry him'. It's a question of what actions the words perform. In semiological lingo, there's no one-to-one link between signified and signifier. A generation after Austin, Roland Barthes echoed this view of performativity in a famous essay on *The Death of the Author*, in which he asserted that a text 'has no other content than the act by which it is performed'. This is to say that in language there is no inherent, fixed referent, in life no behaviour which cannot be adapted or manipulated. In language and in life there is no inherent content, no fixed meaning.[3]

If in a way self-evident, what these philosophical views miss is how a constant shift in expressing themselves makes people feel. If a behaviour can mean anything depending on its context, then people can feel empty. Indeed, once Goffman turned his attentions from institutions like the mental hospital to everyday life, he focused on the negative side of too much role distance. One minute you are behaving like a loyal employee, the next minute you are on the phone soothing an upset child, then you take a call from your bank, trying to sound as though you are confident that you can take care of your overdraft today. As the roles stack up in every life, the performer longs for an anchoring meaning. Or the self is destroyed by seeming at the expense of being, as for Sylvia Plath – smiling outwardly, good at playing mother and wife, responsible citizen, meanwhile depressed and filled inside with murderous rage.

There is certainly a benign side to wearing masks, as when adolescents try out roles to see what they feel like. In school, they'll hold forth as dedicated communists, then equally declaim as libertarian zealots a few weeks later. In each role, as long as it lasts, adolescents are in deadly earnest. But they seem to be able to discard a role in a matter of days, even hours. This chameleon capacity to shed one role and take on another is a legacy of Mr Toad. Moreover, the positive side of passionately performing a role and then dropping it served Machiavelli himself at the darkest hour of his life.

Robed

Machiavelli's life fell apart when he lost power and briefly went to jail in the wake of one of Florence's many political upheavals. Deposed from office, scratching an existence on a farm outside the walls of the city, each evening he put on the robes he used to wear when he was a high official. In a letter to his friend Francesco Vettori, written at the end of 1513, he describes the transformation:

> When evening comes, I return home and enter my study; on the threshold I take off my workday clothes, covered with mud and dirt, and put on the garments of court and palace. Fitted out appropriately, I step inside the venerable courts of the ancients, where, solicitously received by them, I nourish myself on that food that alone is mine and for which I was born; where I am unashamed to converse with them and to question them about the motives for their actions, and they, out of their human kindness, answer me. And for four hours at a time I feel no boredom, I forget all my troubles, I do not dread poverty, and I am not terrified by death. I absorb myself into them completely.[4]

Vettori was a tough old bird and not likely to have been moved by this pathetic scene. But asking for pity was perhaps not Machiavelli's reason for writing.

Donning the robe, he time-travelled backward to the distant past, so as to no longer feel in disgrace. His pain was relieved – if only for a few hours. The robe itself had no individual character – it was just a common court robe (higher functionaries at the time usually wore black gowns with red facings at the sleeve). Once dressed in and transported by this costume, the Renaissance statesman became the brother in spirit of Charles in the hospital, also released from pain – if only for an hour or two.

As his circumstances began slowly to improve after 1515, Machiavelli abandoned his robes and returned to the world; there were no more imaginary sessions communing with the ancients. His situation was a little like that of the adolescent who casts off a role when it no longer 'fits': that capacity both to play-act and to walk away from a particular role.

Machiavelli's mask represents the malign side of role-playing, his robe the supportive side. Role playing is thus is a deeply Janussian phenomenon, since both faces derive from the same childhood source – the ability to throw oneself into a role, then switch to another. Role distance figures in both sides: the Prince makes use of role distance to manipulate his subjects, in ordinary life role distance can be corrosive, and yet it can also liberate people, relieving them temporarily of pain or allowing them to try out new experiences, new identities.

On the professional stage, role distance takes a further turn.

III. The Passage

The Two Diderots

An eighteenth-century text notably sought to figure out the puzzle of investing and then divesting in a role: Denis Diderot's *The Paradox of Acting*. Too much personal involvement in one's roles is, Diderot asserted, counterproductive for the professional performer. He tried to show why that should be so by framing role distance as a paradox: the less deeply a performer feels, the more they can make an audience feel.

Suppose you have a contract from the Comédie Française to perform *Phèdre* thirty times. You might be full of fire for the first couple of these performances, but you are going to burn out during the other twenty-eight unless you hold back your own emotional investment from the start. Diderot had an example of burnout in French *mélodrame*, a form of theatre layering impassioned verbal declamation on top of highly charged music. Performers, especially young performers who threw themselves wholeheartedly into *mélodrame*, quickly became stale, and for this reason impresarios preferred hiring seasoned troupers who had learned how to give themselves some inner space.

New Yorkers my age may recall an instance of Diderot's paradox in a film of the seventy-year-old Ida Kamińska playing, in Yiddish, the young Ophelia in *Hamlet*. Mrs Kamińska was so affecting in this role, pouring her soul into the part of the doomed young girl, that no one thought about her barely disguised wrinkles or prominent veins. In a film of her performance, as the curtain falls, the audience weeping and clapping, the camera follows Mrs Kamińska walking off into the wings. There is a brief glimpse of a poker game set up there, a game to which she was said to be addicted. Diderot's argument might be that the poker game was an essential ingredient in Ada Kamińska's power on stage; it provided her with a release from passionate, deep investment of herself in the role of a young girl.[5]

In contrast, in another essay, *Rameau's Nephew*, Diderot imagined an actor's ability to play many roles as a deformation of self. He describes the nephew of the composer Rameau, a performer who could do almost anything:

> He jumbled together thirty different operatic melodies, French, Italian, comic, tragic – in every style. Now in a baritone voice he sank to the pit; then straining in falsetto he tore to shreds the upper notes of some tunes, while imitating the stance, walk and gesture of the several characters . . . [He was] being himself both dancer and ballerina, singer and prima donna, all of them together and the whole orchestra, the whole theatre; then he re-divided himself into twenty separate roles.[6]

Goethe remarked that this kind of virtuosity embodies the very sickness of modernity: people are adept at playing many parts, committed to none. So too *Rameau's Nephew* is the forerunner of Erving Goffman's critique of empty role-playing.

There is a technical side to Diderot's *Nephew* which is etched in every musician's experience. In a musical performance, switching from one voice to another has to happen quickly; musical performers have to invest and divest in different expressive voices within the course of two hours. A cellist may need to pass from being inside Bach's First Gamba Sonata, full of Italian sun, to inhabiting Samuel Barber's Cello Sonata, full of angst. You have to stop feeling one way to feel something else – quickly. You walk off stage, get a minute to change gears, then go back on. At most, intermissions give you twenty minutes to change expressive roles. Diderot's paradox comes into play because if you are overwhelmed by what you have performed, it's not easy to move on.

For me, absolute silence was required to cross the threshold from one expressive voice to another. I couldn't stand visitors to the dressing room during intervals. My wonderful piano partner, a chatty young woman from Chattanooga, Tennessee, did allow people backstage, acting the Southern belle as she received them. However, if asked later, she confessed that she couldn't recall a single word of what she and they had talked about. For us, the threshold was crossed by, as it were, scraping clean consciousness. Like a Zen moment of feeling nothing, this temporary blanking-out enabled us to move forward.

It's easier to explain the disinvestment, the disrobing, though, than to explain the new investment, the re-robing.

Temporary Identification

In Diderot's time, the actor David Garrick embodied the ability to change character or mood with lightning speed; a century ago, Laurence Olivier, by performing both Romeo and Mercutio in Shakespeare's *Romeo and Juliet*, was another quick-change artist. Both were masters of re-robing.

It might be called more abstractly 'temporary identification'. Konstantin Stanislavski struggled with this concept when creating the Moscow Art Theatre in 1897, a company dedicated to the principle that an actor should be honest and true to him or herself in performing a role. Yet how can a chameleon be honest? Stanislavski's response has sometimes been reduced to a crude caricature of identification. You draw on your own experience: your childhood memories of a toy that resembles the prop you are now holding in your hand, or the smells and sounds which come to mind of streets you once walked in order to bring to life the meanderings of a character meandering in the city, or your feelings if your father – like Hamlet's – were to die suddenly. Personal projection of this sort, Stanislavski soon realized, runs into a problem. Simply telling what you are feeling is not expressive. This is just what went wrong when Allen Ginsberg put *Howl* on stage – unmediated, raw identification of the player with the part.

As an actor himself, Stanislavski suffered from acute bouts of nervous self-consciousness. He met this challenge by developing a set of exercises in rehearsals to enable concentrating on the Other rather than on Me. These focused on the physical relation of characters to one another: why am I looking at her? Why am I standing three metres away from her rather than five? How slowly should I turn my head to acknowledge someone entering from the wings? Asking such questions was, for Stanislavski, a way to overcome self-consciousness. The body does the work of turning outwards.

In a way, his procedure resembles Toad-study. At first, children identify with imaginary figures, as though the doll is a reflection of themselves. In time, they explore imaginary characters who do not reflect themselves, a metamorphosis occurs, as in my grandson's experience in the garden, from toad to bird to angel. Now the child will flap his arms differently, his posture will assume new forms. It's by these bodily changes that he transforms himself, rather than just by thinking 'now I am an angel'.

In terms of the contemporary stage, Stanislavski's aim might be to enable a Black performer to play a slave-owner convincingly, or a white performer to play the role of a slave. If a Black actor is cast in the role of slave-owner, he will need to blank out temporarily all the cruelties he may have suffered due to his own skin colour. The Stanislavski exercises assert that, for example, how close a slave-master would stand to a slave, or how he would chain two slaves together, matter most in creating the role. The actor will not cross the threshold of expression from Self to Other through sheer introspection.

And yet, Stanislavski was uneasy about his exercises aimed at becoming someone else, and he was right to be uneasy. Like Diderot in *Rameau's Nephew*, and like Goethe responding to it, the director worried that the person who is the actor becomes hollowed out in this passage. How then does the player acquire conviction, become passionate, about the new part, if it is not an expression of themselves?

Rightness

Imagine a conductor who mounts the podium, turns round to the audience and announces with a slight smile, 'Well, I could open Beethoven's Pastoral Symphony either as Toscanini or as Erich Kleiber did [their tempi are quite different]; it could go either way . . .' Without inner conviction, the performance will certainly be limp. She will get out of herself by believing that she's playing Beethoven correctly. Toscanini and Kleiber were podium bullies who each insisted his way was correct – that is, what the long-dead Beethoven would have wanted if only he could have heard the conductor. She too will have to make choices about tempo (there are few metronome markings) or she will have to decide just how fast to perform a passage marked *teneramente* – 'tenderly'; it's her decision what that word means in terms of speed. She cannot be a slave to the score, but still her choices have to seem to her what Beethoven *should* have wanted.

The same decisiveness will help for the Black actor impersonating a slave-owner: to carry it off, he's got to believe there's a right way to play it – as he is doing; he's got it right. However, artistic conviction is an odd phenomenon. Stanislavski's method is liberal in impulse: get out of yourself, engage with the world with all its variety, its different roles, scores, choreographies. This impulse combines with an authoritarian streak: each time you impersonate, you need to feel that your way is the way it should be done.

This duality in Stanislavski's method appears early on in everyday life, in the child's experiences of performance. I remarked perhaps too casually that my grandson wanted me to perform Mr Toad just as he had heard the story before. This is one version of rightness; a tradition has to be observed. Once my grandson became the actor, he enacted many variations and transformations on *The Wind in the Willows*, no longer tethered to one way of being Mr Toad. He believed in each new version, throwing himself passionately into each new part. The duality allows the performer to experiment freely, yet act with conviction that they are doing it right – whether it's a boy at home, or a professional artist on stage.

Considered largely, the duality of performing poses an ethical dilemma. It is anything but innocent.

IV. The Tears of Judas

In Caravaggio's *The Taking of Christ*, painted between 1602 and 1603, three figures dominate the picture's centre: Judas, Jesus and a soldier. As Judas embraces Jesus, his kiss signals that the soldier should move in to arrest the god. Jesus looks down, lost in thought rather than surprised that he should be arrested. To the side of them, out of the inky dark the arm of the soldier thrusts forward, seizing the god. So far, the painting tells a story familiar to any biblically informed viewer. But Caravaggio adds a twist of his own.

He paints a little sliver of white between the eye socket of Judas and his nose, a sliver which appears to be light glistening off a stream of tears. Visually, this detail is disorienting: Judas's tear ducts seem to be spurting out a horizontal wet stream rather than dripping drops down the cheeks. But it works in this painting, which, like many of Caravaggio's canvases, features a telling but ambiguous detail. *The Taking of Christ* is lit by different spotlights, rays of light shining into pools of dark; one of these rays shines on the tears.

The white line of tears is puzzling. Why is the betrayer crying? Are his tears fake or real?

The case against Judas is that his tears are like his kiss, put on for show. The weeping Judas wants to convey his own regret, display his own feeling: 'what a pity we have to kill him'. This line of interpretation turns Judas into a figure like Machiavelli's Prince. The betrayer's mask is just for show – though Jesus, whose downcast eyes express the god's foreknowledge of his fate, is not deceived.

The case for Judas is that the tears are sincere because the act of betrayal has made him miserable about what he has done. Tears are often taken as a sign of sincerity: Roland Barthes writes that 'by my tears I tell a story'; tears are 'the 'truest' of messages, that of my body, not that of my speech'. The lyrics to Schubert's song 'In Praise of Tears' (*Lob der Tränen*) declare: 'Words, what are they? One tear will say more than all of them.' The body of the betrayer demonstrates his real feelings.

Are these tears indeed the 'truest' of messages? Here the acting out of crying enters the picture.

Staged Tears

Shakespeare reflected on this power of staged tears in the second act of *Hamlet*, a play written at the time Caravaggio painted *The Taking of Christ*. Hamlet commands a troupe of actors who have come to the castle of Elsinore to put on a play. He is powerfully affected by the principal actor's crying – 'the fruitful river in the eye', as he describes it. After the performance, Hamlet reflects on the nature of stage tears:

> Is it not monstrous that this player here,
> But in a fiction, in a dream of passion,
> Could force his soul so to his own conceit
> That from her working all his visage wann'd,
> Tears in his eyes . . .

How can it be, Hamlet asks, that he cannot cry in the same way for the death of his own father – that tears can appear at the command of an actor but do not flow in a real-life tragedy. 'What would he [the actor] do,' Hamlet asks, 'had he the motive and the cue for passion / That I have? He would drown the stage with tears.' But Hamlet does not cry, and the inability to cry only intensifies his grief and rage. He has no cathartic moment.

Some psychologists explain the impulse to cry as an automatic, instinctive response to pain, and more specifically to the sound of weeping. But Hamlet is getting at something more complex: that crying is an artful performance. Crying on stage, on command, can be as simple as concealing an onion in a handkerchief, then raising it to the face to well up. Professional mourners, employed at funerals in some cultures, rehearse choral crying. In Morocco, where I witnessed them at work, they practised wailing sequentially rather than in unison, one mourner taking up just on the last notes of another, the timing linked to starting and ceasing to weep. Just this staging of tears among the paid professional mourners allowed others at funerals to release their emotions.

The tears of Judas show another kind of performance. Though he acts out remorse as a public display, he may actually feel it once he starts to cry. He might be transformed by his own role-playing; the performance moves him as well as put on a show for his audience of soldiers and townspeople. The transforming power of a staged scene on the performer makes Judas more compelling a figure than if he was taken to be an unalloyed villain, crying for show.

We can't know if Caravaggio himself meant to convey this message; it's something which can be read into a little daub of white paint. But taking up this suggestion made by the painting illuminates the moral ambiguity that attends the act of performing. Performing that transforms the performer can be good, as it was for Charles and for the robed Machiavelli, or perverse, as it was for Machiavelli as counsellor to his Prince. In adult life, striking a distance from one's roles can be a necessity, as for the patients in the asylum studied by Erving Goffman, or self-destructive, as it was for Sylvia Plath, depressed by the divide between her seeming and her being. On the professional stage, Diderot believed it was dangerous for performers to identify with their roles, and he also thought the performer becomes a superficial technician without some emotional relation to the parts they play. Stanislavski warned about self-referential performances, about how to turn performers outward. Yet they had to invest personally in these varied performances, they had to believe in each of them as right, correct, the only way to do it. All these complexities are, I think, embodied in the painted tears spurting from Judas's eye.

3.

The Most Troubling Performance

Dramatizing violence

I. Cut Free from Reality

Hand

When it first came out, I went with a friend who had fought in the Vietnam War to see *The Green Berets*, a blood-and-guts film made in 1968 by John Wayne. My friend had come straight from some sort of military event in army dress uniform. It could not disguise Jamal's war wound; a bullet had shattered his left forearm, and the military surgeons had been obliged to amputate the arm at the elbow. Now Jamal wore a mechanical device fitted with metal fingers and thumb which allowed him to hold cutlery and to type.

My friend sat impassively through the gory war epic, occasionally offering technical comments. The movie patrons by contrast were aroused throughout the two hours of blasted and ripped bodies, applauding particularly good hits. In *The Green Berets*, bloody encounters occur every minute, whereas in actual warfare, Jamal observed, violent episodes happen sporadically over days and weeks. Boredom is the soldier's daily lot. Moreover, if soldiers fought heroically in life the way they fight on screen, they would very likely die or cause others to die. Discipline rather than cowboy bravery is the key to survival. But these facts would make for dull theatre.

When it was over, we lingered outside. Jamal lit a cigarette slowly, then held it up steadily in his claw to his lips. People streamed out around him, a visibly wounded soldier, glanced at the metal hand, and moved uneasily away. Soon we were a little island in the midst of the crowd.

Screen violence is sometimes thought to give rise to violent behaviour in everyday life. A similar argument is made about porn: viewers watching women abused in online videos will become abusers themselves. Dramatized violence can work in the opposite way, however, as at the showing of *The Green Berets*. Outside the cinema people do not want to see signs of the real thing. Our experience there was not, I think, at all unique. The Vietnam War, a cruel and useless conflict which people wanted to forget prompted my generation's great act of amnesia. Staged violence perhaps helped them do so by erasing the reality of pain.

Hood

I thought again about this split forty years later when visiting the studio of my friend Susan Crile. The most political painter of our generation, Crile has created a series of large panels about the barbarity of the Iraq War. Many of the paintings show a theatre of cruelty staged by the soldiers themselves. Sometimes the display meant stripping prisoners naked, and forcing fifteen to twenty naked men to form a human pile, smothering those at the bottom. Photographs were then distributed online to buddies. Crile's paintings focused on a kindred form of staged violence, depicting hooded and blindfolded prisoners, wearing dirty gowns, being subjected to irregular electric shocks, not knowing when the pain would come next. These performances were put on for a live audience of soldiers, standing or lounging around the victims.

In photographs taken at Abu Ghraib which Crile had pinned up on her studio wall, the torturers often present themselves full-face to the camera. The most famous of these photos is of a grinning female soldier jabbing an electric cattle prod into the groin of a hooded prisoner.

The hooded gown has an old provenance as a magician's costume, images of hooded magicians appearing as early as the eleventh century in France. At its medieval origins the magician's hood was a disguise – in an odd conceit, meant to hide him from the sight of God. But the hood also meant that an observer could not see any emotion on the wearer's face. Here, in the torture at Abu Ghraib prison, hoods meant that the victims' expressions could not be seen as they screamed and writhed when 'juiced'. The evidence of a human being's suffering was literally covered up.

Horns

Now, ten years later, I am watching on TV the storming of the American Capitol in Washington on 6 January 2021. The most famous image of this violent event is of Jacob Anthony Chansley. Booted out of the navy thirteen years before, he became a self-described shaman. At the Capitol, Chansley wore a shaman's costume: he was bare-chested, his face painted red, white and blue, and framed with the fur pelt of an animal, a pair of horns strapped on his head. Shamans often dress to dramatize their half-human, half-animal persona, so Chansley was in character.

Chansley's horns, like the Abu Ghraib hood, helped dispel the reality of this event – that the marauders were threatening to kill people in the building. The divide between staged and actual violence perhaps explains why so many of those arrested for storming the Capitol were surprised that they had been arrested for committing a real crime. The event had seemed to them more like a carnival.

I was struck by how carefully Chansley had kitted himself out. The sexy bare chest with its traces of hair was a fleshy sign that contrasted with the abstractly painted hard face; the fur and the horns were, again, a pairing of soft and hard. Any make-up artist would have admired the pairings: they did indeed make him look half-man, half-beast, seeming more menacing than he was in fact. His aura was dispelled as soon as he, a stumbling speaker, opened his mouth.

Our culture avidly consumes dramatized violence of the hand, hood and horn sorts. This consumption may seem to mark a divide from the nineteenth century, which did not eroticize violence to the same degree – at least in public. Think of Tolstoy's descriptions of the battle of Waterloo in *War and Peace*; gore for gore's sake is not the point. Massacred bodies dot the giant canvas which Félix Philippoteaux painted to show the revolutionaries of Paris in the uprising of 1848; blood is everywhere, but it's not, so to speak, prurient blood. But the Vietnam movies, the Abu Ghraib torturers and Jacob Anthony Chansley have one link to that era: the violence they savour is larger than life – not like a stab in the back in a dark alley, but big, lurid, improbable. Nineteenth-century opera shows some of the techniques by which this kind of dramatized violence can be accepted, and enjoyed.

Larger than Life

The very title of Verdi's *La forza del destino* tells us we are in for something big, larger than life; indeed, the opera's plot beggars belief. The father of the heroine, Leonora di Vargas, shuts her away in the country, in order to keep her from Don Alvaro, her lover. Later, Don Alvaro accidentally shoots Papa and kills him. Leonora's brother, Don Carlo, wants to avenge this death but, due to a set of chance meetings, disguised identities and the like, lover and brother actually save one another's lives. The action eventually moves to a monastery, where Leonora and Don Alvaro are separately in hiding, not aware the other is inside. The brother discovers where they are – don't ask how – fights the lover outside her cell door, and is mortally wounded. She tries to comfort her brother, but with the last of his energy he stabs her to death.

All opera, it might be argued, transcends the everyday in order to grip us, but this argument is certainly untrue for Verdi. *La Traviata*, written in 1853, is a drawing-room-sized tragedy; a decade later *Forza*, composed in 1862, belongs to Verdi's middle period, in which he sought big stage effects like those of Parisian grand opera. As he said about *Aida*, composed in 1871, it has '. . . bite and if you'll forgive the word . . . *theatricality*'.

Drawing on ancient models, operas in the seventeenth century dramatized the doings of classical gods and goddesses. The art began to descend to earth in the Enlightened eighteenth century, but it landed lightly and gently. For instance, Jean-Jacques Rousseau's *Le Devin du village,* first performed in 1752, evokes a prettified countryside of shepherds and shepherdesses. The music – Rousseau wrote both libretto and music – is also faux naïf, with relentlessly pleasing melodies and harmonies, without the tensions which animate Handel's operatic art. Mozart's feet are more firmly planted on the ground; he's interested in the world as it is and people as they are. Though *Così fan tutte* draws on an 'exotic' Albania, the characters are recognizably ordinary people doing the unfortunately ordinary thing of lying to those they love. Even an opera like *The Magic Flute,* filled with masonic mysteries, is rooted in experiences audiences can recognize as their own. The masonic rite at the end translates without much filtering as an initiation into adulthood.

In the nineteenth century, larger-than-life plots returned. In contrast to Wagner's allegories of power, Verdi's libretti are more lightly disguised depictions of the politics of the day. Still, they are not direct representations, and here lurks a production problem. The inflation of scale, as in *Forza del destino,* requires a kind of theatrical cunning to pull off.

In the crucial scene in which Papa is murdered, directors are challenged by how to manage the gun. Should the gun fall, does Papa grab it, are hero and father far apart or in a clinch? The action needs to resolve these questions, otherwise the puzzled audience may disconnect with the stage. In one production in Chicago, the director of the Lyric Opera, Carol Fox, made the murder scene work by a simple device: she painted the gun red and let it clatter to the ground, highlighted by a spotlight above. So too, in the stabbing scene she staged for Puccini's *Tosca,* she made cunning use of a seemingly absurd detail. The heroine, Tosca, stabs the evil Scarpia, who is a menacing rapist, and presumably stronger than she is. The challenge is to make credible on stage that Tosca could summon the immense strength required to kill him by stabbing him in in the chest. Fox had Tosca hold up her hand, staring in disbelief at the dripping blood; she appears as surprised as we are about what has happened. Then Tosca licks her fingers to taste the blood.

Just as there's no reason why the gun is red, so there is no dramatic logic to explain why Tosca would lick her dripping fingers (it would make sense only in an opera about vampires). In both operas, an object or gesture which has nothing to do with the plot arrests our attention; it is intriguing in itself. The staging deflects attention from the logic of the plot or, rather, the lack of it. The very strangeness contributes to the suspension of disbelief.

Aristotle is, as always, willing to explain. In the *Poetics* he asserts that these plots come in two forms: 'probable impossibilities' and 'improbable possibilities'. In the case of *Forza*, lovers living in the same monastery but unaware of each other is a situation of 'probable impossibility', since the chances of the two lovers arriving at the same place at the same time are pretty low, and the plot gives no indication of how this could occur. So too, guns aren't red; it's another probable impossibility. Whereas a revolver discharging accidentally is an 'improbable possibility', since we know revolvers can do so, and lover killing father accidentally at a crucial moment may be unlikely but still could happen. Spotlighting the red gun lifts the scene into a fantasy realm beyond unlikely coincidence. And this stage device helps convince us to suspend disbelief about another probable impossibility: that Papa can manage to sing *forte* while bleeding to death.[1]

Music itself can do the work of deflection and arresting detail. That's true for Wagner, Verdi's great adversary, in an opera like *Tristan und Isolde*. Wagner dug deep into the medieval past for his story, making use of newly unearthed manuscripts of the Tristan legend. Considered just as a libretto, *Tristan*, like Verdi's *Forza*, is a bit ludicrous: there is a magic love potion, a ship which fails to arrive in the nick of time and neatly symmetrical killings. But the music makes these stage devices powerful to the ear in a way they could never be on the page.

In this opera, written midway through the composition of the four epics of his *Ring* cycle, Wagner delves deep into the possibilities of chromaticism, the half-tone steps which are the fundamentals of Western music. Long melodies pour forth from narrow half-tone movements. Wagner sets this chromatic thrust against both common harmonic shifts, for example the plagal cadences of church music, and more recherché harmonics, such as hanging 'Neapolitan sixths' – a harmonic adventure of which Debussy later became the master.

This chromatic palette helps Wagner the musical dramatist achieve the intensity which transforms a creaky libretto into a compelling stage work. The great love duet in Act II is carried forward on chromatic melodic waves that are dissolved then recomposed, again and again. We are hearing a small-harmonic shift which becomes more and more arresting in itself. Where will it lead? Will it ever resolve? The unconsummated chromatic shifts deflect us from thinking that Tristan and Isolde are taking a long time, a very long time, to climax their love. No matter. We are entranced by the endless, minute chromatic steps. We take on board, or so I think, Wagner's Goth-religious, larger-than-life librettos because of such finely calibrated, unresolved, micro-movements in the music.

How do opera's ways of inducing us to suspend disbelief relate to the sort of violence dramatized by hand, hood and horn? Displacement through an arresting, displacing detail is one connection. In *The Green Berets* the director, John Wayne, makes use of a cigarette lighter in just the way Carol Fox uses the red gun in *Forza*, as a prop which deflects the viewer's attention. The lighter had belonged to a Green Beret but was found in the possession of a captured Vietcong enemy. The Vietnamese is tortured to extract the story of how he came to own it, but, rather than focusing on his screaming, the camera homes in on the Zippo lighter, flicking on and off. Why is the lighter sometimes not firing? This visual detail takes over while the torture unfolds.

But the willing suspension of disbelief has a larger relation to dramatized violence.

III. The Willing Suspension of Disbelief

Gertrude is only ten feet away from Hamlet, but she doesn't hear him musing out loud. A soliloquy asks the audience to believe that they can hear an actor speaking while the characters around him cannot. A soliloquy differs from stage irony, when the audience know that things are in fact different from how they seem to the characters in the performance, as in Shakespeare's *Othello*: we know Desdemona is innocent, but Othello doesn't. A big issue lies behind this difference. Whereas our actual knowledge enables stage irony, the soliloquy requires our willing suspension of disbelief.

The Romantic-era poet Samuel Taylor Coleridge invented the phrase 'the willing suspension of disbelief'. The phrase might seem merely to describe escapism, as for the audience at *The Green Berets*. But when Coleridge first used it, the 'willing suspension of disbelief' had a far greater sweep. He maintained that people need to believe in religious truths that can't be proved or disproven. Religion requires the willing suspension of disbelief.

Coleridge's Truth

In the wake of the eighteenth century's rational investigation of the world, Coleridge worried that science was weakening the impulse to take things on faith. Deists such as Thomas Jefferson treated the Bible as a collection of inspired allegories and moral myths, as divine fictions rather than as historical facts. A generation after Coleridge, the philosopher T. H. Huxley coined in 1869 the term 'agnostic'. This word, he said, 'simply means that a man shall not say he knows or believes that which he has no scientific grounds for professing to know or believe'. Huxley's agnostic inclined to suspicion rather than neutral open-mindedness. Once you had read Darwin, Huxley thought, how could you ever imagine that God had created the world in seven days?[2]

The poet feared science's power to erode religious faith, as did many others then and now. More particularly, Coleridge feared that disbelief would spread to the arts, dulling people's imaginations. This fear sparked Coleridge to write a certain kind of poetry. He asked himself: how could art suspend scepticism and stimulate people's capacity to believe? Such a work of art would have to be so out of the ordinary that it would overwhelm the claims of cold fact. It had to be larger than life. The poet thus entered the realm of *La forza del destino*; he created what we now call science fiction, an art of the 'hyper-real'.

Coleridge's poem 'The Rime of the Ancient Mariner' is such a hyper-real voyage. It describes the journey of a ship travelling from an imaginary Antarctic to the tropical torpor of the Equator. At the outset of the voyage, the killing of an albatross lays a curse on the Mariner. During the trip the crew of the ship morph between ghosts and flesh-and-blood presences. The reader takes on faith that travel to strange places can cause this alternation of solid and shadow bodies. Coleridge's friend Mary Shelley plotted something similar in her novel *Frankenstein*: Dr Frankenstein, the scientist-artist, creates a living human being, somehow, in his laboratory. For both writers, art should rise above the laws of normal science.

Coleridge's fear that modern society would become chained to facts might have disappeared had he spent a few days on the London Stock Exchange. There, the tulip mania of the early eighteenth century served as an example of secular credulity among hard-nosed businessmen. The bulbs of this ordinary tuber traded for vast sums for no good reason until the bubble of belief burst and traders came to their senses. But only until the next magical thing came along. Observing such madness, the sociologist Max Weber disputed the assertion that scepticism reigns in modern life; in economics as in religion, people need to believe, he thought; fact will always fall victim to desire.[3]

The willing suspension of disbelief had a personal side, one which is perhaps the most compelling aspect of this concept. The American psychologist and philosopher William James thought of it as a remedy for depression.

The Therapy of Faith

Tone deaf, his eyesight, back and stomach weak, William James fell prey to neurasthenia, the nineteenth-century name for depression; he suffered badly as a young man, feeling suicidal for months on end. In his first effort to combat melancholy he took refuge in science, seeking in its hard facts an alternative to self-preoccupation, and entered the Harvard Medical School in 1864. Still he was depressed, and sought a more extreme flight from self. The following year he travelled with the scientist Louis Agassiz up the Amazon river. Yet travel would bring no release. After eight months, he caught smallpox, suffered from dysentery, and returned home, falling into yet another bout of suicidal despair.

It was only in 1872 that he found relief from what he called his 'soul sickness', a release that involved exchanging medical research for philosophical writing, a profession he could pursue or put off as the waves of depression came and went. It was at this point that he began to turn away from agnosticism as Huxley framed it, and to embrace the sheer leap of faith made by religious believers.

In a long essay written in 1902, *The Varieties of Religious Experience*, James spelled out the psychology of belief. The force driving people to believe comes from 'the divided self'. You fear that you are worthless, that your life is meaningless, even as you matter to others and pursue worthwhile activities. In what James called 'healthy-minded religion', relief from feeling worthless comes by being 'twice born', shedding an old self for a new one. In making this passage you don't justify yourself by works, by evidence drawn from your experience; you make a leap of faith in your new self under God.

Such a rebirth didn't speak to James personally; he was attuned to religion that doesn't promise redemption. Faith in God will not make your inner demons go away. Yes, you are unhappy, and nothing can be done about it; even so, you believe in God. The leap of faith is to believe even though you can marshal no evidence to prove that faith will do you good. You live with rather than transcend your depression. Still, there is a higher reality outside yourself. Turn outward.

The Varieties of Religious Experience belongs on the same bookshelf with many of the novels of the philosopher's brother Henry James. *The Portrait of a Lady* is, among other things, a study of the afterlife of disillusion. Its heroine, Isabel Archer, makes a disastrous marriage to a cad; almost immediately, she begins to realize she has made a terrible mistake; but she does not fall into self-pitying victimhood. She remains engaged with her needy stepdaughter and with a dying cousin. The novel affirms her will to keep going rather than fall prey to neurasthenia. For Henry James the leap of faith involves committing to other people, even though you are scarred; for William James there is a commitment to God, even though you remain depressed. 'Faith' itself comes down to the same thing.

These versions of the willing suspension of disbelief may seem far from the realm of violence. But not so: the individual experience of belief throws into relief the collective experience of violence.

Wordsworth Objects

In an account of discussions with William Wordsworth twenty years after the publication of their celebrated book of poems, *Lyrical Ballads*, in which 'The Rime of the Ancient Mariner' appears, Coleridge observed that his fellow poet had now withdrawn from this inflamed realm of fantasy. The reason for this parting of the ways lay in Wordsworth's experience of how the 'willing suspension of disbelief' could lead to street violence.[4]

Helen Maria Williams, a young activist who was William Wordsworth's partner, quit Britain for Paris in 1791. She described the Fête de la Fédération, an outdoor festival celebrating national unity, as 'the most sublime spectacle which, perhaps, was ever represented on the theatre of this earth'. So too Wordsworth at first greeted the French Revolution with open arms, famously declaring, 'Bliss was it in that dawn to be alive . . . to be young was very heaven.'[5]

As the Revolution unfolded, Wordsworth's initial enthusiasm

darkened, as recorded in his long poem *The Prelude*. In September 1792 he crossed the Place Central in Paris 'heaped up with the dead and dying', who were shortly to be burned by a mob. The reasons for this violence seemed unfathomable, 'being written in a tongue he [the poet] cannot read'. That's not quite right. He knew he was in the grip of collective violence made worse by being dramatized. He'd had a foretaste of how this violent theatricalization worked earlier at Versailles; here the *sans-culottes* mob had massacred fifty political prisoners one night, then built a pile of the bodies around which people danced. In Paris one night, unable to sleep, the gore in Versailles mixed in his mind with images of the bodies about to be burned in the Place Louis XV as a public spectacle, '. . . the fear gone by / Pressed on me almost like a fear to come . . . I felt a substantial dread.'

The theatre of violence in the Revolution was exemplified by the guillotine. Though there were British antecedents of this instrument, its technical perfection was owed to the physician Joseph-Ignace Guillotin, who sought to devise a relatively humane method of capital punishment – one which would be swift, unlike the prolonged tortures of the *ancien régime* death, and impersonal, since the victim kneeling with face down would not see the blow fall.

As the Revolution of 1790 turned into the Terror of 1793, the guillotine mounted on a stage became the principal prop for a mass spectacle. As countless novels relate, just before kneeling the victim was allowed to make a last speech to the crowd gathered to watch. About 17,000 people were guillotined during the last year of the Terror. Guillotines were originally set up in small squares in Paris but, as time went on, moved to places which could accommodate huge crowds – ultimately in the largest square in central Paris, the Place Louis XV (today's Place de la Concorde).

Wordsworth came to fear the theatre of the streets from scenes like those which occurred at the guillotine. Coleridge – good-hearted, idealistic, his imagination flying – seemed unable to grasp the nightmare. A century after the discussion in which they talked past one another, Wordsworth's fear of theatricalized violence was articulated more analytically, by a theory which continues to shape our understanding.

III. Violent Street Theatre

Collective Suspension of Disbelief

At the end of the nineteenth century, in 1899, the writer Gustave Le Bon wrote a book on crowds, called simply *The Crowd*, which sought to explain how people inflame each other violently in the street. Le Bon was a royalist who both hated and feared 'The People'; he believed a violent mob lies waiting to spring forth in every crowd. Theatre's power to suspend disbelief is a large part of the reason, Le Bon argued, the mob could be unleashed.

Le Bon's *The Crowd* starts with the premise that people will together commit atrocities which they would never think of committing alone. This was not an original thought; Nietzsche said somewhere that 'madness is rare in the individual . . . but in groups it is the rule.' Le Bon brought this idea down to earth, specifically to the city. The crowded street provides anonymity, so that no one can recognize individuals and hold them responsible. Aggressions usually held in check in private life can then be released in public; 'I' hides behind 'we'. Le Bon thought this was why, during the Terror of 1793–4, ordinary Parisians turned into revolutionary killers: they were protected by anonymity. Had he lived today, trolling online would have served him as a digital parallel: the troll never reveals him- or herself personally, and so avoids being held accountable.

According to Le Bon, the release of crowd inhibitions in the street takes shape in three stages.

First, a dense mass of people gathers. Rather than gathering inside buildings like churches, Le Bon's mob takes form outside in town squares, and also bars and cafés – anywhere people can enter and leave at will.

Once a crowd is assembled, its swirling mass tends to inflate rumour and word of mouth, and these fantasies spread like disease contagions in the collective body. Rather than think concretely, people surrender to events which seem larger than life: the melodrama of enemies and heroes, wild tales of courage and cruelty – these lurid imaginings release demons of hatred and aggression that individuals usually keep in check.

When people are baying for blood, a third stage emerges. Not so much looking and speaking to one another – their gaze indeed averted from each other, as to single out someone individually would break the spell – as looking for an innocent bystander. Attacking someone together will bond the mob. Thus in the French Revolution anyone could be attacked on the street as an 'enemy of the People', just as now a Black person, a foreigner – anyone who looks different – will serve.

Freud was an avid reader of Le Bon. In *Group Psychology*, published two decades later, he embraced the proposition that, once an individual meshes into a crowd, they lose any restraint on the self. A crowd has no super-ego; it's all id. And the id is credulous; it has no analytic inner resources to check its willingness to believe anything and do anything. This insight might explain the puzzled, often guilty reactions of the rioters at the Capitol in the days following 6 January 2021, when people were no longer under the spell of the crowd and had returned to themselves as individuals – as though waking up from a collective bad dream.

Like Freud and Le Bon, Theodor Adorno, in exploring sustained collective violence, believed that collective psychology operated differently from that of the individual. Reflecting on the Nazi crowd, he suspected that few of the Germans, 'in the depth of their hearts [believed] that the Jews are the devil, [nor] do they completely believe in their leader'. Rather, being assembled in a crowd gave Germans the opportunity to loosen the bonds both of accountability and of thinking. Adorno writes: 'if they [the Jew-baiting crowds] would stop to reason for a second, the whole performance would go to pieces, and they would be left to panic.'[6]

Perhaps the least known of Le Bon's heirs was Elias Canetti, who was most attuned to the physical theatricality of a violent crowd rather than its existence verbally through rumour or slogans. His book *Crowds and Power* (1960) drew on personal experience of Nazism in Vienna in the 1930s, and particularly on that ever-so-proper slice of Vienna, its petite-bourgeoisie. How did they become vicious Nazis? Canetti's answer was that saluting, cheering, marching turned them into Nazis. The gestures had that power in themselves and took on a life of their own. When a crowd chased a Jew down one of Vienna's streets, the sheer joy of running motivated the chase – just as, in hunting, horse and rider are absorbed in the visceral pleasure of moving. About the Nazi salute, Canetti observed that this forward-thrust arm gesture happens spontaneously when a mass of excited bodies faces forward; it does not take a specific Jew-hating ideology to make people salute in this way. By performing Nazism physically, Canetti thought, the crowd came to identify with it ideologically.

All these analyses of the violent crowd emphasize that individuals lose awareness of themselves. How does theatre serve that blotting out of self? One answer came from Canetti's contemporary, Antonin Artaud.

History remembers Artaud as a writer of novels, and of a work on drama, *The Theatre and its Double*, but not as an actor. In fact, he was a gifted performer who searched for ways to rouse audiences physically. At the Théâtre Alfred Jarry, which Artaud founded in 1926, he sought to induce a sense of visceral release in audiences, at the expense of logical or critical thinking. His own acting involved rapid movements around the stage, extremes of shouting and whispering, of pointing with his feet and his bottom. About the violence of release Artaud wrote: 'The Theatre of Cruelty has been created in order to restore to the theatre a passionate and convulsive conception of life, of violent rigour and extreme condensation of scenic elements . . . the cruelty on which it is based must be understood.' Jean Genet, in plays such as *The Maids,* also wants to suspend resistance among an audience so that it plunges emotionally and without reserve into its own scenes of degradation.[7]

Wordsworth said he had no language to express the violence he had witnessed on the streets of Paris, and these theories of collective violence help explain why. The violence was created viscerally not verbally. The willing suspension of disbelief on the street happens in the body.

The dramatizing of violence is undoubtedly the most dangerous of all performances. Which might dispose us to think that a return to sanity and civility requires that we stop performing. Civilized life might require dispassionate discourse instead. Huxley might seem to have won the argument; the willing suspension of disbelief might be fine inside an opera house, but is destructive in society. But if we believe only what can be proved, by avoiding fantasy we would do another kind of violence to ourselves. The imagination would wither. The lessons of *The Varieties of Religious Experience* and *The Portrait of a Lady* are better guides; like depression and betrayal, violence is a fact we have to live with rather than transcend. And the spaces of performing suggests how we might do so.

BOOK TWO

Stages and Streets

4.

The City's Three Stages

The elemental spaces of theatre

'All the world's a stage' has an urban meaning. In cities there are three kinds of space in which performances occur. These are the open stages, closed stages, and hidden stages. The three spaces are more than background settings. They shape how performers perform, and how spectators spectate.

The three forms became evident early in Western history in ancient Athens. The open stage was the agora: in Athens, a ten-acre town square combining law courts, food markets, shrines to the gods and spaces to dine, gossip and flirt. On this stage, everyone put themselves on display; there was no distinction between actor and spectator.

The Pnyx was Athens' second stage, basically an amphitheatre built on the side of a hill, where originally people sat on the ground watching dances and listening to recitations of odes and stories performed at the base of the hill. Then it became a more formal place, with stone seats and a paved stage. In time the amphitheatre came to be used for political meetings; it could hold nearly a third of the citizens of Athens. Single speakers held sway over a mass of listeners, deploying many of the gestures and rhetorical devices used in performing plays; in the Pnyx, the political actor separated from the spectator citizen.

The third stage space for performing lay hidden away. From the origins of Western civilization, caves were considered sacred places where the powers of the gods over everyday life outside could be revealed by priests who were keepers of the mysteries. The encounters involved terrifying rites, sound echoing off the cave walls and smoke billowing from ceremonial fires, with the oracle often masked or dressed as a wild creature. Spectators were transfixed by larger-than-life forces rather than human actors.

These three ancient forms have endured for thousands of years.

I. The Open Stage

The agora was a terrain of about 10 acres, on a level plane. It housed the city's central market, functioned as a dining and social hub, and additionally contained law courts and several shrines devoted to the gods. Low walls around the courts meant that shoppers passing by could casually toss in their opinions on a murder trial within. Men swirled around the agora at all hours, going from activity to activity, gossiping, strutting, making their presence known. Women appeared early in the morning to shop, and later in the day during certain festivals, but it was essentially a male space. The 'street' in its richly symbolic sense is an area the ancients would have identified with the agora; the actual streets of Athens were narrow and mostly faced with blank walls.

The space was framed by stoas, boxy buildings that lined the open space. The walls of the stoas facing the open space were removed, so that the buildings were closed on three sides. Within them, people dined or visited prostitutes or snoozed. They were private in the sense that you couldn't just wander in but came by invitation.

The open space of the agora enabled men to put their naked bodies on display; in ancient Greece men did it without shame. Equally important was posture. Men stood in the agora, whereas they sat or reclined inside the stoas. *Orthos*, upright posture, was a posture of pride. A man sought to walk purposefully and as swiftly as he could through the swirl of other bodies; when he stood still, he made unflinching eye contact with strangers, which continued as a sign of manliness as he moved towards another man. He was supposed to radiate personal pride and control by exposing himself, by standing upright, by looking straight at others.

In a modern theatre, when an actor comes down to the footlights, confiding thoughts about what's happening or just dangling their feet over the edge of the stage, seeming to take a rest, they occupy a liminal space – the footlights zone marks a space in between, both on stage and withdrawn from the main space of action.

In the agora, the edges between enclosed stoas and the open space were similar liminal spaces, and were governed by special rules. A person standing on the steps of the stoa on its open side could be seen both from the backstage and the forestage, but could not be spoken to. Once a Greek standing at the edge of the stoa took a step in either direction, that convention no longer applied; the person could be addressed, and they had to respond.

Does it make sense to call the agora a theatre? The ancients certainly thought it did. In ancient Greek, the word for theatre is *theatron*, which means a place for seeing; the placename derives from the verb *theaomai*, which means 'I see'. (Our word 'theory' descends from *theatron*; what theorists see is in the mind's eye. The Greek word *praxis* means doing something about what you see in the mind's eye, that is, translating theory into practice.) In the agora people behaved as though they were on stage, seeing and being seen. But it was a complicated scene. You could enter it, withdraw from it, or contemplate it at will, just by moving from outside to inside. There were harsh limits on participation; in this slave-owning society only a minority were free. Still, it contained the DNA which has endured for a certain kind of theatre: a participatory theatre in which there is no distinction between actor and spectator.

II. The Closed Stage

Most ancient amphitheatres began on hillsides where a crowd of people sat, in order to see and hear clearly the performers at the base – but these observers were not yet spectators, and the people below them not yet singled out as performers. In the beginning, people switched roles, notably during festivals. In an ancient Athenian festival called the Rural Dionysia, for instance, a rite celebrating the grape harvest in the countryside, a parade of people snaked through country lanes carrying jugs of wine, loaves of bread and clay statues of phalluses (the clay phallus being a symbol of the farmer's physical vigour), ending up in a hillside clearing in the city where the celebrants performed verses and musical odes. People watched others do the dances, play the music or recite the poetry they would themselves perform.

In time, the City Dionysia, a more sophisticated affair, signalled the specialization of spectacle. Everyone could still be a celebrant, parading through the street, carrying the traditional loaves of bread, jugs of wine and clay phalluses, to which was now added a wooden statue of Dionysius, as the deity presiding over theatre. At the culmination of the City Dionysia in the amphitheatre, famous playwrights and poets declaimed and competed for prizes, replacing the simple dramatic expressions of farmers in the Rural Dionysia. The stage then became the territory of skilled performers, signalled in one way by Sophocles' triumph in the City Dionysia festival, taking the first prize in 468 BCE over the older playwright Aeschylus; Sophocles' play *Triptolemus* requiring highly skilled actors and elaborate staging.

Both Dionysia terminated at a site named for Dionysius himself, built on the south slope of the Acropolis. From that temple, looking down today, we can see remnants of the theatre as it was at the end of the fifth century BCE, with a rising fan of stone seats, a regular, round space at the bottom on which to perform, and further down the hill a building storing masks, costumes and scenery. This articulation of space enabled the closed theatre to take form.

The Scenery of the Imagination

Originally, beyond the performers, the mountains outside the city were visible to the audience. Drama could not be physically separated from Nature. Starting around 500 BCE, though, this exposed view became partially blocked. A back wall called a *skene* was added to the *orkhestra* performing space. This sight-blocker was originally just a curtain made of cloth; later the barrier became wood, still later, stone. Behind it, actors prepared and masks were stored. The more solid and bigger the front wall became, the better it reflected the voices, strengthening the sound, but the more it blocked out the natural view behind.

Here we might take a quick jump between past and present. A blank surface like a *skene* or colourless backcloth invites the viewer to project, to imagine more freely than if an audience is shown a scene which represents what the performance is about. The spectator sets the scene in the mind's eye – which was the original idea of the *theatron*. Today, *skene* space appears, for instance, in the solid colour backgrounds for many of George Balanchine's ballets; they show you nothing. You aren't asked to imagine a specific place, instead you are invited to imagine the space formed by dancing bodies intertwining, separating, organizing themselves into patterns on the stage floor.

In the fourth century BCE, theatre began to erode this primal act of imagination, putting representation in its place. Actors declaimed against the front wall of the *skene*, called a *proskenion*, and painted panels called *periaktoi* started to be mounted on it. The chorus became a less important element of the theatre, changing into a sometimes seated, sometimes standing layer of voices between audience and stage. The *proskenion* itself grew more prominent, because its actors were raised over the heads of the chorus, on a stone platform. And as the building, the *logeion*, became a solid piece of architecture, actors began to declaim from its upper windows, or use the roof, which was taken to be a *theologian*, a place where actors impersonating the gods spoke at the beginning and the end of performances.

Thus the free play of a spectator's imagination was gradually limited by staging; it's not that imagining flagged, but rather that now it was organized, shaped and defined visually for the spectator. Freely imagining yielded to controlled imagining.

The Powers of the Dominating Voice

The control of the ancient audience's imagination derived from a seemingly unrelated fact about the ancient gods. They did not expose themselves directly to men and women. The gods were felt but unseen powers, and so needed messengers. The divinely inspired messenger was at first a rhapsodist, a reciter-singer on their behalf, 'the god speaking through me'. Over time and in practice the performer passed from a rhapsodist to a more self-aware interpreter; the performer's goal now focused more on training and technique, which meant that he (always then a 'he') could perform the complicated parts written for him. The power of the political performer in part reflected this specialization; then as now political speakers needed to learn the arts of rhetoric, movement and voice control.

But this explains only partly why the difference between actor and spectator arose. It was also due to the fact that spectators sat. They sat according to the neighbourhood tribe (the tryttis) to which each citizen belonged, and if you weren't in your proper place, your vote didn't count. They sat for hours at a time. Male citizens – who were only about 15 to 18 per cent of the total population of the city – passed hours immobile, listening to speeches given in the *orkhestra* by a succession of speakers, and then voted. When exactly votes would occur was not fixed, so, rather than come and go, people remained in their places.

In the agora, where everyone was on display, people stood, and standing had a positive value; *orthos*, upright posture, was as we have seen the posture of pride. By contrast, the seated posture of spectators in an amphitheatre was thought to render them passive and vulnerable. Greek science imagined that a moving body heats the blood, and hot blood stimulates the brain, whereas the immobile body just receives and takes in sensate impressions. They drew an analogy: just as a crouching body is vulnerable in warfare, easily attacked, so in the Pnyx it could be attacked by the rhetoric of the standing orators.

To be sure, the crowds in the Pnyx were not at all silent, unlike the figure standing and observing in the liminal space between stoa and open agora. Spectators in the Pnyx were highly vocal, but reactively so: they cried out in response to what a speaker said, they did not break away in huddles to discuss it among themselves. This is one reason why ancient writers on the theatre feared its power over spectators, whose judgement was overwhelmed and passions manipulated by a persuasive performer, a dominating voice.

The Two Voices

In the simultaneous and shifting activities of the agora, the babble of voices easily scattered words, the mass of moving bodies experienced only fragments of sustained meaning. In the agora, many things happened at once, crying out for separate attention, and diminished the dominating power of any one activity. Experience in it was not coherent, whereas in the Pnyx the single voice shaped itself into sustained expression. A political performer skilled in rhetoric could go on and on, his victims sitting for hours on end, the weight of words gradually accumulating, judgement sinking under their weight.[1]

Here we can make another connection between past and present. In the ancient city, the Trumps of the day were particularly feared. Cleon, for instance, was an ancient, wealthy Greek who, like Trump, posed as a 'man of the people' to pit himself against the aristocrat Pericles during the Peloponnesian War. Aristotle observed him even dressing down to play the part of a man of the people, by tying his cloak around his waist the way farmers wore theirs. Cleon sought to grab attention, Aristotle said, by using 'abusive language', by insulting others personally. The attacks singled out individuals who were then physically menaced and sometimes killed.

Demagogues like Cleon were thought to flourish in ochlocracies, which were cities or states inflamed by fickle, spontaneous mobs running amok in the streets. Polybius invented the word 'ochlocracy' in the second century BCE to distinguish this crowd violence from tyrannical rule, in which a despot imposes his will on people, who submit in silence, passively. On the whole, however, the powers of the voice lay elsewhere. For every Cleon, there were a hundred others who spoke down to the people, rather than in their name – each speaking with authority, certainty, conviction, followed by others with other views speaking with authority, certainty and conviction. Gradually the people became exhausted or bored; worn down, they then voted.

The Pnyx thus showed enduring elements of the closed theatre. It is closed in space and place. In space, the spectator's imagination is controlled by carefully contrived staging. As a place, the actor proves stronger than the spectator. These two elements combine in closed theatre to create an aesthetic of inequality.

III. The Hidden Stage

The ancient cave was, like the modern church, a space that put human beings in touch with cosmic forces; its rites and rituals were larger-than-life performances. Even so, an effort arose to demystify the rites, to understand how the magic was constructed.

The most famous effort to understand caves in human terms was Plato's 'Allegory of the Cave', which appears in Book VII of *The Republic*. He imagines a cave where prisoners sit, shackled around the neck and legs, facing a wall. Behind them a fire burns. Between prisoners and fire runs a low wall, and on it statues parade, manipulated by invisible puppeteers. The prisoners see images cast by the parade on the wall in front of them. The reflected images are larger than life, but, since the prisoners have been chained up all their lives, they know no other reality than what they see on the wall; they imagine these shadowy shapes and echoing voices are real beings and cry out to them.[2]

For twenty-five hundred years this allegory has endured. In part this is due to the projection machinery which casts shadows, shadows that are taken as real because the spectators do not understand the mechanics which produce them. And Plato gives a new, political meaning to the use of puppets.

The Puppet

To investigate the power of image theatre, Plato first had to change the normal understanding of puppets. Basically, puppets come in two forms: glove puppets, like my Aunt Sylvia's Ollie dragon, manipulated by a hand inside, and marionettes, manipulated by strings above the puppet. A marionette can be made to fly suddenly through the air because its walking, arm gestures and head movements are more flexible than the human body, whereas the gloved hand is more physically limited. The Greek word for puppet, *nevrospastos*, refers specifically to a marionette. In Plato's allegory, though, the puppets employed are statues held by hand; it's the flickering fires illuminating them from behind that make the shadows jiggle and appear marionette-like.

Puppet theatre in Plato's time was familiar in China and India. Shadow puppetry in Europe became popular ages later, during the seventeenth century, when it was imported in the course of colonial expansion. Plato's puppets, a thought experiment, were a prescient anticipation of these actual theatres. However, the non-Western puppet theatre had a quite different relation to illusion than did the kind of puppet theatre Plato imagined.

There's a contrast, for instance, with the use of puppets in Japanese Bunraku theatre. Each Bunraku puppet requires three puppeteers shrouded in black and fully visible to the audience; a chanter recites the parts of all the puppets, accompanied by a musician playing the three-stringed shamisen. In Bunraku, the illusion is transparent; the mechanics of illusion are not hidden. We see these mechanics exposed yet still fall under the puppets' spell, whereas in Cave theatre, illusion depends on being impenetrable, hermetic, inaccessible. As a consequence, puppet power becomes larger than life.

The veil cast over the puppets comes from a technology which is the precursor of the film camera and ultimately, the mobile phone screen.

Camera obscura

In Latin *camera* means a room with a vaulted roof, *obscura* means dark. Inside this space, if you shine light through a pinhole, objects in the path of the light will appear on the wall opposite upside down. Some evidence indicates that the humans in the Neolithic period already had puzzled over the workings of the *camera obscura*. Plato's Chinese contemporary Mozi also probed these workings, wondering how an image could pass through a small pinhole and then reappear super-sized opposite on a wall; Plato's student Aristotle wondered how an image passing through a round hole could reappear as a square.

It was another two thousand years before Huygens, in the sixteenth century, advanced understanding of the visual mechanism of a *camera obscura*. He did so by inserting a lens into the pinhole, which enabled him to better analyse the process of refracting an image. A *camera obscura* fitted with a lens was the ancestor of the photographic camera, in which the process of reflection is reversed. And by the middle of the nineteenth century, optical science had a pretty good understanding of how the human eyeball works like a *camera obscura*, the pupil being the pinhole and the retina the wall on which the image registers.

Shadow theatre resurfaced a century ago. The German artist Lotte Reiniger played with the physically larger-than-life dimensions of the *camera obscura*, in abstract shapes which appear monstrous on a white screen, looming over the spectator visually but soundless, huge ghosts all the more frightening because these silent shadows are larger-than-life abstractions which move, nonetheless, like human beings. The artist William Kentridge has reconfigured the shadow theatre in a different way, as in a recent production of Alban Berg's opera *Wozzeck*, where the live singers and the shadow projections of faces, larger than life, appear to merge – as though the projections were themselves singing. Both these modern shadow theatres trace back ultimately to Plato, in that in both we aren't aware of the means by which the illusion is generated.

There is a digital analogy to Plato's Cave that you hold every day in your hands.

The Digital Cave

The LCD, or liquid crystal display, is the screen used today in most computers and hand-held devices. The crystals lie in a slice; behind them is another slice, a reflector flashing pixels (micro-square bits of image) which the crystals project and fuse, with the aid of a polarizing element. What you see on the screen thus is a digital version of the *camera obscura*, an image backlit from behind. The OLED screen, an expensive replacement for the LCD, has a single slice of light-emitting diodes, with a passive rather than active reflector behind. As in the *camera obscura*, so on the screen, a very small image is recomposed so that it looks big.

The digital cave follows the Platonic allegory in that the hand-held device, hermetic as it is, exerts a hypnotic power. In the metro, a hundred people packed together are each lost in their mobile phone. Above ground, in the process of walking, lunching, taking a meeting, people are also glued to the machines – no matter where they are, their attention is gripped by the magic small screen.

These, then, are three elemental architectures for performance: the open stage, the closed stage, the hidden stage. Of the three, the hidden stage seems to me the most insidious, because there are performances with no tangible performers who can be held to account.

The open stage is, moreover, yielding today to the closed. The modern town square is weaker than its ancestor, because modern agoras tend to be single-function places – the campus, the office tower, the shopping mall; mixed-use is a kind of garnish on public space. People do not connect much to difference, to strangers. Nor do we treat our bodies on display as civic exposures, as in the richly coded experience of *orthos* – the ancient citizen's posture, gait, eye contact, even nakedness establishing his presence as an actor in the public realm. The code of the closed stage – spectate and submit – has become the guiding principle of modern politics.

But the closed stage also has its own inner history. Over the years it has drawn ever closer to the hidden stage, to seem like a cave of art, divorced from the street. This evolution did not happen in a straight-line manner; it involved a great rupture spread over the course of centuries. To understand how this happened we are going to time-travel – perhaps regretfully – from sun-drenched ancient Athens to Renaissance Vicenza, a small, rather dark and grim town near Venice.

5

The Stage Withdraws from the Street
Architecture encloses the imagination

I. The Sealed Theatre

Teatro Olimpico

In the late 1570s Andrea Palladio designed the first fully roofed, walled-in theatre in Europe. It has since become the prototype for most closed stages – performance spaces withdrawn from the street.

Palladio's Teatro Olimpico still stands in Vicenza and has been beautifully restored, so that it's clear to see how the architect worked. Like his peers, Palladio believed that theatres were founded on ancient, classical models. He relied particularly on the ancient amphitheatre of Dionysius in devising the plans for this theatre, but he also innovated, for very practical reasons.

Open or closed, theatre was problematic outside. Our ancestors got very cold sitting outside on stone seats in winter; no matter the season, they got wet when it rained. Night-time posed another problem: light from a campfire, used in the performance of Berber stories, couldn't supply anything like the light required to illuminate an amphitheatre holding several thousand persons. Enclosing theatrical space seemed to Palladio to solve these problems, but the project proved challenging on the site he was given.

This was an old tumble-down prison, built on a narrow plot of land. The compression of the site meant that the stage was shallow, the actors obliged to move more laterally rather than forwards and backwards; it also limited dancing, and there was no room for anything like a modern orchestra pit. Yet constraint proved a blessing in one way, in that the flattened auditorium created an intimate connection between audience and stage.

Palladio used the inner shell of the building to reinforce the experience of hermetic closure. The Teatro Olympico's walls were stuccoed, because the architect understood that stucco is a good diffuser of sound. (The set designer John Ross, who a generation later created the acoustic cloud, found that a stuccoed panel detached from the ceiling was a better spreader of sound than a ceiling panel painted on canvas.) The plastering of the Teatro Olympico's walls was unusually thick, the mass abetting sonic reflection. Finally, to make it possible for the theatre to function at night, Palladio devised a system of lighting with torches arraigned on the back wall of the auditorium as well as in the stage wings, spreading light strongly and evenly throughout the interior.

An enclosed stage, then, but its architectural bones do not feel oppressive due in part to the lighting and in part to the theatre's sheer height; its plaster columns reaching upwards make it feel as though the roof is floating away.

A telling contrast to Palladio's work was the other great theatre of this era, Shakespeare's Globe Theatre. The Globe, built in 1599, then rebuilt in 1614, was a huge round building resembling a bagel; actors performed in the hole in the centre. The Globe could seat nearly 3,000 people, the more intimate Olimpico about 1,300. A roof protected more privileged spectators sitting at the perimeter; closer to the centre there was a ring, open to the heavens, where poorer spectators stood, sometimes in the rain. The Globe stage jutted out in the centre on a platform, with a two-storey, *skene*-like building at the back. This 'thrust stage' achieved intimacy by shoving actors out towards the audience, whereas there was no room in the Teatro Olimpico for performers to move forwards.

In the Mind's Eye

These contrasting architectures created different spaces of illusion. The scenery and stage props used in the Globe tended to be sparse:

a chair, a table, little more. As in the ancient theatre with its cloth *skene*, spectators had to set the scene in their own minds.

Mind's-eye imagination figured equally but differently in the temporary stages set up within palaces, which was how privileged Renaissance spectators usually watched plays. The court spaces were boxy constructs, like Inigo Jones's Banqueting Hall in London, built two generations after Palladio. During theatrical events, servants cleared the centre, and courtiers and ambassadors sat or stood on raised bleachers on both long sides. In the middle of one short side the king had his chair or throne, surrounded by his sitting or standing intimates; on the other short side could be found the queen, dowager-queen or officials of special rank.

In palace theatre, scenic decor such as painted flat panels was pushed around the room in carts drawn by the servants, as were special effects like the wave machine, churning paddles in a box of water simulating waves. As in Kabuki theatre in Japan, the illusion was self-evident. The slopping water was meant to prompt people to imagine a wavy tempest in their mind's eye, it was a symbolic prop. The wet stage floor, menacing the shoes of the spectators, was just that: wet.

The Teatro Olimpico sought to create a different sort of illusion, neither spare, as was the Globe stage, nor symbolic, as were the props in the Banqueting Hall. The Teatro Olimpico's stage scenery emphasized withdrawal from the reality of the street.

This was not the work of Palladio himself, who died a few months after the project was in the ground. His son initially carried on; then in 1582 Vincenzo Scamozzi took over. He completed the theatre inside by erecting a fixed stage set in plaster and wood, painted to simulate marble. Through this stage set we look through seven doorways which give out, seemingly, on to the city – views which are painted. These imaginary views are amazingly detailed long perspectives, which was a feat of trompe-l'oeil, because the backstage is only a few metres deep.

When Inigo Jones visited the finished theatre and looked at the seven windows on to the street, he was struck by the fact 'that wherever you sat you saw one of these Prospects'. Nothing stood in the way of seeing – but they gave a clear view of a fantasy. The shapely streets looked nothing like the stinking, irregular mess which actually lay outside. The view of the city from inside the theatre was of an orderly, clean, harmoniously coloured place. As seen in the mind's eye of art, life had been corrected.[1]

Such idealization departed from how an earlier architect, Sebastiano Serlio (1475–1554) thought the street should be represented on the stage. He wanted stage scenery to make spectators think harder about life.

In 1545, he published *Regole generali di architettura*, a book which in part explains how stage backcloths could play this role. Shakespeare's *As You Like It*, set in the Forest of Arden, is the sort of romance in which Serlio might have used a pastoral backcloth and stage props to suit, had it been written a half century before: 'The trees on stage should be clothed of silk, so that they shimmer.' Bathtubs on wheels, the tubs coated in painted plaster, were to be made for 'Nimphes, Mermaids, divers monsters, and other Strange beastes'.[2]

For comedies, Serlio draws a scene which shows the city as a jumble of buildings in the background, with the foreground an open town square. The comic scene must include a 'brawthell [brothel] or bawdy house, and a great Inne, and a Church' – it's an agora of sorts. Following the laws of perspective with which Renaissance designers were experimenting, in Serlio's design the background buildings diminish in size, the square in front is magnified. The point of his drawing is to bring comedy close up to the audience – its bustling and crowdedness should, he thought, look like the packed streets outside.[3]

In the staging of tragedy, Serlio reverses the imagery. 'Houses for Tragedies, must be made for great personages . . . you must make none but stately houses' – tragedy of the classical sort does not happen in brothels. Serlio's backcloth leads the eye along these grand streets to a vanishing point on the horizon, away from the square, from the scene of the everyday. Rather than orient the eye, in the Tragic Scene he disorients it by placing different vanishing points, marked by two obelisks in the distance. It's quite disturbing; the eye moves restlessly from one to the other, unable to resolve the distance. Which was Serlio's point: visual disturbance conveys the idea of tragedy as an unsettling of order.[4]

To a man deeply immersed in the difficulties of his time, it would have made absolutely no sense – I am speaking on behalf of Serlio's ghost – that the tragedies performed at the Teatro Olimpico were staged with pretty views of streets in the distance as decor.

As a place devoted to staging tragedies, the Teatro Olimpico worked well practically, always dry and well-lit. But Scamozzi's elegant scenery disconnected tragedy from the street. The issue isn't a lack of 'realism', as we might term the connection of stage and street in Serlio's 'comic scene', a stage backcloth which would visually bring real life close up to the audience. Rather, in Scamozzi's backcloth for tragedies, the action on stage becomes more gripping, more real, than the decorous illusions outside. The stage tells a truth the street does not.

II. A Parting of the Ways

Enclosed theatrical space after Palladio followed two contrasting paths. Along one, the space became full of the audience's own actions. Along the other, the enclosed theatre focused the audience's attention to the stage rather than on one another. The contrast was between the theatre as an interior agora, with people very aware of one another, or as an interior Pnyx, whose spectators concentrate more submissively on the performers.

The Open Stage, Inside

In 1720, an imaginary Persian attends the Comédie Française. Montesquieu, the author of *Persian Letters*, has created a sophisticated Persian traveller, Rica, who marvels at the crudity of the natives, called 'Frenchmen', whom he encounters. Their social pleasures are as puzzling, as their belief in God is simple-minded. Here, in a place in Paris the Frenchmen call a 'theatre', Rica is rather confused:

> The main action is on a platform . . . [but] on either side you can see, in little alcoves called boxes, men and women who together enact scenes without words . . .

What confuses him is that the real action in the theatre happens not on the platform, but in the boxes:

> every passion is depicted on those [seated] faces . . . all the more intense for being wordless . . . these actors are visible only to the waist . . . Rather than a response to the stage, these actors – ladies – are flirting with gentlemen in other boxes, who dash about in corridors, flitting from box to box if they see any sighs or smiles if eyes meet.

The poorer spectators are below the boxes:

> Standing on the floor below is a group of men who jeer at those that are above . . . they in turn make fun of those below.

Whatever happens on the formal stage is much less interesting than the sexual intrigues and the verbal aggression between rich and poor in the audience.[5]

Montesquieu's picture was nearly, but not quite, right. When the Comédie Française was founded in 1683, the social world of the theatre was akin to that of Shakespeare's Globe at the beginning of the century: all classes were in the building. By Montesquieu's time in the 1720s, the proportion of poor spectators had diminished relative to the rich. The upper classes frequented it more, rather than attend court theatres, because it was easier to be naughty in a box for hire. Still, the place had elements of a low-grade joint. The Comédie Française stank, more than Shakespeare's Globe, simply because it was an enclosed, airless space. Throughout the theatre, people bought chicken wings and sausages from roving vendors, and peed in the plentiful pissoirs located in the corridors. The audience was noisy. Everywhere everyone talked to their neighbours whenever the mood struck. If sexual intrigue in the boxes reached a certain point, a curtain at the side of the box could be drawn. Though the Comédie Française drew on the lighting and sonic innovations of the Teatro Olimpico, the French theatre now served as restaurant and bordello as well as temple of art.

The audience at an eighteenth-century theatre ruled the stage. Because people went so often to plays, key lines were etched in the spectators' memories, and audiences acted on this familiarity. On the stage of London theatres, when an actor belted out the line 'To be or not to be?' the audience would answer him equally loudly, 'that is the question!' If an actor performed a particular speech well, the audience would call out 'Point! Point!', demanding that the speech be repeated. Opera performances were also often pointed, French crowds shouting 'Bis, bis!' ('Again, again!') even before an aria had ended. Pointing was a feel-good moment in the theatre. Sometimes this became gross, as when crowds pointed the Queen of the Night in Mozart's *Magic Flute* to hit its famous high F note over and over. (Josepha Hofer, Mozart's first Queen of the Night, could perform this feat, driving audiences wild.) But if the actor or singer delivered the familiar phrases or melody badly, the audience began to speak or sing along, needling the performer by slowing down or speeding up the lines, hoping to drive the poor wretch into the wings. This process was called 'settling'.

Settling was a feel-bad moment in the theatre, leaving the public, as one *Spectator* article put it, 'baying for blood'. Feel-bad moments were limited to public theatres. In court theatre, as in aristocratic salons, settling was considered vulgar, and an audience expressed dislike or distaste simply by no longer paying any attention to what the performers were doing.

The Spatial Transition

At the time Rica attends the Comédie Française, the architectural envelope for the theatre as an agora was already morphing into a Pnyx. That change appears, for instance, in two great theatre buildings constructed in Germany.

The Schlosstheater in Celle dates from about 1670, and was later somewhat altered during the era in which Montesquieu set the *Persian Letters*. The Schlosstheater is a two-storey hall with boxes of equal size ringing the semi-circular interior. As in the Comédie Française two generations later, there were rows of seats on the ground floor, rather than the standing room for Shakespeare's plebs. And as at the Comédie Française, the most aristocratic patrons or royalty would be found in the boxes close to the stage, or actually seated on it, amid the actors themselves, as elite attendees did at London's Covent Garden – built in 1732 principally for the performance of Handel operas and oratorios. In Celle and in London, proving Rica's point about Paris, the audiences were on display, chatting, munching, flirting, pointing and settling.

In contrast to Celle, the Residenztheater in Munich, constructed in 1751 by François de Cuvilliés, points forward to a condition in which the audience is more orderly and controlled. The royal box, a two-storey affair encrusted in rococo froufrou, was at the back of the auditorium, the royals removed from display on stage. The boxes were ranked by size: stalls level, good; parterre level, great (being on the same level as royalty); then up a level, less good; and, above that, space in the gods for those who cannot afford a box or a chair on the ground. The seating at ground level was for the bourgeoisie and fixed in rows, so that the general public could not see the royals behind, and nor could the flanking aristocrats without turning their necks, which was thought bad form.

The Disciplined Audience

By the end of the eighteenth century, sausage vendors started to disappear from the interior of this more orderly kind of theatre, the chamber pots were moved out of the corridors into special rooms and, most important of all, the audience began to shut up. The rituals of pointing and settling withered; so did the spontaneous outbursts of clapping, in musical performances, after a keyboard player executed a particularly demanding flourish. And, though the change was gradual, talking to a neighbour while an actor or musician performed became frowned upon. You watched, you listened, you kept still. The spectator's command of the stage receded.

Bourgeois self-discipline is often contrasted with the *gaucherie* of the uneducated classes below when in the presence of Art. E. M. Forster's *Howard's End* depicts that contrast. In the novel, the well-bred Schlegel sisters interpret the clumsiness at a concert of the clerk Leonard Bast as a sign of his not belonging there, even though he is deeply moved by the music. The image of the loud and raucous working class at the theatre, in contrast to the self-controlled bourgeoisie, did not fit the facts of working-class behaviour. As in the Yiddish Theatre District of New York's Lower East Side, so in the working-class theatres in Paris and London players performed to hushed audiences, particularly when acting in classics like Shakespeare. In Paris, for instance, the Théâtre des Funambules, opened in 1816 and originally showing acrobatics, by the 1840s had become the home for the first high-art mime, Jean-Gaspard Deburau. The film Marcel Carné made in the Second World War about the Funambules, *Les Enfants du Paradis*, is a faithful reconstruction of the silence of the public following Deburau's silent gestures on stage.

Again, the Schlegel sisters might have been surprised if they had attended concerts in London at Toynbee Hall, the first of the city's 'settlement houses', which sought to settle rich and poor together in a communal setting. The music played in the halls of the settlement houses was more advanced, more edgy than the repertoire of most 'polite' stages.

The history of claques provides a further insight into the disciplined audience. A claque is a group of people determined to make a performance succeed or fail by ostentatiously displaying their reactions to the stage, and so influencing other people in the audience. In the Renaissance, during a performance attended by an aristocrat or a king, the claque aimed to influence one or a few individuals in the crowd. Around the time that Montesquieu sent his Persians to the Comédie Française, when the public began to support performers, the claque sought to influence the spectators en masse, instead.

The nineteenth-century claque turned claquer influence into a fairly well-organized business. Members of a claque reported to a *chef de claque*, who in turn extorted funds from the house management, star performers or composers. Members of the claque were seeded throughout a theatre singly rather than grouped together, so that they appeared to be ordinary spectators. *Claqueurs* and *claqueuses* played specialized roles: there were women who were experts in weeping, men good at belly laughs.

As audiences became more self-disciplined, it was harder for the claque to get an audience to hiss rather than applaud. Of course sometimes, once started, the people couldn't stop. For instance, the Paris claque hired to ruin Verdi's *Don Carlo*, a very long and demanding opera, had to work hard in the first act, but by the opening of the last act the public was booing even before they heard a note. Helped over this barrier by hired hissers, the spectators had lost their inhibitions, along the lines sketched out by Le Bon. But they recovered them quickly. The Goncourt brothers, great chroniclers of Parisian public life, observed that the men leaving the theatre resumed an air of 'staid, dour propriety'. Which is to say that, thanks to the claque, the public could enjoy a temporary release – a safe, short catharsis.

The Street Becomes a Spectator Space

Just as the theatre became a pacified space, passivity began to rule the theatre of the streets. Spectacle was created commercially in a particular way.

In early nineteenth-century Paris, both in its small shops and in the larger *magasins de nouveautés,* when you went to buy a pasta pot you saw a mass of pots of different sizes and shapes in the shop windows, and you haggled over the price once inside. By 1852 the department store did business a different way. The price of every object was fixed; there was no more haggling. Take it or leave it.

Amazon follows a similar rule: you can't negotiate the price online. Again, take it or leave it – the consumer no longer has independence.

Haggling is the classic form of economic theatre. Buyer: 'The weave is uneven; I won't pay what you ask.' Rug merchant: 'You are ruining me, this is my rock-bottom price.' Buyer: 'I'm leaving.' Merchant: 'OK, let's split the difference.' Buyer: 'It's a deal.' The department store deployed theatre in a different way.

The classic big department store sprouted in Paris in 1838 with the founding of Le Bon Marché, a huge emporium selling everything from clothes to food to household furniture. Part of the genius of Aristide Boucicaut, the founder of Le Bon Marché, was to deploy huge plate-glass, steel-framed windows to display his wares to the street – the first use of this staple of modern construction. It was a spectacle behind glass. Le Bon Marché put on display a prosaic cooking pot next to cheap costume jewellery, with a stand holding men's cravats behind them and, as a backcloth to the whole thing, a sensuous textile from one of the new French colonies. These juxtapositions suspended the sense of ordinary reality, endowing utilitarian objects with a kind of glamour by association, aiming to stimulate the buyer's imagination. 'Fantasy sells,' declared Boucicaut, 'utility does not.' That was also Marx's point about commodity fetishism. The department-store window realizes these precepts; it functions as a theatre set.[6]

There was an eerie parallel between shopping as spectacle and the *flânerie* of the nineteenth century, when people strolled through the streets in search of arresting scenes of life – which they observed rather than participated in. They were *flâneurs*, spectators of the city. 'By "modernity",' the poet Charles Baudelaire wrote, 'I mean the ephemeral, the fugitive, the contingent . . .' The street embodies the essence of this modernity with its comings and goings, its stray noises, its accidental encounters. Baudelaire's *flâneur*, a wanderer in the city, is in search of these stimulations. In his *Tableaux Parisiens*, the *flâneur* walks the streets of mid nineteenth-century Paris, often at night, greedily devouring these scenes and their characters, who are mostly needy outcasts. He ventures forth, looks, and then goes home.

> I see only in the mind's eye that camp of shacks, those piles of roughed-out capitals and sections of columns, the weeds, the great blocks turning green in the water of the puddles, and, reflected in the windows, the nameless jumble.[7]

The street as a spectator space paired nicely with the idea of spectacle inside the closed theatre.

The Closed Aesthetic

'The concert is . . . myself,' Franz Liszt declared in 1841. His long flowing locks, his soulful stares into the wings, his wild hand-plays, became not only onstage showbiz but caused audiences to fall silent, hanging on his every note, not wanting to miss anything. Chopin lacked any of Liszt's antics on stage, but still had the same power to comand a hush. Many accounts of his performances emphasize his apparent remoteness on the concert platform, as though he was somewhere else in a space all his own. He barely acknowledged the presence of the audience, bowing only briefly to them, and disappearing as soon as the concert ended.

In instrumental music, there's a particular reason for this hush appearing when it did. Perhaps surprisingly, trained amateurs in the eighteenth century were able to play much of the music professionals played – not masterfully, maybe, but at least well enough to perform for others. Notably for cellists, Mozart's three Prussian quartets have technically demanding and prominent cello parts, which Mozart's patron, King Friedrich Wilhelm II, could pull off himself.[8]

This amateur capacity didn't suddenly disappear. Up to the First World War, many of those who listened to high art music could also play it. However, a parallel track of instrumental music developed which only professionals could play with any satisfaction. The technical divide translated into an emotional inequality: the art is triggering in you feelings you can't express yourself. The price for this revelation is not missing a note, disciplining yourself to keep still and take it in. Technical inadequacy produced the hush of art.

The musician who best drew on this hush was Richard Wagner, who grounded the hush of art architecturally. His theatre in Bayreuth consummated the closed aesthetic which began in the Teatro Olympico.

In 1876 Wagner built a theatre intended only for performances of his own operas. Though the Festspielhaus was his own conception, the design drew on a project the architect Gottfried Semper could not pull off in Munich. The building was completed in time to prèmiere Wagner's four-opera cycle, *The Ring of the Nibelung*. By modern standards, this is a medium-sized hall, holding just under 2,000 spectators. The Opéra Garnier in Paris, completed the same year, was a giant confection of gilt and marble, where people fondled their partners in the dim recesses of tier after tier of boxes. By contrast, the Festspielhaus is mostly plain brick outside; the inside is also relatively severe. The auditorium holds its spectators in a compressed, raked wedge with a row of boxes behind the rake. As in Palladio's theatre, everyone has an equal wide-angle sightline of the stage.

Proponents of stage realism, like Denis Diderot in the eighteenth century, had a scenic imagination rejected in Bayreuth. For Diderot, the front face of the stage should be treated as the 'fourth wall' of a room which has been removed so that the audience can watch the people and the unfolding action within, spying on real life. In Diderot's plays, such as *Le Fils naturel* (*The Bastard Son*) of 1757, the spying is on scenes of everyday life, meant to draw people into the action occurring on stage. To pull this off, the director should eschew off-stage action, and the wings on the side should be treated as doors opening into the room. Architecturally, the proscenium should be well defined both at both the top and the sides so that it functions as a picture frame. Unframed, ambiguous or ill-defined space was to Diderot the enemy of realism. Bayreuth rejected this architecture of realism in two ways.

First, quite directly, through a double proscenium framing the stage, the inner frame being smaller than the outer, so that the illusion is created of looking at events deep inside the space, events that are as far away in space as they are in mythological time. And second, in a more complicated distancing device, Wagner sought to make the music appear to come from nowhere we can see. This trick of mystification he accomplished by covering the orchestra pit with a leather hood, a device which hides most of the musicians from audience view and disperses the sound so that it seems to come from everywhere in the hall. Wagner described this leather hood as creating a *mystischer Abgrund*, a mystical abyss.

Even to me, who doesn't much like Wagner, the architecture of the hidden sound and the shaping of the stage transform what is to my ears dull music into a magical experience. The architecture cannot, of course, explain all of that transporting power. If you happen to love Wagner, *Siegfried* might grab you even if staged in a concert where the singers stand in front of an orchestra and belt it out. But the architecture explains something about the hold of an interior over the imagination.

In his famously total theatre (*Gesamtkunstwerk*), Wagner sought to combine music, blocking, lighting and costuming. The closed stage made possible the *Gesamtkunstwerk*. Its coherence denies the very idea of a street – the many activities happening in a street, the often senseless disorders, the distractions at every new turning. This muddy stimulation is what Baudelaire's *flâneur* craved. In Bayreuth, the audience, silent, seated uncomfortably on bleacher-like seats for hour after hour, concentrates on a marvel that is many-layered but which coheres. The spectator is meant to be transported to a higher realm. But both the *flâneur* and the worshipper at Wagner's shrine are essentially the same. They are spectators – to life, to art.

III. The Sports Stadium and the Opera

Contrast the performing space in which you can hear Wagner's work with nearly any sports stadium. The stadium is today's version of a spectator-empowering space; at a stretch sports stadiums can be taken as the descendants of the old Comédie Française. The scale of Bayreuth, of course, can't compare with sports stadiums like the Emirates in London, which holds tens of thousands of spectators. Once play begins, you might say the fans are as engrossed as the Wagnerian devotees. But were the fans to be transported to Bayreuth, they would shout 'Go, Wotan!!' when the god steals the sacred Ring from Alberich in *Das Rheingold*. Or, if belonging to the Alberich Avengers Football Club, they might rise up at the theft, urging Alberich, 'Watch your back!!' Again, much more is going on in the audience at the Emirates stadium than just watching the game. People are eating and drinking, as in the old Comédie Française. And though the Emirates is located in a desolate part of the city, people are in and out of nearby pubs and shops at all hours, just as the Comédie Française never seemed to close.

Architecturally, the Emirates' seating is a raked amphitheatre, as was Bayreuth and, long before it, the ancient Pnyx in Athens. In the Pnyx the seated body was thought to pacify the spectator, making him receptive and focused on what he saw. The men and women attending the Comédie Française were usually too busy with themselves to attend properly to the stage, but once they did pay attention, they were active, not to say vociferous, 'pointing' and 'settling' the singers or actors. This engagement becomes visceral in the Emirates crowd, and fans jump up from their seats whenever action on the field heats up.

There is a psychological difference between spectators in the opera house and those in the sports stadium, and perhaps this difference is the most fundamental. There are two ways a spectator can identify with performers. I'd wager few in the audience at Bayreuth would identify directly with Wotan – 'I am a god' – but at the Emirates it's as though the fans themselves are playing the game. Wagner did everything he could to create a tangible divide between actor and spectator – the double-framed stage, the *mystischer Abgrund* hood covering the orchestra seating; identification with the stage thus involved a leap of imagination, a convoluted interpretation, whereas in the Emirates physical identification – 'I feel the kick,' or 'I am running' – makes identification more direct.

These contrary forces have shaped more largely the long history of stage and street. Along one path, the theatre has sought to integrate itself into the city by joining actor and spectator. Along another path, art has sought to withdraw from the street, which is enabled by separating actor from spectator. The one path leads to open art, the other to closed.

Missing in this too neat summary are the performer's own feelings. They may suffer from the same divide between open and closed. To understand how this might be, we have to retrace our steps to the Renaissance.

BOOK THREE

The Turning Point

6.

Making a Life On Stage

The performer became free, and vulnerable

The term 'Renaissance' means 'rebirth'. Around 1450, an educated elite began looking backward to the culture of antiquity for models of how they themselves should live. Deep changes in science, economics and warfare meant actual return to the antique past was impossible. The savants knew this full well. 'Renaissance', rather, applied to their passionately held belief that people might follow other models for living than those they had inherited from the immediate past. Idealizing the distant past in order to make a new life in the future is part of what the Shakespeare scholar Stephen Greenblatt calls Renaissance 'self-fashioning'.[1]

Could performing enable self-fashioning? Certainly not by looking back to antiquity. Dancing, flute-playing or acting were arts mainly practised by slaves; male musicians and dancers were often abused as effeminate; and it was thought indecent for women to perform in public at all. Professional performers in the Renaissance sought to self-fashion so that they had more dignity and more freedom. Their struggles foreshadow more modern, more general difficulties of identity.

I. Self-Fashioning through Art

Jaques's Big No to New

Jaques's famous speech in *As You Like it* declaring that 'all the world's a stage' might seem to elevate the status of acting.* But the speech

---

* See the full speech on p. 107.

is in fact a strong condemnation of the very idea of self-fashioning. Nothing in life is new. Just as actors belt out their lines, night after night, so people act out roles, generation after generation, following a script not of their own making. A young man in love, for instance, is

> Sighing like furnace, with a woeful ballad
> Made to his mistress' eyebrow

The young couple imagines that no one can guess at their happiness, no one has felt such passion before – think Romeo and Juliet – but love's sighings and searching looks are to Jaques standard-issue performances. You think your love is special? Forget it, your life isn't going to break the mould.

Jaques's conviction that life is always the same has biblical roots: 'What has been is what will be, and what has been done is what will be done, and there is nothing new under the sun' Ecclesiastes 1:9 states. In the Hellenic world, this conviction was applied to the arts; Aristotle sweepingly declared – he always declared sweepingly – that 'All extraordinary men in philosophy, politics, poetry, and the arts are plainly melancholic,' because their creations prove so often futile; it's all been done before. This too became a commonplace among certain Renaissance writers. Timothy Bright and Robert Burton ascribed the artist's melancholic temper to the fact that all human works are 'vain strivings', as Bright put it.[2]

To set Jaques in a wider cultural frame, the speech might be compared to a Zen Buddhist critique of life as theatre, written in Japan around the same time as Shakespeare's play. The Rinza Zen master Bankei also disliked dramatizing the 'new' in the arts and harboured 'great doubt' about performers who drew attention to themselves at the expense of tradition. But Bankei's response was to shrug: it doesn't matter one way or another. He taught his followers to become indifferent to what's new in order to see life clearly. Jaques lacks Zen. The emotional punch in his great speech comes from its anger at the idea that people imagine they could be different from those before them; 'new' is a fraud. Unlike Bankei, he has not learned the art of indifference.

The religious powers of the European middle ages also lacked Zen: the theatre particularly raised their ire. The twelfth-century theologian John of Salisbury, an apostle of Christian modesty and humility, asserted in his *Policraticus* that the saints 'despise the theatre of this world from the heights of their virtue' because of theatre's seductive, ego-inflaming powers. This loathing again traces back to Western antiquity. The stoic Zeno of Citium rejects theatrical expression as demeaning. Early Christians feared 'all the world's a stage'. Saint Augustine sits in the circus, draws his head down to the scenes of blood and lust performed below. Then faith intervenes, and slowly his head turns away.

John of Salisbury, if I may say so, was talking nonsense, because theatre became in his time ever more important to the practice of religion. Within the Church, priests studied gesture and rhetoric as integral to practising their profession. John of Salisbury's spatial domain was nothing like the plain, unadorned worship of the first Christians which took place inside houses at dinner. The intricate design of stained-glass windows, the elaboration and luxury of vestments, the use of incense, all increased the theatricality of churchly experience. If theologically 'all the world's a stage' meant wickedness, in fact the Church by Shakespeare's time had put theatre in the service of faith.

Jaques's jeremiad has one striking feature which breaks with the Church moralists. Neither God nor the Devil, vice nor virtue, figure in his speech; 'all the world's a stage' is about the body, about the seven ages of the human lifecycle. Each person thinks they are the star of the show, then dies. A new person takes over as the star, performs exactly the same roles, then dies. Life goes on as before.

Which was an odd speech to be delivering in 1603, when *As You Like It* was probably first performed. That was the year in which Queen Elizabeth I died. She had been an icon of self-fashioning, a female monarch who, breaking with custom, refused to marry, lived independently and ruled actively, defying the belief that only men had the will and understanding to govern. Her era had been a rebirth for the country as well; the Tudor reign of terror during the time of Henry VIII ended in hers. Now in 1603, since she died childless, there was to be another reinvention of the regime. But Jaques's speech denies that great changes like this matter much in the way people actually lead their lives.

Pico says Yes to Now

Sourpuss Jaques embodied one strand of Renaissance ideas about making a new life. A more complex strand of self-fashioning came from the Renaissance philosopher Pico della Mirandola, who declared in 1486, in his *Oration on the Dignity of Man*, that 'Man is his own maker,' meaning that you are 'free to be the shaper of your own being, fashion yourself in the form you may prefer'. You make you.[3]

He had in mind transformations of self that differed from those depicted classically in Ovid's *Metamorphoses*. Ovid writes stories in which the gods inflict sudden and unexpected changes on each other or on humans, as when Daphne is magically turned into a bay tree in order to escape being raped by Apollo. Shakespeare drew on Ovid in writing *Romeo and Juliet*. The star-crossed lovers recall Pyramus and Thisbe in the ancient Roman's tale, each lover's blood turned magically into the dark red fruit of the mulberry tree.[4]

Pico's idea of self-fashioning is of change coming not magically from the gods but from people's own actions. The idea made sense particularly in creative work, as for the metalworker Benvenuto Cellini, who embodied Pico's version of self-made metamorphosis. In his *Autobiography*, Cellini tells us he began as a modest goldsmith's apprentice, his ambitions channelled traditionally by the craft: apprentice to journeyman to master. But he jumps ship as a young man, and his own self-fashioning begins when he moves from making jewellery to making sculpture. From being a craftsman he becomes an artist.

The nineteenth-century historian Jacob Burckhardt first sought to generalize about self-fashioning from stories like Cellini's. Burckhardt saw the Renaissance as a profound moment of change in culture, one which inaugurated the idea of the Individual, the individual who self-fashions. In the medieval era, he writes, both sides of human consciousness – the side turned to the world and that turned inward – lay, as it were, beneath a common veil, dreaming or half awake. The veil was woven of faith, childlike prejudices, and illusion . . . It was in Italy that this veil first melted into thin air . . . man becomes a self-aware individual and recognises himself as such.[5]

If he was wrong-headed in likening medieval people to credulous children, Burckhardt leaves out the perils of becoming a self-guiding, self-aware individual – perils to which Cellini was attuned.

Cellini suffered in making his own life. Liberated from the guild's traditions and protections, on his own, Cellini was often afflicted by anxiety for no apparent reason. His art had earned him the right, so he believed, to recognition, it was a source of self-belief, but anxiety suffused his dreams, as he feared that everything could collapse like a house of cards.

Such inner unmooring the sociologist Emile Durkheim would later call *anomie*, meaning that something feels empty inside in people who, no longer bound to the station and beliefs of their parents, have carved out a life for themselves. So too for Pico, self-fashioning is not a smooth unfolding with predictable results. He knew it was like peering into the dark. And in this, he was joined by Shakespeare, outside the frame of *As You Like It*.

In Shakespeare's *King Lear*, sheer self-assertion is portrayed as an invitation to disaster, as when Edmund declares in the first act:

This is the excellent foppery of the world, that, when we are sick in fortune, often the surfeit of our own behaviour, we make guilty of our disasters the sun, the moon, and the stars . . . An admirable evasion of whore-master man, to lay his goatish disposition to the charge of a star.[6]

Pico too feared this surfeit of self because he was a devout Christian. Without God's guidance, people cannot rightly reckon themselves morally. Yet still he believed in 'man as his own maker', in the sense that people *should* try to take responsibility for how they live and

think hard about who they are, rather than rely on blind faith or tradition. They should act as though they were free to choose – that
piece of Zen wisdom Pico would well have understood. It would
become the ethos of modern existentialism. Try to make your own
life as though you are free, even if, like Cellini, it depresses you, or
daunting circumstances stand in your way. Try.

On a less metaphysical level, there's also a difference between
Jaques's 'nothing ever changes' and Pico's 'man is his own maker'.
On his side, Jaques is really talking about rituals – the same roles
played out, generation after generation. On Pico's side, it is a matter
tied more to changing ways of living in cities.

Self-fashioning in the Streets

Shakespeare's London was full of outsiders and migrants who had
swelled its population over the course of the previous three hundred years. As in its contemporary, Venice, or modern New York,
internal population growth was weaker than inflows from outside.
And as in all migrations, many of these outsiders refashioned their
lives as a result of moving. In Renaissance London, self-fashioning
sometimes occurred through a fraud: migrants stole the identities
of established inhabitants of the city, acting as members of guilds to
which they did not belong.

By the early 1400s, guilds in London had adopted distinctive clothing which identified their members in the street – a ceremonial sash,
scarf, or badge indicated you were a carpenter, a baker, a goldsmith.
The costumes brought some order to civic life; if others didn't know
who you were, at least they knew what you did. In the course of the
next three centuries, many of these costumes were counterfeited by
people who had no right to wear them; in a flea market, an
immigrant could buy the badges of a dead guildsman, and in the
city's back-streets it was possible to commission guild scarves from
shady tailors. The counterfeit allowed young people to get credit in
shops, conferred recognition in churches, and answered the night-
watchman's challenge, 'Who goes there? Who are you'? To survive,

the young migrants had to play more than one role. If found out one day as a bogus tailor, the following day a kid would appear as belonging to the ironworkers' guild.

Impostors could get away with multiple impostures partly because London had grown so large that people in guilds no longer knew every member personally. Even so, to carry off these deceits required a certain artfulness. If challenged, or just in the banter of conversation, the street performer had to balance credible references to his craft without being too specific about what he did. It was like script study – the actor learning how to play a part. In London, the migrant faking a part would do best to insert himself in crafts like goldsmithing, which was taking in many new members owing to the expanding scope of metallurgy. The crafts involved in goldsmithing were not fixed and codified. Disguise did not work so well for the old guilds, just because their practices were quite well understood, and thus it was fairly easy to judge if those who wore the robes of the craft in fact knew the work.

A big prize was involved in this street theatre. If the imposture was successful, it could set someone legally free. A feudal master held you in a lifelong grip in the countryside. If you could remain inside the city walls for a year and a day, the master could no longer reclaim you as his legal property. The year-and-a-day rule gave weight to the medieval phrase *Stadtluft macht frei* ('The air of the city sets you free'). Authorities inside the city were not friendly to the migrants, however; it was a matter of keeping your head down. The costumes of belonging and of being gainfully employed helped shield the immigrants from the authorities ever on the lookout for people who stood out.

There's nothing unique to the Renaissance about street imposture. Balzac, for instance, would have instantly recognized the kids' game. His novels set in Paris during the 1820s and 1830s are peopled with those who are making themselves up. A penniless youth from the provinces who acts like a young mogul on the stock exchange or a criminal from the slums bludgeoning his way to power: Balzac conjures up a huge cast of such self-inventing characters. Vautrin, the criminal turning himself into a policeman; Lucien de Rubempré, the provincial klutz remaking himself into an urban elegant – each novel features characters like them donning masks of self in the city. An audience of strangers cannot know whether or not these roles represent who the character really is; they can only judge the performance.

There was one thing, though, about the young imposters in Shakespeare's London, something which sets them in a more favourable light than Balzac's performers on the make. The mask of identity in London was more than a con. The performers developed an attachment to their roles, and in a quite specific way: they wore the ribbons, sashes and badges even after a year-and-a-day, that is, after danger had passed. Performing gave them an identity which they prized, even though it was fake. Like Judas in Caravaggio's painting, they identified with their part.

II. A Life On Stage

People who worked professionally in the performing arts could make a life for themselves in two ways. Their careers could smoothly unfold their inner potential, or their art could develop in fits and starts.

Gradual Unfolding

In 1603, when James I became King of England on Elizabeth I's death, a certain kind of dancing marked the change of regime. Masques were traditional performances mixing dancing, singing, speech and costuming to celebrate the coming of age of a young person in a wealthy household, or a change of master on an estate. These performances were rooted in an old ritual in which masked players made a surprise visit to a family to celebrate a birth or a marriage, presenting gifts of food as well as performing. The revels, which could last all night, concluded only when the revellers decided to unmask. Now the new regime stimulated change in the art, and the masques became the province of professional performers.

Elaborately scripted and staged, they required highly skilled dancers, costumers, decorators and stage designers.

One of those who seized this professional opportunity was the young Inigo Jones. He did not train as any sort of artist; his father was a cloth worker and tradesman. The backstage realm of costuming was an even lower class of labour because it had no guild to protect its workers. Jones may have fallen in status to enter this realm, but once employed he transformed and elevated the status of costuming in the performing of masques. He created extreme, David-Bowie-like extravaganzas, with tall ostrich feathers stuck into men's helmets, rope upon rope of jewels draped across women's bosoms. With hats and helmets, capes and robes, sandals and boots, he created a total architecture of the body.

In 1603, the young Jones made his first trip to Italy in order to take in the creations and ideas that had already germinated there. Jones was able to study the work of Palladio near Venice, and made contact with Giulio Parigi, who combined the career of architect and stage designer in Florence. These experiences Jones brought home and expanded upon, step by step.

The biggest of these steps was to take theatre as a guide to making architecture in the Banqueting Hall of 1619–20, a room used for masques as well as for banquets, its players costumed in his Bowie fantasies. Then he moved from individual buildings to urban design, notably Covent Garden in the 1620s, the first regularly designed square in Britain, with three sides of houses around an open market, capped on the fourth side by a church. Covent Garden was shaped by Jones's experience of theatre in Italy; it looks like a big stage set. But by now Jones had evolved far beyond Parigi, conceiving of Covent Garden as open and porous, rather than the tight and sealed public spaces drawn by the Italian.

There's no evidence to show that Jones had heard of, much less read the *Oration on the Dignity of Man*. But his was one model for 'man as his own maker'. The narrative of his life was of an unfolding, each step expanding his horizons and his creations. That a single artist would develop from within in the course of their lifetime, like a flower opening, was in the Renaissance something new. In traditional guilds, skills evolved over generations, more than within individual lifetimes. It took about eighty years, for instance, for tailors to learn how to cut clothes on the bias. Now, evolution sped up. The unfolding of change could occur in one lifetime, in one artist, as it did in the masque costumes fashioned by Jones. In this, Jones's path is like that of Cellini, and also of Stradivarius the master instrument maker, who evolved steadily into his old age.

Jagged Unfolding

Unfolding development of oneself requires a nurturing framework which allows one's inner capacities to flower. Traditionally, guilds were spaces of male privilege; so on the stage. It was a space which belonged to men. For women to make a life in art required greater struggle, and the path of making that life was more jagged. Still, the Renaissance stage offered women a chance to develop as performers.

Up to the mid sixteenth century, women's roles were played by 'beardless youths and clean-shaven men', as the playwright Goldoni later put it. Women players were thought by the Catholic Church, so the Inquisition proclaimed, to either behave like whores or actually be whores. This remained the prejudice of the Protestant world longer, extending from Shakespeare's time to as late as Congreve's theatre in the eighteenth century, so female roles were still often played *en travesti*.[7]

Musical performance was similarly male-dominated. St Paul had declared, 'let the women keep silence in the churches' (1 Corinthians 14:32), which meant that, until their voices broke, boys sang soprano parts in church music, as well as in madrigals and motets. Among adults, counter-tenors took on high voice parts, inhabiting a different palette of vocal colours from boys singing high or alto; the castrati produced yet another shading of high notes. Neither of these voices could be mistaken for a woman's.

The musical realm open to women lay instrumentally with the virginal and the lute. The virginal is a box-shaped, often beautifully painted instrument, its keyboard running parallel to a set of strings plucked in the middle. Vermeer's painting around 1670 of *A Young Woman Seated at the Virginal* shows a woman in a small domestic space sitting at the instrument (in fact, a more flute-sounding variant of the virginal knows as a muselar). The virginal, whose volume was slight, could only be audible in such a setting, and this sheltered space was thought to suit female 'modesty'.

A new form of art disrupted these gendered distinctions. Commedia dell'arte began in spoofs and skits organized by high-born players. Associations of young aristocrats in Venice – called 'Companies of the Hose' because of the tights worn by these gentlemen – from 1487 on employed jugglers, dancers, musicians and actors of both sexes to provide impromptu amusements, both inside their palaces and outside in the city's squares. The generic name 'commedia dell'arte' was later coined by Carlo Goldoni, probably in 1707, to cover what were by then more than twenty troupes mixing dance, music and skits.

The challenge to gender coupled with the impulse to mock. The performers burlesqued tragedies, mocked politicians, were rich in fart jokes, made graphic comments on cock and bosom size. They refined mockery into a high art as they became more practised players. A company called the Junior Royals thrived on sending up the elite who were their own sponsors.[8]

One aspect of commedia dell'arte touched the self-fashioning of women in the city. Because it had become popular art, with performances sometimes improvised at street corners (the Renaissance version of pop-up art), the Church and the authorities had neither the power nor, really, the interest to prevent these temporary eruptions. Pop-up theatre created an opportunity for women: from the mid sixteenth century, wives began to substitute for ailing husbands, or were used as extras to thicken the sheer numbers of people on the open, urban stage. By the 1570s the revolution of women playing women was under way.

This transformation was notably embodied in the person of Isabella Andreini. She married at sixteen, in 1578, into a troupe of commedia actors who became known as the Gelosi. In succeeding decades, she became a distinguished actress in tragic roles, then morphed into a playwright. A contemporary, Giuseppe Pavoni, was struck by her abilities to mimic other actors and to do so with all sorts of sexual innuendoes. She also improvised crude stage business, as in a skit which made the blasting sound of the ancient god Saturn farting. This freedom to be raunchy was a mark of gender equality; lewd innuendoes and jokes had been spoken before on the commedia stage by women characters, but it was considered all right because the actors were really guys. It was striking that a woman playing a fishwife on stage swore like a real fishwife in the market. The female actor was self-fashioning as a female.

Yet Andreini wanted to be, on stage, more than this. She fought to be allowed to play in tragedies, then fought again to get her own plays mounted on stage. Though she was brash and aggressive in spirit, even so the world often got the better of her. She was frequently depressed, feeling she was not understood. Her path contrasted with that of Inigo Jones, who developed – at least as far as we can judge from his works – in a smooth linear way.

Andreini confronted a deep-rooted prejudice that also afflicted certain male performers. In the ancient Western world, the only arts which could claim elite privilege were verbal – notably poetry; every upper-class child in Athens learned to recite by heart large swathes of Homer. Words destined for the stage had a similar prestige, Sophocles being honoured variously as the treasurer and military commissioner of the city. But dancers and musicians were servants or slaves, their art enjoyed but their persons not counting for much. In the Renaissance, they were more visible presences. This visibility could be a danger.

III. Surviving

Commedia dell'arte players were, as we would now say, 'transgressive'. They mocked the politically powerful, though to avoid the master's lash the mocking had to be indirect and allusive rather than a head-on confrontation. The allusions had to be framed in such a way that if the actor was challenged, they had some room for deniability. In America, African slaves spoke a pidgin patois that the master could only half understand, and so the slaves could avoid challenge. The commedia dell'arte players tried to use non-verbal gestures, costumes and stage blocking to transgress – but this kind of theatre, meant to be allusive, the powerful could often understand only too easily.

The Gelosi depended on aristocratic supporters who could humiliate actors even as prestigious as Andreini. In 1582, for instance, the near-dwarf Duke of Mantua had condemned three actors in the troupe to hang for mocking him by bending over so that they appeared his size on stage. Fortunately, the ropes at their execution broke, and the Duke then forgot about the condemned, though not about the potential power of the stage to insult him. In 1596, he dismissed Andreini from his service in response to one of her pantomimes, which he found too 'pointed': she massaged her crotch while bowing low before his courtiers. The penalty now was not death, but she had to grovel before him as though pleading for her life.[9]

The story of patron humiliation extends in high-art music from Bach to Mozart and onwards into modern times. One consequence of patron power in the later Renaissance was that more popular art sought safety in the streets, performers choosing the alternative of playing to a larger public who paid for individual performances. In theory, this should have been a big step forward, the artist setting him or herself free by selling art on the open market. In theory.

Isabella Andreini died in 1603; her troupe, the Gelosi, lasted only as long as she lived. One of her sons, Giambattista, created a new troupe early in 1604, the Fideli, which continued for nearly half a century. The Fideli, like other commedia troupes, took to the streets to get away from the threats of individual upper-class patrons, and travelled from city to city, sometimes finding empty theatres, sometimes setting up impromptu in vacant open spaces. Itinerant performers were in Italy, France and Britain classed as 'masterless men' – which may seem to mark them positively as free people. In fact, 'masterless men' were treated as unruly vagabonds. Precisely this negative prompted kids migrating to cities to adopt craft costumes, to show that, rather than being 'masterless', they belonged to an institution. No city was particularly keen to provide places for free, 'masterless' artists to perform, so acting troupes in the first part of the sixteenth century usually set up in places that could be abandoned quickly.

Travel diminished their art. Commedia del arte audiences demanded well-worn routines, and itinerant companies could not afford to alienate them by performing strange, demanding or unpleasing pieces. Andreini's successors repeated exactly the same fart-jokes she had thrown off on the spur of the moment, since these were surefire crowd pleasers. Innovations in costuming and masking withered. In the early sixteenth century there were hundreds of variations on the mask worn by Il Dottore, a commedia dell'arte stock character; by the end of the century the mask had become standardized. Most important of all, the players had to be careful not to offend the authorities who didn't want strangers in town, so the political digs were erased and there were no more of Andreini's pointed remarks. The fact that the travelling performers were good offered them no protection; if anything, the more original, the more forceful, the more threatened they felt. 'Liberated' from aristocratic or royal patronage, on the market, they were pushed toward conformity; free agents, they became compromised artists.

Collective Defences

'Here today, there tomorrow,' a member of the Fideli, Domenico Bruni, wrote in 1623; 'forever living in inns . . . I wish my father had consigned me to another trade.' The last being the telling comment. Troupes held together against the humiliations of freedom because they were formed of families. Though actors might dart occasionally from one company to another, the family bond was the performer's core professional unit. Family alone, however, was not strong enough to protect them from the market.

By the end of the sixteenth century, in London and Venice, the two theatre capitals of the Renaissance, performers sought to shield themselves collectively in contrasting ways.

The London shield was an institutional hybrid composed of patrons, families and unrelated artists. The first Baron Hunsdon and his son gradually put together a theatre company in the mid sixteenth century called the Lord Chamberlain's Men, which they protected from having a single patron-humiliator by making it a joint-stock company in which anyone could invest, including those who acted there. In 1576 James Burbage built the first dedicated performance space in London, called simply the Theatre, which he part-owned and passed down to his son, but again with outside investors. Shakespeare's Globe, constructed in 1599, was a largely actor-owned company, the actors investing also in the Lord Chamberlain's Men.

These hybrid arrangements limited liabilities but did little to stabilize the theatres themselves. The Globe, which survived until the Puritans shut it down in 1642, was the exception that proved the rule. Being dependent on selling tickets to a fickle public meant that the fortunes of most places see-sawed just like those of the travelling troupes.[10]

The other shield appeared in Venice, a generation after Shakespeare, and was stronger. This was protection by the state institutionalizing the market. The city ran theatres open to anyone who could afford a ticket, and in that sense state-run theatres were indeed market operations. In Venice, the first of these opened in 1637. But the state-owned theatres could afford to offer performers written contracts and, by 1682, permanent positions, independent of ticket sales. The same was true in Paris of the Comédie Française, opened in 1680. State-supported art could, occasionally, be receptive to creative innovation. Monteverdi's amazing, innovative opera *The Coronation of Poppea* was performed in such a new, state-run theatre – the bureaucrats evidently accepted for the sake of prestige the losses it incurred. The personalized humiliations inflicted by aristocrats shifted to the more impersonal diktats of bureaucrats, with their endless committee meetings, their jealousies and bickerings hidden behind the veil of rational management.

Renaissance self-fashioning in sum looked quite different from the liberated individuality Burckhardt celebrated. In the realm of performance, the 'self' was a twisted domain. The melancholy Jaques thought the idea of self-fashioning was a fraud; 'all the world's a stage' to him meant that people are players, generation after generation after generation, in a tragicomedy not of their own devising. Pico's declaration that 'man is his own maker' implied that you are responsible for your own life, which is a burden for people – too heavy, in his own view, for most to bear. It was true legally that the late medieval and early Renaissance city acknowledged the individual's right to the city: *Stadtluft macht frei*. Imposture of the sort practised by the young kids moving to London in the later Renaissance would earn that freedom after a year-and-a-day, but then they became attached to roles which marked them as belonging to a collective body, the guild, rather than appearing as 'masterless men'.

In the realm of performing, self-development unfolded like a flower, as for Inigo Jones, but it could also become a more difficult, jagged pursuit, as for Isabella Andreini and her heirs. Her path was the one most artists followed then, and follow now. Their self-made careers did not release the voyagers from humiliation or the degradation of their art; rather they travelled from one territory of control to another, from scenes where autocracy ruled to scenes ruled by the capitalist market. Their art could thereby be demeaned. Collective resistance through stock companies did not stabilize their lives. The state bureaucracies which brought artists stability did so at a price: imagination became ruled by committee.

All the World's a Stage

(spoken by the melancholy Jaques)

All the world's a stage,
And all the men and women merely players;
They have their exits and their entrances;
And one man in his time plays many parts,
His acts being seven ages. At first the infant,
Mewling and puking in the nurse's arms;
And then the whining school-boy, with his satchel
And shining morning face, creeping like snail
Unwillingly to school. And then the lover,
Sighing like furnace, with a woeful ballad
Made to his mistress' eyebrow. Then a soldier,
Full of strange oaths, and bearded like the pard,
Jealous in honour, sudden and quick in quarrel,
Seeking the bubble reputation
Even in the cannon's mouth. And then the justice,
In fair round belly with good capon lin'd,
With eyes severe and beard of formal cut,
Full of wise saws and modern instances;
And so he plays his part. The sixth age shifts
Into the lean and slipper'd pantaloon,
With spectacles on nose and pouch on side;
His youthful hose, well sav'd, a world too wide
For his shrunk shank; and his big manly voice,
Turning again toward childish treble, pipes
And whistles in his sound. Last scene of all,
That ends this strange eventful history,
Is second childishness and mere oblivion;
Sans teeth, sans eyes, sans taste, sans everything.

As You Like It – Act II, Scene 7

7

A Change of Clothes

Self-fashioning led to new ways of appearing

I. Tragic Clothing

Had Sebastiano Serlio lived in Venice during the early years of the Renaissance, he would have witnessed a tragic scene acted out on the streets in the way people dressed. Their apparel became inseparable from the great tragedy in their lives, the arrival of the plague. Commedia dell'arte would mock this apparel of woe, just as it mocked power.

The Plague

By the fifteenth century, Venice had become the greatest global city in Europe. Thanks in large part to its watery location, it connected Europe to the Far East, from which came spices and cloth; the city financed the slave trade in Africa; it funnelled food, crafts and skilled workers from the Mediterranean into Northern Europe. Global money meant people came to the city to trade, and by 1507 Venice was the only city in Europe where foreigners outnumbered natives. As a result, it also imported diseases from all over – particularly the plague, an urban disease seen in all places where people lived tightly packed together, and made worse in Venice by the foul state of its canals and its resultant immense population of rats.[1]

Rather than rat-borne, the plague was at that time thought to be air-borne, transmitted by people breathing on others. Just as during the modern Covid pandemic, the remedy was largely isolation, with people fleeing cities as soon as signs of plague appeared. Doctors, however, were not supposed to leave, and they had close physical contact with the patients who, for reasons yet unknown, could infect them.

The Doctor's Mask and Gown

Doctors protected themselves largely by wearing masks and full-body gowns, as health workers do today, but those masks were quite different from ours. Theirs consisted of a full-face mask shaped like a bird's head, with an immense beak, and the doctor breathed through the beak's nostrils. Doctors' masks were made of two materials, leather for ordinary consultations, and papier mâché when treating air-borne diseases; the latter could be discarded after each use. The papier mâché mask originated in research into air-borne diseases by the Persian physician Ibn Sina, commonly known in the West as Avicenna. The breath of a plague sufferer, Ibn Sina thought, interacted with putrid vapours in the doctor's own body. The beak-like mask lessened the chances of air getting into the lungs.

The doctor's gown aimed at a similar sort of protection. It draped all the way down to the feet – indeed swept the ground in folds – so that no vapours could get within. The gown was made of thick cloth; it was not meant to breathe and was therefore hot and sweaty in the summer. It was washed frequently, but, still, the doctor smelled.

In themselves, these were not at all complicated costumes, just largely useless ones. Mask and gown acquired a more complex character when the doctors wearing them were Jewish. Expelled from Spain in 1492, Jews and Muslims flooded into Venice, the Jews in greater numbers and causing greater alarm. In 1516, the authorities consigned Jews to an island within the city which formerly housed metalworks. Jews were imprisoned in this ghetto at night, and no light was permitted to shine from the windows; it was as though the Jewish community literally disappeared in the dark. Yet during the day the city needed its Jews, particularly if they were doctors.

They brought Islamic science from Spain to Venice. Before the expulsion of 1492, Jewish and Muslim doctors had mingled. Jewish doctors learned from their Islamic colleagues, for instance, the close examination of the eyeball. Ibn Sina had discovered the elemental structures of cataracts and devised the first surgical treatments for them, at a time when the received Western treatment was to apply cold compresses to the forehead. If you really wanted to cure your sight, you had better go to the Jews.

But this meant close contact with a Jewish body – a Jewish doctor examining Christian eyeballs close up. In Christendom the bodies of Jews were considered disgusting, their blood impure, their breath full of foul odours. This prejudice inflected the meaning given to a doctor's mask; during an outbreak of plague, the mask's beak served not so much to protect the doctor from disease as to protect patients from the contamination that was thought to emanate from the alien breath. The papier mâché mask had to be disposed of by the Jewish doctor in the presence of a Christian man, to be sure that the Jew had thrown away his mask, rather than saving money by re-using it. In ordinary medical practice, the mask served the same prophylactic purpose. Impurity and purity have to be taken together to make sense of most cultural practices. In Venice, the masks worn by Jewish doctors mediated between the pure and the impure.[2]

The Jewish doctor's costume figured in the most charged of all occasions, the last moments before death. At this time, deaths were public occasions, a 'choreographed ritual', as the historian Philippe Ariès writes. Family, friends and servants crowd into a room, knowing where to stand, what to say, when to weep and when not. A priest has been called to administer the last rites, and kneels at the side of a dying woman's bed, but does not touch her, nor do family members turn her body or clean it. These physical comforts are delivered by household servants.[3]

Looming behind the kneeling priest is a bird-man wearing leather gloves. He feels her heart, opens her mouth, smells her urine. This alien bird-man has taken charge of the old woman's body in the actual passage from life to death. The grieving family, friends and the priest do not understand what he is doing, because it is an alien, an un-Christian, science. The moment she is gone, however, the bird-man doctor is expelled from the room, so that the family can grieve, guided by the priest.

II. A Brief but Important Note on Masks

Like toys, masks such as the Jewish doctor's are potent objects. The Greek word for mask, *prosopon*, is also the word for face. Machiavelli's distinction between mask and face was at the origins of our culture, ambiguous in some ways, in others clear-cut. In the ancient theatre, wearing a mask separated actor from spectator; the spectator was never masked. Spectators were thus directly exposed to the power of those who wore masks, whether in caves or on stage. In *Oedipus Rex*, to emphasize the King's self-blinding, an actor would don a mask with enlarged eye-holes. When the actor entered wearing his blind mask, before he had spoken a word, audiences panicked, so it was said, the masks having a terrible power themselves to blind those who looked at them.

Ancient masks were made of stiffened linen, leather and cork, and designed so that the mouth opening was small. It used to be thought that this small hole permitted the mask to function as a megaphone; modern mask research leans to the view that the mask instead strengthens the 'head voice' (the sound an actor or singer makes at the top of the windpipe), which increases the intensity but not the volume of sound.

Originally, Greek drama employed only two masks, one for comedy, the other for tragedy: the mask of comedy with its satyr's mouthing leering up in pleasure, and the mouth of the mask of tragedy drooping in woe. All the characters in the Greek chorus were masked in order to separate them from spectators, but the masks, more neutral in expression, were undifferentiated, to mark out their collective personae as commentators. By the time of Aeschylus, actors' masks became more varied in form tied to particular roles. By wearing different masks during a performance, two or three actors could create many characters on stage. And because the

Greek stage permitted only men to act, masks transformed men into women; the mask had a gendering power.

We can expand this outside the European context. Among the Senufo people in the Ivory Coast, half-animal half-human face masks carved out of wood mark both male initiation rites and male deaths. When worn at a death, they signal that the wearer is both putrid and a healer. With the more abstract painted wood and fibre masks donned at funerals among the Dogon in Mali, the mask itself has the power to heal or to kill, echoing the potency of Greek masks. In the Noh theatre of Japan – an art form a thousand years younger than the Greek stage – fans open or shut, pointing or held close to the chest, expressed a particular character's feelings, whereas the masks were simply character types: demons, young girls or boys, old men. The Noh fan had the same emotional power as the Greek mask, which is perhaps hard for Westerners to feel when attending a Noh play today; the slightest flick of a fan might be so insulting that another character becomes bent on murder.

The anthropologist David Napier finds the potent power of masks 'curious', since behind the physically 'unchanging visage' a character usually evolves, swinging from rage to sorrow or fear to courage in the course of an evening. The shifts would register graphically on a naked face, but not on a static mask; at most, the masks would identify what sort of person a character was, rather than his or her specific evolution during the course of the action.[4]

But that is the point about some masks, even though they might not arouse specific feelings of terror, for instance, like the ancient mask worn by the blind Oedipus. They can be arousing in another way. Who is behind the mask? Who is the 'real' person covered up? Just as in George Balanchine's ballets, the blank stage backcloths stimulate the spectator's imagination. But Napier is pointing to a change which occurred in the Renaissance of the potency of masks, and equally of make-up and costumes. The ethos of 'man as his own maker' changed the meaning, on stage, of bodily appearance.

III. Comic Clothing

Dottore's Mask

The Jewish doctor's mask morphed into a stage prop in commedia dell'arte plays of the late 1530s and 1540s, thereby transforming the character of the man who wore it from a terrifying personage into a whimsical guy full of fun.

The figure of Dottore in the plays hailed from Bologna rather than Venice, and was an academic rather than a medical doctor, since Bologna was the principal seat of learning in Italy at the time. Still, the gown Dottore wore, black and full length, was the same colour as the Jewish doctor's. Dottore sometimes wore gloves as well. The Jewish doctor sported a yellow rosette; all Jews in Venice could be identified at sight because they were obliged to wear something yellow. A few images of Dottore portray him as festooned with badges, ribbons and medals, but these were gaudy and came across as just more mockery of his puffed-up importance.

Dottore wore a mask whose nose is a beak, just like the Jewish doctor's mask, but the beak was now extended to be as long as the rest of the mask is tall. Pantaleone, the character with whom Dottore was paired on stage, also had an extended nose. Pantaleone's mask had a pointed beard which was sometimes as long as his nose, and a huge moustache, made by pasting hair onto a strip of leather. The pair were not identical, because Pantaleone typically dressed in red and black vest and hose, which set him apart from Dottore with his long gown. But their shared noses differ from the masks of the Zanni, who were crazy servants, by being hooked rather than jutting straight out – the hooked nose even then being taken to be a typically Jewish trait.

The stage mask did further transforming work on the Jewish doctor. Whereas Pantaleone's mask covered the full face, Dottore's was a half-mask, exposing the cheeks as well as the lips. The cheeks are rouged, to show that Dottore drinks, a lot. The mask thus explains why Dottore speaks in an incomprehensible way. Dottore's knowledge, like the Jewish doctor's, is abstruse, expressed in smatterings of foreign languages unintelligible to other characters on stage. But in commedia dell'arte this knowledge is ridiculed rather than feared. In some commedia dell'arte scripts, Dottore performs seemingly magical cures of the sick, but even then, death is something the plays usually joke about.

Dottore in his mask thus broke with the real-life scenes in which the Jewish doctor – gloved, masked, gowned, a bird-man standing behind the kneeling priest – appeared as an emissary from the Grim Reaper. The commedia dell'arte players improvised lines, riffing on Dottore and Pantaleone. Beneath their masks they were not imprisoned in their symbolism, as was the Jewish doctor. The theatrical figure had detached from the ritualized figure, and the tragic scene had morphed into a comic scene, enabled in part by how people dressed.

A Christian Parallel

This transformation is not just a Jewish story. Had we time-travelled a generation earlier we could have witnessed it on the London stage.

If in 1491 you attended a performance of *The Play of the Sacrament*, by John Croxton, performed by a touring company of actors crisscrossing the English countryside, you might well have been shocked. The plot involves Jewish villains who steal the Host from a church; the bread is then rescued by a bishop. No surprise there. The shock is that a sacred object, the wafer taken in communion, has become a stage prop.

Up to the sixth century, bread and wine were shared in the communal meal of the Eucharist, recalling the fellowship of the first Christians. These appear to have been easy, informal occasions, with prayers and blessings offered spontaneously during the course of the meal. In the sixth century the formal rite of the Latin Mass began to replace the sacred supper party. In pre-medieval celebrations of the

Mass, both bread and wine came from offerings brought to church by the congregants themselves. After four hundred years, by the tenth century, with the growth of monasteries, these offerings were replaced by special bread from priestly hands. The people's bread had been confected from rye and spelt; the priest's bread consisted of unleavened white wafers made purely of wheat. Only this special bread, the 'oble', could be transformed into Christ's body during the Mass.

As with bread, so with wine. The chalice of wine in the pre-medieval era passed from the lips of congregant to congregant; by the tenth century the wine was imbibed through a straw; in the twelfth century, frequently only the priest drank the wine, on behalf of the congregants.

This Christianized rite saturated the meaning of bread in a way that contrasts with the matzo used in Jewish ritual. The unleavened matzo, eaten annually at Passover, recalls the story of Jews eating on the run as they fled persecution in Egypt, lacking the time and the ovens to bake raised bread. The matzo is a mnemonic symbol; it awakens that memory, but, crucially, matzo has no magical properties in itself, whereas the Christian wafer is a 'real presence' in the Mass – the bread and wine of the Eucharist are actually the flesh and blood of Christ. The spell cast by the Mass turns consuming these food staples into the living experience of God's body. Thus was the doctrine of 'transubstantiation' codified by the Catholic Church in 1215.

As the schism between people and religious performer widened, the rite itself became more of a spectacle. Inside the church, the priest used special gestures and tones of voice to act out Christ's last days. The elevation of the Host was performed with raised arms so that the event would register with those who might not hear or understand the priest's words.

It thus might be said that using an oble as a stage prop merely carried religious spectacle to an extreme, rather than constituted a break. But a real separation occurred, because the stage prop, unlike the parading of the Host, no longer aroused piety. As the historian

Andrew Soper remarks, 'the wafer as stage prop aims mostly to characterize the actors – the savagery of the Jews, the cleverness of the Bishop. Unlike medieval mystery plays, the *Play of the Sacrament* does not incite the audience to pray.'[5]

This historical shift, in which bread and wine become just stage props, or masks no longer give meaning to the deathbed, seemed to Max Weber what he grandly called, in *The Sociology of Religion*, the 'disenchantment of the world'. Traditional societies, he said, inhabited an 'enchanted garden', due to magical and mythological thinking, embodied in the magical powers of objects like masks. In his view, as for the poet Coleridge, modernity, with its scientific rationality and its cold-hearted materialism, did the disenchanting.[6]

It would have been news to Dante that he lived in an 'enchanted garden', but Weber's sights were set on a certain strand of Protestantism. Church reformers such as Wycliffe did doubt the magical powers of a piece of bread. Calvin's followers sought to eliminate from the ritual of the shared supper any belief in the physical presence of the divinity at the table. A line can be traced in Protestantism from this refusal of the physical, bodily presence of the divine to the repudiation, in Quakerism, of ritual itself. You do not need to sip a glass of wine representing God's blood to believe in God.

Venetians did not stop seeing Jewish doctors because they had laughed at Dottore on stage. Nor did Christians in London stop taking communion. Culture does not work like a zero-sum game in which you have to diminish one thing in order to increase another, more comedy at the expense of less tragedy, more science at the expense of less religion. Rather, the culture added to its expressive repertoire in reformatting these 'enchanted' objects into stage props.

One consequence of this expanded repertoire was political. At the debut of modern society, the manipulation of bodily appearances became a tool of power.

8.

The Art of Charisma

Performing domination

The pages which follow may seem an odd story, that of a king who danced in order to rule. Louis XIV danced amazingly well, and his prowess helped legitimate his aura as a charismatic figure. His dancing entailed a new kind of costuming, hair-styling and make-up, all meant to reinforce the appearance of 'majesty'. This is not in fact such an unusual story. The charisma of the modern ruler also relies on creating a commanding personal appearance. Louis exemplifies how political performance presence could be taken to an extreme.

I. A King Dances

The Ballet de la nuit

In the late winter of 1653, the First Minister of France, Cardinal Mazarin, assembled for the court a thirteen-hour ballet. The *Ballet de la nuit* started at dusk and ended at dawn, and its star performer was the fifteen-year-old king Louis XIV. The storyline resembled an off–on switch: during most of the night the dances dramatized chaos, nightmares and disorder; then, at the break of dawn Louis suddenly appeared arrayed in rubies and pearls and diamonds – a glittering young king banishing darkness and misrule.

The First Minister was not in search of amusement. He meant to send a message to his aristocratic audience. During the Fronde, a period of upheaval in France, the boy Louis, waiting to become king, had been driven from Paris when aristocrats rebelled against the increasing iron grip of the centralized state. These same noble rebels now, in 1653, watched hour after hour in a vast, smoky chamber dimly lit by candles as demons and furies represented their own brief era of revolt. When sunlight broke through the room's windows, order returned symbolically in the sudden appearance of the dancing king. Louis was cast as Apollo, the guardian of light. Mazarin summoned the old god to symbolize a new configuration of power: a Sun King around whom planets of aristocracy revolved.

The *Ballet de la nuit* played eight times in one month. It was literally a command performance. The doors of the court chamber in which it was performed were closed each evening and guest lists strictly checked. By the eighth performance, though, they came voluntarily. This exclusive audience was exhausted by a decade of near civil war. Tired of violent disruption, the aristocrats wanted a return to order. They found something reassuring about the royal display of physical prowess, repeated night after night.

To make this display work, Louis had to dance unusually, indeed supremely, well. At the end, the young king had to dominate the stage as soloist for more than an hour. If the boy stumbled or tired, the message would implode and the aristocrats' attention wander. Like his predecessor Louis XIII, the young Louis XIV had spent more hours of each day learning to dance than reading books, and, to judge by the result, he took to the discipline brilliantly.

Choreographers from the early Renaissance onwards worked with thick 'plot-books' drawn from classical mythology to create the stories for their dances. But our ancestors suffered from something like narrative fatigue. The doings of gods and goddesses had become such commonplaces by the seventeenth century that they did not provoke. Now, the performing body had to do the work of arousal.

Louis danced in public from 1653 to the early 1670s. During this period, writes the modern historian Philippe Beaussant, the evenings of dance shift 'from the sovereign mingling with his subjects, and among and with them, to the sovereign as director of a choreography centred on himself alone'. Or, in Louis's own famous words, the art symbolized his boast that 'L'état, c'est moi' ('I am the state').[1]

This form of self-fashioning on stage may seem to share little with artists like Isabella Andreini who were struggling to survive. At the very pinnacle of power, though, the performer had to draw on a kindred repertoire of non-verbal expression.

Bodily Charisma

The word 'charisma' literally means a 'gift of grace', and in religious terms the gift comes from God, who endows the charismatic figure with something of his holy power. Whereas in Louis's case, charisma became a physical presence created by art.

The Christian Middle Ages drew a distinction between a king's two bodies: the body of flesh, confined to the cycle of life and death, and the body of blood, passing from generation to generation. It was this bloodline body that gave legitimacy to the succession of kings. By Louis's time, though, the claims of authority established by bloodlines were beginning to be challenged, as in the Fronde. The regime was not so naive as to believe that the verbal promise of 'peace in our time' would be convincing just because the king uttered it. The king had to make his right to rule felt viscerally.

Before and into Louis XIV's time, bodily charisma was exemplified by such activities as 'the king's touch', the supposed power of a king to cure scrofula or leprosy by laying his hands on the head of the sufferer. (The magic of touching a star's body happens today in crowd surfing during a rock concert, the performer held aloft by the mass of raised arms of the fans.) Louis continued the tradition of laying on hands in audiences with the ill, yet his dancing established another code of touching. He did not partner, grasping the hands of the women dancers moving on the spatial perimeter around him. His solo dancing meant to make him stand out by touching no one else.

Charismatic Space

Louis took control of the stage space by colonizing its centre and pushing lesser figures to the back and sides. We now take for granted the
spatial configuration of power which puts a dominant figure front and
centre – whether on stage or on screen, the most important space is in
the middle. The visual organization of dominance was not always
thus; it was a product of a historical change in the Renaissance.

The sixteenth-century stage floor was strictly ordered into
imaginary squares and diagonals, foregrounds and backgrounds,
reflecting Renaissance neo-Platonic beliefs about the rule of geometry and perspective. Geometry disciplined the dancer because he
or she had to learn to place the feet precisely, in order to follow
straight lines or move around the circle's perimeter. The precursor
to the *Ballet de la nuit* in this was the *Ballet comique de la Reine*, a celebration of the queen's marriage in 1581, choreographed by
Beaujoyeulx. He derived from the Renaissance geometry on the
stage floor a trajectory of 'supreme power' – a route reserved for
the star's path on entry to or exit from the centre. Dancing the route
correlated with a certain kind of gesture. In the *entrée grave*, for
instance, a man announced his presence by gradually, steadily
unfolding his arms, walking forward into the centre with deliberate
steps, accompanied by stately music.

The *Ballet comique de la Reine* nonetheless mixed star dancing with
ordinary social dancing, and with acrobatic displays and buffoonery.
At Louis's debut seventy years later, the clowns were expunged, as
were the country dances; the aristocratic dancers were compressed
at the edges, the centre left empty for the king to dance in. No one
should occupy his space, and so distract from his appearance.

Charismatic Scenery

The same principle of purging space so that the king could stand
out framed the architecture of the king's palaces as at the Palace of

Versailles. In 1674, for instance, he gave an entertainment making use of Versailles's grand canal to celebrate the conquest of the Franche-Comté region; 20,000 candles illuminated the lightly rippling water on which Louis appeared in a gondola, dancing in place.

The iconography of the 'ship of state' was as obvious and stale as the mythology of the Sun King. So the creators of this dance framed the scene to focus attention on the king alone. Along the huge waterway, the carefully hooded candlelights reflected Louis's jewels; the very darkness into which the spectators themselves were plunged contrasted to this Sun King now appearing in the dead of night, in a gondola towed by hidden ropes so that no gondolier shared the boat with the king.

Performing Hierarchy

Louis XIV was tall, and this natural fact was transformed on stage into a sign of hierarchy. Costumiers underlined his height to emphasize that he stood, literally, above others. They stuck in his hair the tallest ostrich feathers they could find, so that when the towering king nodded towards other dancers, his feathers covered his partners like a priest's benison.

His costuming reinforced the gesture of the *reverence*, an acknowledgement of other dancers while maintaining the separateness and distance of the star. It deployed lesser or greater bows from the waist, depending on whether the person greeted was another important character or just part of the mass of dancers. The *reverence* combined recognition and inequality. Other mimed gestures first developed in this period sought for the same combination, as when arms stretched out in making an appeal – outstretched more fully among the minor characters than the principal dancer, who had to make only the slightest movement to arrest the attention of others.

Gestures like the *reverence* also created the same hierarchies off stage. The Duke of St Simon noted, for example, that 'to ladies [Louis] took his hat right off, raising it more or less high; to titled people, he half raised it, holding the hat in the air or level with his ear for a more or less marked instant or two; to gentlemen, he was pleased [just] to touch his hat. He doffed it, as he did for ladies, to princes of the blood.'[2] The king bowed to his subjects, he recognized them, he was polite, but he condescended from a height; courtesy was his to give, and he expected deference from those to whom he bowed. Even if old and crippled, they were meant always to bow as low as possible.

Almost all of the dances of earlier times could be performed by anyone who put their mind to it. Certainly there were better or poorer performers, but the quality of the performance didn't depend on which class you came from. Whoever you were, you could learn how to dance a passable gigue. By the king's time, graceful physical movements had become coded more unequally.

For instance, the turn-out of the feet. Dancing treatises define 'noble' turn-out of feet from the hips as forty-five degrees (whereas modern ballet training aspires to a more extreme turn-out of eighty to ninety degrees). The dancing masters contrasted nobility of turn-out to ordinary folk dances in which little turn-out occurred, so 'base' characters like peasants or shepherds were depicted on stage with their feet turned awkwardly inward.

In Louis's middle years, the choreographer Beauchamp elaborated the distinction between noble dancing and people's dance. He sorted out the noble dance steps into the five basic positions of modern ballet, and developed a dance notation (the Beauchamp-Feuillet system) that allows choreography to be passed on from generation to generation. Noble turn-out was not a normal stance, and much work with a mirror and criticism from a master was – and is – necessary to master it.

We know Louis practised in front of mirrors as part of the rigorous lessons he took aged twelve to fourteen. He was capable of stern self-critique, took criticism more seriously than praise, and was proud of what he could achieve on the dance floor. But the real mark of class was to hide this hard work, making it all appear a matter of effortless mastery.

In Britain, effortless mastery is stamped into the class system as an Etonian ideal, boys taught to behave as though they don't sweat or strain, but ace their exams casually. Eton is rooted in the Renaissance. The Renaissance writer Castiglione had, in *The Book of the Courtier*, defined effortless mastery as *sprezzatura*: an assured lightness of bearing which distinguishes aristocrats from merchants, whose movements were, so Castiglione claimed, clumsily assertive, due to the rude circumstances of making money. Castiglione idealized *sprezzatura* as an entire way of life. As in the ballroom, so on the battlefield, the aristocrat evinced 'grace' under fire.

Of course few aristocrats measured up to Castiglione's ideal courtier, and most Eton boys are gifted only with privilege. Louis was the real thing, and so was exceptional. Certainly few if any other rulers could or would follow his example by attempting to dance their way into power. But many would understand the need to create a charismatic aura for themselves which is non-verbal – a matter of how they move, their tone of voice, their clothes, how artfully they are made up for the cameras. Carefully crafted, coherent policy isn't going to produce a halo around them.

In the famous scene in *The Brothers Karamazov* in which Dostoevsky's Grand Inquisitor confronts Christ, whom he has put in prison, the Inquisitor says that people 'hunger for someone in whom to put their faith'. It doesn't matter what the leader does; as long as he does it with conviction, the public will follow. This view can be traced back to the seventeenth century, to Étienne de La Boétie's *Discourse on Voluntary Servitude*, the first essay on mass society, which argues that the desire to believe and submit 'dominates the passions'. Those who have subscribed to the classic doctrine of voluntary servitude think that submission is more important than the particular characteristics of a charismatic figure: the hunger is to believe and to obey rules.

Louis's charisma argues the opposite case – that the personal appearance of the ruler matters, and that this can be constructed both physically and artistically. The result was, in the words of the modern dance historian Jennifer Homans, 'veneration of the King's body; art sharpened autocracy.'[3]

II. Another Brief but Important Note about Puppets

We are not quite done with effortless grace. Any ruler needs to display self-confidence and assuredness on stage. 'It's really hard for me,' or 'I don't know,' are fatal words for a politician to speak. But these words characterize a human being, a flesh-and-blood, thinking and feeling human being. By contrast, there are creatures who can show effortless grace, whose movement can be absolutely, reliably programmed. They are puppets.

Readers will recall that, in the Cave, Plato's jailers put on a puppet show for their prisoners. Puppets play a role also in discussions of charisma. To Heinrich von Kleist, writing in a celebrated essay in 1801, they seemed endowed with the 'gift of grace'. These are puppets of a certain sort. Hand puppets like the Kukla puppet used by my aunt are limited by the hand strength and fatigue of their human puppeteer. The marionette has no such limits. As we have seen, it can be made to suddenly fly through the air, and its movements are more flexible than those of the human body. These puppets, Kleist declares, 'have the advantage of being for all practical purposes weightless'.[4]

Kleist thought that any device that works like a puppet is superior, not inferior, to human beings. The puppet theatre of Kleist's time had evolved far beyond the Punch and Judy shows put on at country fairs for children. The eighteenth-century doll was technologically much more advanced. Jacques de Vaucanson, for instance, perfected mechanical dolls that could make minute gestures with their hands and feet – as in his Flute Player, which seemed actually to play the flute with its fingers, and opera tunes with expression. In fact there was a wind-up device inside that did the playing, with a midget puppeteer pulling strings attached to the mechanical fingers. But the public wanted to believe, it wanted to submit to the illusion, to enter the Cave.

Diderot, we recall – don't we? – believed that the professional actor had to separate him or herself from investing too much emotion in a role, in order to perform it over and over. Kleist raises Diderot: a puppet is an even more reliable actor than a flesh-and-blood pro. Kleist explains this human frailty as a matter of self-consciousness. He describes a beautiful young dancer who becomes increasingly ungraceful the more he studies himself in the mirror, too self-conscious about what he is doing. 'A year later, nothing remained of the grace which had given pleasure to all who looked at him.' Whereas mechanical beings like puppets don't suffer from stage fright or nerves; un-selfconscious, they are not afflicted by 'trembling'.

Power enters Kleist's argument in the form of a Baltic bear. This imaginary creature is a slight fly in the writerly ointment, because the bear is a flesh and blood creature. But it shares with the marionette a lack of self-consciousness. Trained to fence, it also does not 'tremble' when facing a human opponent and is not fooled by the human fencer's feints and jabs; indifferent to the acting of the other, the fencing Baltic bear invariably and accurately thrusts home. It is like the puppet in having no independent being, or in Kleist's words 'no soul'. Because there is no 'trembling', it embodies the Eton ideal of effortless ease. And because neither puppet nor bear suffer from self-consciousness, they are full of grace as Kleist understands it, as a purity of gesture, of expression: 'Grace appears most purely in that human form which either has no consciousness or an infinite consciousness. That is, in the puppet or in the god.'[5]

Kleist's parable could thus be read as being about the mechanization of charisma. Flute players, flying marionettes, Baltic bears are more commanding presences than human beings. But this conclusion seems to me to get charisma wrong.

III. The Paradox of Presence

The Halo of Uncertainty

Perhaps stage presence is the aspect of theatre most difficult to describe. But it is real for all that. We feel the moment an actor walks on stage a vivid sense of their presence, we hang on their every word, even if we know the words. 'To be or not to be . . .' sounds just as though they'd thought of it for the first time. Similarly, the amazing thing about Charles's rendition of 'all the world's a stage' was that we were spellbound by him, wondering what he would say next, his slight pauses seeming as though he were grasping for a thought (even though I'd heard him rehearse these pauses dozens of times when he staged the play near Washington Square). In a musical performance 'presence' has this same character. Even with master technicians such as the pianist Vladimir Horowitz, you hang on every assured, perfect note: what comes next?

Kleist's bear is a master technician, but it has no stage presence of this sort. The bear's mechanically perfect gestures happen again, and again, and again, identical each time. After the first few feints you are no longer filled with wonder that the bear fences perfectly. So too with Vaucanson's mechanical Flute Player: people watched it go through the motions, at first amazed, then bored. We might observe in passing that this is what's wrong about Etonian 'effortless mastery' or Renaissance *sprezzatura*. The performances impress only once or twice; after that, they seem rather empty, self-satisfied displays . . .

There are ways to explain, in music, how this vivid sense of 'What next?' can be created. It is not a gift of the gods. We can work, for instance, on air-pauses, so that the player learns to break metronomic regularity, instead letting the phrases 'breathe' with slight irregularities of pulse. Or we can alter the dynamics of a phrase each time it repeats; Wagner's leitmotifs, for instance, should never sound exactly the same – quite a demanding thing to pull off in operas where they may appear dozens of times. The choreographer Frederick Ashton once said to his dancers, 'You've practised that turn to death, but on stage you will perform it like you are surprised by doing it.'[6]

Louis XIV had just this halo of uncertainty around his dancing. Yes, the leaps, battements and twirls seemed were superbly done – but could he pull it off, time after time? That question hovered in the background as the eight performances of the *Ballet de la nuit* unfolded. This question differs from the uncertainty Machiavelli believed his Prince should cultivate, the people asking what's in his mind, is he feeling vengeful or in a kindly mood? That's a question about mood rather than mastery.

Liveness in a performance comes from the halo of uncertainty. Equally, the halo of uncertainty is part of the reason that people are drawn to live performances. Is the song, the score, the soliloquy going to sound fresh? Uncertainty frames the moment of truth in live performances.

The Inevitable Withering of Charisma

In his writings about charisma, Max Weber argued that, in politics and religion, most charismatic figures are disrupters of the state or of established religion. They too are haloed by uncertainty, nobody knowing what they will do or say next. The essence of the charismatic figure is that they are unpredictable. Of course, that wasn't true for Louis XIV, since the point of his charismatic performances was to restore order in the state. But the sociologist and the king are on the same page about the durability of charisma. For both, the halo fades. In Weber's account, a charismatic figure becomes gradually domesticated, their message flattened into rules and procedures, a process Weber grandly calls 'the routinization of charisma'. Jesus serves as Weber's great example, a divine challenger and disrupter whose message became codified for an established Church. The princes of the Church will convert the story of Christ into doctrines. Jesus will no longer be a disruptive personal presence.

Louis XIV's charisma faded for a different reason. By the age of forty he had to invite others to dance his old roles. The choreography and costuming, the stage setting, the mythical tales, remained in 1680 just what they were in 1653; but now, with surrogates dancing his roles, the power of the stage no longer magnified his own person. By the 1690s Louis was a bewildered king, not understanding that the art which had once served his majesty no longer seduced. His courtiers began to chafe again, but this time emotional disengagement, disinterest and boredom took the place of revolt. By 1700, they fled Versailles for Paris whenever they could.

The Legacy

In sum, three elements of Renaissance performance have come to us. First, tradition and ritual no longer seemed to give people a sense of themselves; they had to generate their own life narrative. It was, and remains, a difficult if not impossible task.

Second, the effort to make a life applied to all people but took a particular form among those who made a living on stage. In ancient times, performing as a profession had been of low status, and, even as the Renaissance unfolded, the professional actor, dancer, singer or instrumentalist was too often treated as a servant whose purpose in life was to entertain the elite. Now, though, performers began to push back; they wanted to be treated with dignity, precisely because they were artists. But there was a puzzle contained in being *performing* artists. The actor impersonated others, the musician played scores not of their own making, and these scores were increasingly detailed; the dancer followed directions laid down by a choreographer, and these too were ever more complex. How could you shape yourself if you were enacting art not of your own making? The performer served a new master: the creator.

Finally, changes in the realm of appearances contributed to this personal dilemma. On the streets of London, there was no truth in appearance, as evinced by the clothing certain young people wore, but in time they clung to these costumes of self. The divide between seeming and being widened on the professional stage. In Renaissance Venice, the Jewish doctor's plague told a grave story about how Jews and Christians related at the moment of death; the mask morphed into a comic piece of decoration, its symbolic weight lightened. What were then the appearances that truly expressed the 'real you'? What are they?

Subservience to creators and the value given to appearances might seem divorced from the realm of power, as they did to Machiavelli during his time in office. Louis XIV's dancing tells an opposite story. In the realm of power, appearances matter more and more, appearances which are carefully contrived, which are artful, The content of power – policy – mattered less and less in comparison to a charismatic personality. Which is a legacy, passed down from the Renaissance, that has only grown stronger over the centuries.

We turn next to explore how this political legacy is now being spent.

BOOK FOUR

Malign Performances

9

A Theatre of the Defeated

The failed performer becomes a spectator

Imagine a play called *Defeat*. The actors are manual labourers, and the script lays out the trials they suffer in getting work. They become angry and rightly so, because circumstances beyond their control have caused them to fail. At a certain moment a demagogic politician appears to them, playing on their hurt. What makes *Defeat* a distinctive play, however, is that nothing then happens. The demagogue exits stage-left, and the workers return to their preoccupations with paying what bills they can, or taking on temporary jobs to fill in the days. The curtain falls without a catharsis.

Defeat is not a fantasy. It is a malign story I watched, uncomprehending, when I was young, and which I have now tried to reconstruct, to understand the workers' failure as real-life performers.

I. *Defeat* is Staged in New York

The Stage

A blinking sign announced only 'Bar' at the entrance to Dirty Dick's Foc'sle Bar next to the West Side highway in Greenwich Village, a building which had once been a warehouse and that after the Second World War was converted to a bar on the ground floor and small apartments above. I lived one flight above Dirty Dick's when I worked at the Judson Dance Theater, and I was happy in my room; it was full of afternoon sun, and had a beautiful view of the Hudson River just across the West Side highway. You would never guess what the bar was like inside from the street, its walls blank and grim.

But you can see it in a film made a few years ago by the video-grapher Cassim Shepard, just before the bar was torn down to make way for expensive, river-view apartments.[1]

Inside, at night, Dirty Dick's drew in a louche crowd comprising artists living in the West Village mixed with gay men of colour drawn from all over the city. In the 1960s Harlem was a dangerous, intolerant place if you were a Black homosexual, so people came downtown. Dirty Dick's was just a bar – those were pre-disco days – which served food until midnight, so it was mostly a restaurant for these refugees, though serving Irish rather than soul food. Black gay men relaxed rather than cruised here.

Outside, in the morning, the scene was also sociable. A crew of cleaners dealt early with the mountains of beer bottles consumed during the night's festivities. Around the same time a clot of people – mothers who had dropped off children at school nearby and fathers returning from night-shift work – gathered outside, sipping coffee from a bodega next to the bar. Around 8.30, the neighbours went their various ways and the mood of the place changed, as unemployed dockworkers arrived at Dirty Dick's and headed for the back room.

The bar had been well named. The old word 'foc'sle' applies to the front underdeck of a ship, where sailors sleep. The back room was a big, former storage space, furnished with plastic chairs under neon lights, heavy with the odours of sweat, cooking grease, liquor and cheap cigars. Many of those who hung out here during the day, willing and able but with nothing to do, drank themselves into a stupor in this cavernous inner space. The men did swap information about opportunities which might pop up or complain about corrupt practices on the docks, but by late afternoon they had exhausted their talking and withdrawn into themselves.

Defeat

The 1960s was a bad time to be a young stevedore in New York. The port of Manhattan withered as shipping business moved across the river to New Jersey. From afar on the West Coast, Harry Bridges, the union boss of New York's dockworkers, both communist and Mafioso, decreed that whatever work remained on the New York docks should go to older men. The longshoremen's union now privileged seniority over opportunity: because you are younger, you are on your own.

Capitalism has long had the problem of there often being more workers than work. National government had focused on this dilemma since the Great Depression; in the New York area, the Mob dealt with oversupply as well, making work for members of the unions it controlled. *On the Waterfront*, the great film about life on the docks, depicts the reliance of stevedores on the Mafia. But from the 1960s, the memory of the Great Depression began to fade, and Mob unions were beginning to erode. With weaker institutional support, labourers had to face on their own the problem of more workers than work.

The curtain rises in *Defeat* with a 'shape-up'. Each morning at six-thirty, stevedores lined the edge of the West Side highway running alongside the docks. They stood in a single line, while the foreman walked down it, saying, 'You, pier 6,' or 'You, pier 8,' making a first selection of those who would get work that day. Then, at eleven, there would be a second shape-up, when those not originally picked lined up again, and a few more were chosen for odd jobs in the afternoon. The workers presented themselves hoping that the foreman would single them out from the mass, but in the mid 1960s there was no more than one half-day job for every three unionized workers.

The humiliation of the shape-up lay in the unanswerable questions: why was he chosen? Why not me? It's a situation familiar to every young academic. Two hundred people are all qualified for the same job; 199 academics receive a form letter beginning, 'Sadly among such an outstanding group of candidates, we have had to make hard decisions . . .' and then a string of clichés follows. An explanation which is no explanation. At least the foreman made no pretence of offering one.

Today, the dockworkers' dilemma has spread throughout the labour force, as for people working on zero-hours contracts. They are expected to perform, which means that more than just execute a task, they must show they are stand-outs, worth singling out. The presentations they have to make of themselves are emotionally fraught because there are too many of these insecure or temporary workers for the available work. Yet as with the foreman who offered no explanations to justify whom he chose, there is little reciprocity in the presentation of self – why should the boss bother to interact? The onus is on the worker; if you don't like it, there are plenty to take your place.

Around the time the longshoremen were shaping-up and failing to stand out, Herbert Marcuse was putting the finishing touches to *One-Dimensional Man*. In it he invoked 'the performance principle' to explain the experience of being chosen or not chosen. To Marcuse we owe the concept of the labour market as a form of theatre. His idea is in one way straightforward: as in the shape-up, so more generally the worker tries to show they are worthy of being given work, behaving in a way that makes them stand out from the mass. This performance is bound to fail – as the Dean's rejection letter states, there are so many qualified candidates.

The theatre of labour was not simply a metaphor for Marcuse. Like his colleague C. Wright Mills, he was struck by how big businesses and bureaucracies focus on performance metrics – that is, on quantifying how well people act. In the white-collar world, the battery of aptitude and personality tests, the endless assessments on the job, the psychobabble of 'personal development' all mask demands for ever greater productivity from all, though only a few will be rewarded for it. This is what Marcuse called 'surplus repression' – displays of unrewarded performance dominate modern capitalism. It breeds a double consciousness: on the one hand, cynicism about a system stacked against you, and, on the other, a wounding awareness that the performance is a judgement on *you*, personally.

The Personalizing of Defeat

The personalizing of defeat happens because Marcuse's worker internalizes the roles of hard work. His worker genuinely believes it's a good thing to be productive, efficient, dedicated, loyal, willing to put in extra hours if necessary. The worker's character makes them worthy to be employed. But character counts for little in the selection process. Were Marcuse staging *Defeat*, he would have drawn on this duality: character has nothing to do with economic value, yet good work habits and attitudes are all the unskilled worker possesses. In an office the display of personal worth might consist of showing in meetings just how good you are at teamwork, or your skill in solving a problem. But in the shape-up, look-at-me-how-cooperative-how-capable-I-am moments don't happen: you are just a pair of hands.[2]

Though Marcuse's ideas apply to capitalism in general, he supposed that Americans were more caught up in the personalizing of defeat because in the United States the individual is meant to make his or her own weather in life. The fear of being an invisible individual, lost in the mass, was an American preoccupation of the post-war era. David Riesman wrote about that worry in *The Lonely Crowd*, an analysis of how individuals stand out or are submerged in the mass. The same anxiety appeared in C. Wright Mill's study of corporate life, *White Collar*; and being no one special yet asserting one's desire for recognition formed the theme of John Updike's novel *Rabbit Run*.

The brutal circumstances of the dockworkers' lives suggested they should have walked away, at least emotionally, to protect themselves through role distance. In his *Paradox of Acting*, Diderot had observed that there is something self-defeating about emotional investment in a role. On stage, getting too wrapped up in your role means you will perform it badly. This observation has an obvious parallel in the theatre of work. When people in interviews show themselves anxious or nervous, they send out negative signals;

employers are more likely to respond well to those who can at least mask their desperate need of a job.

A fundamental turning point in our culture came when people began to believe in self-fashioning, believe that they should at least try to shape their own lives. In microcosm, the shape-up showed the negative today of this Renaissance-rooted belief. It is failure which is personalized: you are in a rut because of who you are.

The Defeated Actor Becomes a Spectator

Defeated as actors in the daily theatre of the shape-up, taking the defeat personally as their own failure, the dockworkers retreated to Dirty Dick's to nurse their injuries. They had now become spectators to work.

Becoming a spectator who watches others get a life is a fear which runs through American literature, as in Henry James's novel *The Ambassadors*. The reproach that one is not making a life for oneself comes to the protagonist Lewis Lambert Strether in Paris, where he is trying to 'rescue' a young man, Chad Newsome, who seems to have been snared by the pleasures of the city. In Paris, Strether sees that he is the one who needs rescuing. 'I haven't done . . . enough before – and now I'm too old; too old at any rate for what I see . . .' And so he declares to another young American, 'Live all you can!' Strether himself didn't.[3]

On the ground of everyday life, spectatorship might seem like the condition the sociologist Orlando Patterson calls 'social death'. His phrase was meant first to describe slaves denied standing as adult human beings, their needs not registering with owners whose only interest was keeping the slaves physically alive and so at work. 'Social death' is akin to the idea of 'bare life' in the writings of the philosopher Giorgio Agamben, his touchstone being the conditions in a concentration camp where human beings had lost any civic or legal standing. The dockworkers were not oppressed by these extreme denials. Rather, their plight resembled a white version of Ralph Ellison's description of the legally freed African American as an 'invisible man', present but not seen, or, as the American phrase has it, 'just part of the woodwork'. Sheer indifference is not a mortal threat, but it nonetheless undermines one's sense of self-worth.

II. It Has to be Someone's Fault

In Dirty Dick's, the TV volume was turned up whenever George Wallace appeared on the screen. An avowed racist, Wallace, a governor of Alabama, would go on in 1967 to found a national political movement amalgamating anti-Black prejudice with white working-class resentment. At Dirty Dick's the dockworkers were galvanized by his anger when Wallace declared, 'I say segregation now, segregation tomorrow, segregation for ever!!' Wallace claimed that Black workers were muscling in on the jobs of white workers, abetted by rich white do-gooders who looked down on poor whites. The dockworkers shouted back at the TV as though Wallace were in the room.

'"They" are taking your jobs' is a standard trope about who to blame, made real because Wallace, like Donald Trump, was a very good performer. His voice was rough like sandpaper, he fell into a boxer's crouch in front of the cameras, and he appeared to be so infuriated that he might lose control. The fury was, however, confined to the stage; away from the television camera Wallace proved a cool-headed operator. He differed from the billionaire Trump, who rails in the name of the people against the elite, in actually coming from a dirt-poor white family. Wallace scorned the manners of the faded Southern aristocracy as much as he passionately hated African Americans. He performed the person he really was.

It's common to equate demagogic performances like Wallace's with 'populism', particularly among the right-wing working class. Which is twice lazy. First, because populism does not only apply to the right. The *narodniki* in nineteenth-century Russia were agrarian reformers who called themselves 'populists', as did agrarian socialists in the United States. Second, it's lazy because populism of a rightist stripe has no specifically working-class character. Anti-immigrant zealots, Islamophobes, homophobes, opponents of abortion are as likely to be middle class or wealthy.

Wallace's claims about African Americans taking jobs from whites wasn't true on the docks at that time, and I suspect the white men in Dirty Dick's knew full well that it was false. Old photos of the shape-up along the docks do show the occasional African American face, but it's inconceivable that a Mafioso foreman would have preferred and picked out a Black worker from the shape-up line. Whether white or Black, the manual labourers were paid equally badly.

White workers then, as now, often distinguished between individuals they actually worked alongside and the category 'Black men taking your jobs'. Face-to-face knowledge of individual Black workers would have been of men probably worse off than themselves. But Wallace shouting that 'Blacks are taking your jobs' was not about actual persons, just as his mantra 'Segregation, segregation, segregation for ever!' offered no solution to the decline of the docks. The Black was a fantasy target – the fantasy working Black the reason for the white worker's own defeat.[4]

Yet just here was the most surprising thing about the scene in Dirty Dick's. Wallace appeared and disappeared on screen. Once he finished speaking, the volume of the TV was turned down again, a sports channel was redialled, and people lapsed back into silence. Nobody ran out into the streets to find a Black person they could throttle. Subdued, depressed, their strivings unaccounted and their pain unrelieved: that's how the curtain fell on this performance of *Defeat* in New York. An aspect of dramatic art illuminates why it ended as it did.

III. There is No Catharsis

Catharsis

Defeat lacked a catharsis. A physical catharsis will purge a harmful or painful element from the body, as in vomiting bad food. When we are in pain, we want not some slow release but immediate relief. Tragedy is meant to provide this sudden release as well. At the end of a tragedy a compressed, revelatory scene usually releases an audience which may have been watching violence or cruelty for much longer; it's as though poison has been flushed out of them.

At the origins of theatre, thinkers puzzled why catharses work as powerfully as they do. Aristotle calls the turning point when a character on stage passes from ignorance to knowledge 'anagnorisis', as when King Oedipus suddenly understands that he has murdered his father and slept with his mother. The catharsis is both a moment of truth and a release from identification. We identify with Oedipus the searcher after the truth, doing so to release his city from the plague – until the moment when he – and we – know the gods have sent the plague because he is an incestuous murderer. At this anagnorisis we stop identifying with him; we are not like that. (Or are we?)

Aristotle famously asserted that the result is the purging of pity and fear. Pity, as it figures in his *Poetics*, is what we understand today by empathy: we identify with the protagonist as someone like us. When the moment of truth comes, and we stop empathising, we lose the fear that the bad things happening to him could happen to us.[5]

In a way, Aristotle's formula is too neat. Catharsis requires, as the critic Frank Kermode put it, the sense of an ending, of the story being over. But there lurks in everyone's psyche the desire to kill and the thrill of forbidden sex. These are not going to be erased thanks to a night out at the theatre; the theatre provides only temporary relief from the inner demons. Catharses in art are thus not like vomiting, which truly expels poisons from the body. The inner poisons remain, but thanks to art they stop making us feel sick – for a while.

The psychologist Thomas Scheff applies Aristotle to everyday life by calling catharses 'distancing emotions'. You engage with other people initially because you are curious about who they are, and you have a tendency to empathize with them because you seem to recognize experiences shared in common. Once you know more, you often stop projecting and you draw away; either you share little, or you don't like who the other person turns out to be. You take your distance. There's a pleasure in disengaging from other people, or at least, Scheff says, a feeling of relief. You have then a catharsis.[6]

There were no catharses of this sort on the waterfront. The shape-up allowed no such distancing emotions. In Dirty Dick's back room, at the end of each day, there was no sense of an ending, of a bodily purge, of temporary release. My strongest memory of this back room, when I ventured there late in the afternoon, was that alcohol was not providing that catharsis. The men by that time drank, many heavily, but almost all drank silently. The drama of rejection would be repeated the next day.

10.

A Theatre of Fear

The spectator is afraid of the future

I. The Denial

Young Climate Deniers

About thirty years ago, I began consulting for the United Nations, first for its culture branch, Unesco, then for UNDP, its development arm, then for UN Habitat, the agency specifically concerned with cities. My career at the UN concluded at a 'global climate summit' held in Glasgow in 2021, when I helped organize a group examining how climate change will affect cities. 'It is such a grave danger,' the politician-summiteers agreed before leaving Scotland for other engagements.[1]

In preparation for Glasgow, in the summer of 2019 I had gone to Washington to meet a group of climate scientists who the arch climate-change denier Donald Trump had let go after years of government service. Our meetings took place on the day a group of climate deniers gathered inside the Trump International Hotel, in Washington. That group, called the Heartland Institute, was sponsoring the '13th International Conference on Climate Change'. Founded in 2008 to ratify the so-called 'Manhattan Declaration', which proclaims that 'assertions of a supposed "consensus" among climate experts are false,' the signatories demand that 'regulations and other interventions intended to reduce emissions of CO_2 be abandoned forthwith'. This thirteenth meeting celebrated 'the courageous men and women who spoke the truth about climate change during the height of the global warming scare'.[2]

The local branch of Extinction Rebellion had assembled a small crowd outside the hotel to protest against this event. They were kept well out of sight, but they could be heard inside thanks mostly to a large bass drum which one protester had brought along. Rather cleverly, she played it off the beat in varied tempi, so it was hard to ignore.

Within the hotel, the most striking group were some young people who looked less scruffy than their peers in the street. During a tea break I was particularly surprised by the young woman next in line who helped me to forbidden sugar. Earnest and soft-spoken, she proved nothing like the stereotype of an intolerant right-winger. Perhaps my liver spots and other all-too-visible signs of old age inspired a certain amount of trust in her, even after she asked what I did, and I mentioned the words 'United Nations'. She nodded politely, and to paper over this unfortunate revelation, as Americans will when meeting strangers, began telling me about herself.

A libertarian, she was majoring in 'Ayn Rand studies' at a local college. She had come with a dozen or so classmates, to whom I was introduced in turn and with whom I then had lunch. Ayn Rand, it transpired, had a lot to do with their interest in climate change; Rand's doctrines are all about individual initiative, and students majoring in Ayn Rand studies are likely to discredit impersonal forces beyond personal control.

At lunch, they evinced a certain open-mindedness which went beyond politeness. They asked me, for instance, how much differ-ence a rise in global temperatures from 1.4 to 1.85 would make in the coming decade – one speaker that morning had denied it would make any difference. They did not dismiss as 'fake news' my explan-ation of why each decimal point matters. But the open-mindedness lasted only until we adjourned for the big events in the ballroom. Then the malign powers of theatre seized hold of the kids, turning them into an acid-angry crowd.

Charts flashed by on a giant screen as each speaker proclaimed some version of 'The science is a fraud'. The fraudsters were absent figures – professors from Harvard and MIT, professional do-gooders at the Rockefeller Foundation, and of course UN bureaucrats. Not once did a speaker declare about a climate-change advocate, 'Although she is mistaken, she means well.' Instead, character assassination became the way to push back against scientific fact.

The audience responded by nodding, or chanting 'That's right!' The charts were often too difficult to read, but no matter. Gradually the Ayn Rand study group became infected by the mood of aggressive denial. My companion, so restrained outside, began smiling, then clapping, then calling out. She removed her spectacles, her eyes streaming from excitement. The Ayn Rand study group's response recalled the aroused eighteenth-century theatre in which audiences pointed and settled the actors – here, the applause pointed the speakers on stage, and settled the absent do-gooders. Another historical echo: the claquers in nineteenth-century theatres had to work hard to overcome polite bourgeois propriety, but, once that threshold had been crossed, the jeering public was rabid. So too here. It had taken a while for the kids to warm up, but once they did, bile poured out of them.

This performance was, however, something of a George Wallace event. When the speeches ended, the kids' calm good manners as suddenly returned. Indeed, in another tea-break – I was longing for a martini instead of tea to dispel the taste of rhetoric – my companions acknowledged rather shamefacedly that climate change is a real threat. The transformation from inside to outside was one Le Bon and Freud would surely have understood: massed as an audience, the kids became unthinking, whereas as a group of distinct individuals, they returned to the realm of fact.

As I departed the Trump International Hotel, they promised to write more about Ayn Rand and climate change. I haven't heard from them, and in a way I'm not surprised. Unlike the scene in Dirty Dick's bar, in which the workers could find no catharsis, in the Trump International they found one of sorts. In this version, under the spell of theatre, the purge consisted of denying reality even as they knew there was a real threat. The explanation of this duality came from places far away.

States of Denial

In a remarkable study of apartheid South Africa, the sociologist Stanley Cohen explored what the white Boer community actually knew about conditions in the townships to which the Black majority were confined. Cohen found that the whites knew a lot and were fully aware of the miseries that the apartheid regime inflicted, but at the same time they blotted out this awareness as much as they could, claiming for instance that they had never heard a Black servant complain about the regime. Cohen called this state of denial simultaneous 'knowing and not knowing'. His sharpness lay in perceiving that the liberal, enlightened remedy for changing people's attitudes – information, education – was perversely counterproductive. The more people knew about how awful life was in the townships, the more they denied its reality.

Cohen's study reinforced an observation that Hannah Arendt had made decades before about German concentration camps. Ordinary Germans professed to know nothing about them, which Arendt didn't believe for a second; too many Jews, Catholic resisters, homosexuals, Roma and socialists had gone missing from the streets; it was not possible for the ordinary German to not wonder about how and where they had gone. To Arendt, the ordinary citizen, as much as the camp monster Adolf Eichmann – just following orders and doing his job – dwelt in a state of denial, knowing and not knowing at the same time. Brutally put, the Arendt–Cohen thesis is that the more painful facts people know, the more they feign ignorance.

Their thesis calls into question the project of Enlightenment begun in the eighteenth century. For Montesquieu and Diderot, Adam Smith and James Ferguson, knowledge is liberating; for Cohen and Arendt, knowledge is paralysing. The Enlightenment thought that when people have full information, they will demand action. In this regard it was a big mistake for my colleagues at the UN and me to subscribe to the rhetoric of 'climate emergency'.

The word 'emergency' pulls the trigger on denial. If the facts are overwhelming, then there is nothing a person can do. You are helpless. So you deny what you know.

There's everything right about the Arendt–Cohen thesis, but it's not the whole story. The fear of climate change is about a terrible thing that's just beginning to happen, rather than, as with the Oedipus story, a terrible thing which has already happened. In such a classical tragedy, the audience is pulled in to uncover the truth, to get the right facts, like conducting an autopsy. But the denials of climate change are based on imagination of the future, making sense of projections, possibilities and the like; it seems as though there's as yet not much tangible evidence (even as there is). And if, as Thomas Scheff maintains, a catharsis requires dissociation and 'distance taking', this pushing away of future time has a distinct shape.

II. Foreshadowing and Foreboding

The Distinction

The future forks along two paths in time: foreshadowing and foreboding. In foreshadowing, you can be fairly certain what will happen and you know the actions to take to address that probability. Thus in the recent pandemic, you knew what the outcome was likely to be if someone sneezed in your face – so you wore a mask. In foreboding, the future is less certain; as with Long Covid, its effects appear unpredictably.

Philosophically, foreshadowing derives the deductive way of reasoning from 'if x then y'. If the x in deductive reasoning is shaky or plain wrong, the resulting y will be too, but at least the deduction can be tested, and you can learn from the mistake you have made. Foreboding lies outside the deductive framework; instead, it imagines a variety of possible outcomes, none of which is testable. Foreboding inspires feelings of 'ontological insecurity', a fancy name for feeling continual disquiet, inner unsettlement, due to not knowing what happens next but fearing the worst. The political philosopher Jennifer Mitzen believes that ontological insecurities drive people to extreme politics, usually right-wing politics, in order to quell this inner daily anxiety. You might describe the kids at the climate-deniers convention as suffering from ontological insecurity (I can't quite square that lurid label with their sensible cardigans and neatly pressed trousers). More solidly, ontological insecurity is based on the operations of chance.[3]

Fortuna

Foreboding has a back-story that emerges from how people have thought about chance. Foreboding comes out of the belief that the lived experience of chance is not like flipping a coin, in which things are as likely to come out heads as tails. Instead, in the long term things are more likely to go wrong than right. The cards are stacked against you.

Chance figured originally in our culture as the goddess Tyche in Greece, Fortuna in the Roman world, who wore a blindfold to symbolize that things can equally work out well or badly; in this, Fortuna was cousin to Janus, the god who makes no predictions about the future. In the ancient world Thucydides celebrated *tuhke*, which meant 'Luck favours the daring' or, as we'd say now, 'Who dares wins', whereas the tragedians spoke of *ate*, the doom a person may in fact invite by daring. The classicist E. R. Dodds remarks that tragedy presents 'the spectacle of a man freely choosing . . . a series of actions which lead to his own ruin . . .' There is a third state, *proaisthima*, the fear that we might do ourselves harm, not by acting purposely but rather by chance.[4]

From its origins, Christianity disputed the idea of chance harm, equally of chance as blind. Instead, chance was thought to work like a crooked casino, the wheel of fortune fixed so that you couldn't win. The cruelty of chance resulted from Adam and Eve's sin. Once outside the Garden, things were not likely to work out. In Chaucer's *Monk's Tale*, the narrator observes 'And thus does Fortune's wheel turn treacherously / And out of happiness bring men to sorrow'. In Dante's *Inferno*, chance appears as the trump card in a game of Tarot, casting people into the hellish pit.

It could be said that in climate change, chance appears in just this Christian way. Though many of its immediate workings are unpredictable – as where exactly a storm will strike, or just how hot New York will be on 3 August 2024 – in the long term, the odds are stacked against us because, as with original sin, we are the authors of our own misfortune.

It's quite plausible to think that the speakers in the Trump International Hotel ballroom wanted to lift this Christian burden from their listeners, though they probably wouldn't put it that way. You haven't done anything wrong to make the planet hotter, it's all fake science, buy the biggest car you can afford. What struck me greatly about these speakers is the undertow of violent aggression in their attacks on climate science. This was true of George Wallace as well: he wasn't just a racist, he was a violent racist. I've since wondered what this viciousness has to do with the dramatizing of violence explored earlier in this book. How could denial and foreboding about the future be dramatized so that the refusal and the fear becomes violent?

One answer comes from contemplating the myth of Saturn, who in the ancient world was the companion of Janus.

III. The Scythe of Saturn

In Goya's Dining Room

In 1819, the painter Francisco Goya bought a house just outside Madrid which he began to decorate in a singular fashion. *Saturn Devouring his Son* went into the dining room. It is one of the most grisly images in the history of art: the boy's head and part of one arm have already been eaten, and red blood and white flesh light up the painting. Out of the darkness the only parts of Saturn's face we see are his wide-open mouth and his bug eyes. The god's fingers appear like claws digging into his son's back, as Saturn prepares for another bite.

From early in his career, Goya made paintings like this, dramatizing irrational violence as a counterweight to the decorous portraits which initially made his name. There was nothing perverse about hanging this cannibal scene in the dining room; Goya's public also looked avidly at images of horror; they too wanted to see inside the psyche, especially if the images were framed by ancient myths.

In the myth of Saturn that Goya depicted, the god's violence comes directly from his foreboding about the future. 'Saturn' was the Roman name for Chronos, the Greek god of time who murdered and ate his children because he feared that if they lived they would supplant him. Saturn/Chronos was 'sated with years', said Cicero, meaning he was a god who feared the future. The story takes a further twist when Saturn, exiled for his cannibal crimes, was taken in by Janus and the two then governed lands which would eventually become Rome. It's one of those deep, provocative pairings which occur in myth: Janus, the god of unknown future time, ruling with Saturn, the time-denying god.[5]

As with all myths, Saturn's story is not simple. A destroyer, he was also paired with the harvest, representing the winter, when the productive earth is exhausted. But as a god of foreboding he hovers over the imagination. The cannibal Saturn in Goya's painting is a symbol of the old fighting against loss of control in the future – or, put more disturbingly, fear that the young, our young, are out to destroy us.

The novelist W. G. Sebald was obsessed with Goya's painting, brought the myth into the present and used it to think through the destruction of the environment. In *The Rings of Saturn*, Sebald records a walk through the Suffolk countryside in England when visiting another émigré from Germany, his friend Michael Hamburger. In the course of his journey he notes the scarred landscape filled with discarded plastic bottles, rubbish and senseless buildings, occasionally intersected by sudden eruptions of quicksand and other unforeseen, natural disasters. Then his imagination makes a leap to the Nazi passions of his parents' contemporaries in Germany. Thoughtless destruction, chance destruction, self-destruction – the three elements hold together and compose the power of foreboding, which Sebald calls the 'scythe of Saturn'.

The painting of Saturn in Goya's dining room relies on a myth that is theatrical and fantastical, which Goya's painting is as well. In its depiction of violence, it is larger than life. Here is another form of the connection between theatricality and violence. The scythe of Saturn becomes a weapon in foreboding about the future.

BOOK FIVE

How Art Opens

The Stage Rejoins the Street

Open spaces for art

You and I are of course too wise to believe that for every problem there is a solution. Still, we want to push back against destructive performance.

Repair of broken things comes in three forms. The first is a replacement repair, like putting in a fresh light bulb when an old one burns out. The second is an expansion repair, as when a memory stick with more memory is substituted for a current one. The third type of repair involves more drastic refiguration; for instance, replacing an old computer with a new one often changes the kind of computing you do. This sort of repair expands your understanding.[1]

Repair of performing art follows somewhat similar lines. Your voice is scratchy, so you take a throat lozenge to enable you to sing again just as you did before. Your voice coach teaches you how to hit high Cs, and you have added notes to your repertoire. You listen to a recording of yourself and it doesn't sound right: you've failed to convey the bitterness in a seemingly sweet song. You have to rethink the techniques of phrasing in order to give your voice an edge. You have to learn again how to sing.

This third, most searching form of repair is how the art of performing becomes more open. Which first of all concerns how art touches the ground, its physical presence in the city.

I. The Open City

Accessible

Arts administrators (a dismal tribe) talk about making art 'access-ible', which is one version of 'open'. What they mean is that, if paintings are attractively labelled, if performers make little speeches about 'what it means to me' before playing each piece of music, if choreographers provide dance classes after people watch it done professionally, the art becomes enticing and so swells audience numbers (administrators live and die by audience numbers). Rather than being democratic, this measure is condescending, as though without the packaging, people won't get it. It's also at odds with much of the art the managers are trying to flog – art which is inher-ently unsettling or difficult and so impossible to pasteurize. And the administrators do get the public wrong – at least the urban public. In contrast to a village, a city is filled with people who are not alike, and whose differences are often impossible to reconcile. In musical terms, human dissonances don't resolve in a city; the public lives with difficulty and dissonance every day. The challenge is to engage art as part of urbanite experience, rather than to wrap it in tourist cellophane.

This starts as a problem for architecture and urban planning. In Chapter 5, we traced the long process by which the theatre with-drew from the street, becoming sealed inside special buildings. The challenge today is to re-engage with the street. This challenge exists more broadly. Gated communities are a greater imposition of clos-ure on the city, and their form dominates new mass housing. Most office towers are monofunctional – just for business – sealed at the base so that no one without identification can enter. Withdrawal from the street, messy in form and multiple in function as a street is, marks the modern city. So how would we re-engage the street? One possibility is suggested by the word 'complex'.

Complex

This was a keyword in the development in science of 'open systems' theory. Pioneered by engineer-scientists such as Norbert Weiner and those at MIT in the middle of the last century, open-systems thinking explored how computers, like people, are stimulated by things which are difficult and demand effort to understand. William Mitchell, my colleague at MIT, applied open-systems analysis to the city's transport systems, building codes and strategies for urban regeneration.

I understood concretely what complexity theory was about when, twenty years ago, I worked at the United Nations on a special project. It compared urban spaces in Seoul and Lagos. The contrast between the two cities made strikingly apparent the differences between a closed and an open environment. New parts of Seoul functioned efficiently enough but had little street life; the buildings consisted of uniform apartment blocks, sometimes requiring huge flags with numbers to be hung in front so that residents could tell which one was theirs. New Seoul was the polar opposite to public spaces in Lagos that were noisy, contentious and informal. A district selling used cars, for instance, housed shepherds from the country-side who in the dead of night frequently stripped cars and sold the parts before dawn. To prevent vandalism the car lots stayed open at night, which led to all-night restaurants opening so that customers could eat. Some shepherds then became cooks . . . Unlike the new bits of Seoul that were static and failed to develop economically, the complexities in Lagos eventually stimulated growth.

In an open system, change does not follow a straight path. Things happen which no one expected, leading to further changes, each with their own knock-on effects; the process – in open-systems jargon – is 'path-dependent' rather than 'linear'. To cite another urban instance, Gaziantep, in Turkey, today exemplifies path-dependent development. It was suddenly surprised in the 2010s by an influx of massive numbers of Syrian refugees, the city nearly doubling in size over five years. Rather than shutting out or segregating the incomers, the city scrambled to benefit economically from their unexpected advent. Making use of tech-skilled refugees, Gaziantep expanded its service sector, creating a new regional economy for the city.

In computing, there's a particular connection between complexity and reflexivity. Which simply means that, as things move forward in unexpected ways, a computer system will search its memory to see what can be of use in new circumstances and what is now useless. The feedback loops in an open system inaugurate its third-stage repairs of reconfiguration.

For human beings, the process of reckoning via feedback loop is often the same, but, whereas a computer has no feelings, the results of human sifting are often distressing, especially in an open environment. I was struck by this distress when I first travelled to Shanghai in the mid 1980s. People were freed from the Maoist surveillance culture which had penetrated deep into their lives before. If you were young in Shanghai at that time, you embraced Western culture – its movies, its music, its intellectual fads – you were hipper than hip. But if you were older and you could not simply step outside the frame of your memories – you did not forget the betrayals to the authorities your neighbours practised on you, or perhaps that you practised on them for the sake of survival. The very fact that the city was more open was disturbing. It was harder to ignore the many grave matters being discussed out loud in cafés and bars rather than kept behind closed doors as before.

Which is to say more generally that a city that opens up does not simply issue an invitation to pleasure; the feedback loops can hurt. The challenge of opening up culture is how to engage with these present dissonances and past disturbances rather than repress them. Which in our corner of culture is a particular puzzle. How could the arcane realm of theatre architecture address an issue of this scope, if at all? Isn't it far beyond what a building can do? To find an answer, supposing there is one, we need to consider the guts of the buildings themselves.

II. Porous Theatres

It might seem that the simplest way to open up the performing arts to the city might be to abandon theatre buildings as special places. Everything would then happen in the street. Many city planners now harbour this dream of no barriers, no filters, no walls, everything out in the open. But performances require certain solid barriers to enable people to hear and see well. Specifically, there are good technical reasons for walls of the kind which first appeared in the stone wall, the *skene*, behind the ancient amphitheatre stage.

Walls reflect sound. In a totally walled-in theatre like Palladio's Teatro Olimpico, this reflection takes form in an 'initial time-delay gap'; this is the precise amount of time it takes for a sound bouncing off a wall or a ceiling to register on a listener's ear tympanum. In a totally enclosed space the gap provides a sense of being enveloped stereophonically in sound rather than hearing it directionally as though coming through a window. The acoustician Leo Beranek worked out in a path-breaking study that the gap should be just under two seconds. The aesthetic effect of stereophonically enveloping sound is that the listener feels closer to the stage.[2]

As with hearing, so with seeing. Say you are a broke street musician and you are performing in a corridor of the underground or at a street corner to pay the rent. The flat plane will defeat you because, if a crowd gathers, only the people at the front will be your spectators; the others, unable to see you, tend to move on. One obvious solution to the problem of flatness is to rake the seats, but this solution also has to be applied carefully. Too steep a rake increases visibility at the expense of inducing vertigo, as anyone who has sat in the cheap, upper seats of opera houses such as Covent Garden will attest. As with the Beranek parameters for sound, so the rake parameters are fairly strict, between 2.5 to 4.5 degrees.

For technical reasons like these, simply pulling down a theatre and replacing it with a plaza or other empty space doesn't work well. The challenge is how to use physical elements of enclosure, like its walls or raked seating, to bring stage and street together. Nature has a suggestion.

Membranes and Shells

Living cells are sheathed by two kinds of container: membranes and shells. A membrane is usually a thin, soft wall which takes nourishment into the cell and expels spent materials easily, while a cell shell is a thicker, harder wall, more oriented simply to repulsing elements from the outside. A membrane is not open in the sense of lacking any barriers. It filters matter from passing inside to outside; without this filter, the cells would soon spill out their guts and die. And the cell shell is not inert; some degree of osmosis occurs, though material moves more slowly than through a membrane. Still, there is a big difference in degree; the membrane is more porous.

As in cells, so in urban culture: porosity might serve as a model for making stage and street more open to one another. But how to design porosity? Here are four architectural models for doing so, only one of which really opens up space in a way which addresses complexity, dissonance and discomfort.

Internal Porosity

You are trying to find your way to a concert inside the Barbican Centre in London and are late – but the performers will wait because they know it's not your fault. The entrance is difficult to find, especially from public transport, and it's not clear just from walking in the neighbourhood that any sort of art-making goes on here.

In the medieval era, a barbican was an archer's tower placed at a city's gates; thereafter a barbican came to stand for any fortified, not easily penetrated space. The concert halls of the Barbican Centre are barbican-ized, as is the greatest European concert hall built in modern times, Hans Scharoun's Philharmonie in Berlin, a marvel inside, an uninviting fortress outside.

With this shell of art, however, the space is porous. Drink in hand, you can wander through reception rooms, bars and restaurants, or from inside to a huge pool outside, faced by apartment blocks which enclose the spaces on the other three sides.

What's significant about the Barbican model is that the residents dislike the noise and litter resulting from the public's attendance at art events. My students who examined this conflict noted that the residents stayed inside their flats when the public went outside to enjoy the lake. The City of London, which is the borough controlling the Barbican, has strict rules excluding the art-public from the residential spaces, even though the rules are frequently ignored, and the art-going public – not exactly a scruffy band of looters – stroll the entire site. The larger defect represented by the Barbican is that there are invisible shells confining porosity – the space is not legally porous.[3]

Percement

The most direct action of breaking a planning shell is called a *percement*. *Percement* involves the punching of windows and doors through the solid walls of a building, so that physically there's no barrier between inside and outside; more, this gateway is not policed. Recall that the Janus lintel over doors in ancient houses told people where to move between rooms, but provided no rules about when the rooms were open, nor who had the right to go from place to place. People can become, moreover, doubly conscious, aware of what they are doing themselves at the same time they see and hear people in an adjacent space. This too has an ancient root, in the synchronous activities of the agora, in which many things happened at the same time.

If *percement* makes possible this layered consciousness, a theatre or other performance space whose walls have been pierced can, oddly, weaken the experience of a performance itself. An example is London's Half Moon Theatre, a masterpiece of architectural *percement* designed by the architect Florian Beigel from 1975 to 1985.

The Half Moon was shaped around a courtyard, the space entered through a gate in the heaving and clanging Mile End Road. In the courtyard, Beigel built two theatres, one big, one small, separated by a *ruelle*, a small lane in which people congregated during intermissions. In both theatres Beigel pierced the walls with windows and doors which could be easily opened and closed. Beigel imagined he had created the perfect architecture for commedia dell'arte, in which characters pop in and out of doors at ground level, appear at windows behind the spectators higher up and then disappear.

Things tended to fall apart during concurrent performances in the two theatres. By keeping doors and windows open, the audiences felt as though they were attending two events at the same time. In both houses people couldn't focus and became disconnected. *Percement* is like attending two Zoom meetings simultaneously, neither of which you can really concentrate on fully. Porosity was rescued inside the Half Moon complex by a simple device. Doors and windows were closed, but their blinds were raised; sound in each space was kept in, sight of somewhere else was admitted.

This transformed the *percement* into a more membranous state, by letting in one sensation, filtering out the other; the theatre was now truly porous. But what's the point? *Percement* tends to fragment perception. In a theatre or concert hall, we don't want weak, watery experiences.

Sealed Spectacle

What if you have to control access, and even if you wanted to, you can't break down walls? How can you make the space nonetheless feel open and porous? This was the problem the architects Elizabeth Diller and Ricardo Scofidio faced in renovating Alice Tully Hall. New York City planning law in 2007 dictated that, for security, access to any concert hall had to be controlled. Outside, cars honked all night on Broadway, and a subway rumbled beneath the street. The architects could have built something along the lines of the Barbican, totally enclosed, but instead they sought to make a spectacle of the crowd inside the hall, drinking and eating in the foyer, perfectly visible to those walking outside on one the city's most dense corners. The plate glass used to expose the inside to the outside is of very high quality and beautifully engineered, so that it seems completely one piece. To further the sense of inward-looking spectacle, the architects created on the street corner a little amphitheatre, facing the crowded interior.

Sealed spectacle runs against the logic of the typical corporate headquarters, whose ground-level entrance, even if made of plate glass, shows no crowds inside, just tasteful furniture, the emptiness guarded by receptionists behind a desk. Still, Tully Hall full of people is problematic. It functions like an aquarium. This glass is a visual tease: come on in, buy a drink, buy a ticket. But this is a pricy aquarium, the drinks are costly. Moreover, when no concert is on, there are few people inside. No one, whether a music student at Juilliard, the conservatory abutting it, or the backstage workers at Lincoln Center, hangs out here. Sealed spectacle can create a shell rather than a membrane. Diller and Scofidio knew this full well, but they were given control over how the building looked, not how it was used.

In sum, whether internally bounded, pierced or aquarium-like, the visual display of openness does not enhance engagement. Is the project of porosity therefore futile? A fourth kind of theatre resists that conclusion, by more radically reformatting the meaning of porosity.

The Mobile Theatre

The Romans believed household gods hovered over specific places; Alexander Pope, who helped found the discipline of landscape architecture, thought that the local environment should guide the designer's hand:

Consult the genius of the place in all;
That tells the waters to rise, or fall;
Or helps th' ambitious hill the heav'ns to scale,
Or scoops in circling theatres the vale . . .

The contrast is with landscape designers such as André Le Notre, who in making the gardens of Versailles, developed severe geometries which could be, and would be, imposed everywhere on every sort of terrain.[4]

Today, we often subscribe to the virtues of place-making and place-based art. It's a dangerous move politically, if the place is home predominantly to one kind of person, white or Black, Christian or Jew, excluding people who are seen as outsiders. The local 'genius of a place' can serve as a shell-mantra.

The architect Tadao Ando wanted to counter the idea of 'It's my space' by creating a theatre which, he said, brought 'the outside in,' on the principle that art should be shown which the community would not otherwise see. In 1986 he designed a theatre that could be moved from neighbourhood to neighbourhood. This is the Kara-Za Theatre, whose walls and ceiling are easy to assemble and disassemble, the materials able to be 'tuned' acoustically to the particular shape the theatre assumes in different public spaces, its tent-like walls angled to suit any site.

It isn't meant to be blended into the 'genius of the place', as though it were always there; its black, bulky form immediately labels it as a special structure. Absent also are the interior visual markers of 'normal' theatre in Japan, the zones and gestures to which people have become accustomed. The Kara-Za put on unknown plays and music from abroad. Ando's prestige as an architect drew in people, but still Kara-Za did not play to packed houses. Arthur Miller's *Death of a Salesman* initially met with resistance, as did many of Kara-Za's imports. But in time these pieces from outside came to be accepted locally.

Ando's credo was straightforward: 'Where we live shouldn't determine the art we see.' He was dedicated to bringing experiences to the local community that they would not otherwise have, via a building that can easily be set up and taken down, moving from place to place in the city. Art from elsewhere is addressed to you but not about you.[5]

Of the four porous theatres, Ando's is the most open in the systems sense of that word. The architecture asserts the fundamental value of complexity: that art should stimulate people by exposing them to foreign, alien or challenging ways of expression. Rather than being accessible, or serving as a mirror of the community, Ando's theatre project accepts that the tent is not a space in harmony with its surrounding. The tent is meant to house a message from outside, rather than a much-loved local institution.

Just as a thought experiment, I've tried to imagine what it would have been like for Carl to have performed his difficult, audience-unfriendly music in Ando's tent. It would relieve the curse which informal space can lay on performers, as in the jazz clubs where Carl's music served as no more than background to drinks and talk. Were Ando's theatre erected in Harlem, Carl's group, though they all lived locally, would appear in the same guise as *The Death of a Salesman* in Tokyo, bringing news from elsewhere, news of the Other. Carl's quartet, freed from their identities, freed from representing the community, would have become like the Messenger in Greek tragedy, who enters, makes an important announcement, and then leaves. Ando's mobile tent might enable this role for the players.

III. The Healing Agora

Simmel's Realism

This may be no more than an architect's fantasy. The sociologist Georg Simmel, writing at the beginning of the twentieth century, certainly thought so. The Berlin of his day had a certain resemblance to Lagos. In its centre there were too many things happening at once: crowds shopping on foot, a ceaseless flow of horse traffic, noise from workshops mingling with the smells of cooking in apartment blocks next to the industrial sites; homeless people begging or sleeping in the niches between buildings, frequent outbursts against Jews or against foreigners who seemed to be flooding the city . . .

Berliners responded, he thought, by donning a mask of indifference, not reacting visibly or engaging socially on the street. People can't handle, Simmel thought, urban overload; they may put up with Lagos-like conditions for a time, but in the end environments like nothing-is-happening peace-and-quiet Seoul are more bearable. Because people can't bear too much complexity, the open city inevitably gives way to a closed one. A tent theatre isn't going to change this.

Some modern ethologists have supported this view in studies of dense animal environments, such as E. O. Wilson's writings on insect communities. These are order-maintaining, dissonance-repelling habitats, particularly hostile to intrusions by others. Biologically, according to this view, human beings' disposition is to stay with their own kind and repel others; we are more 'shell' than 'porous' creatures. To put it another way, this is the elephant in the room of liberal, mutually accepting cosmopolitanism.[6]

Though Simmel's realism may seem just common sense, his withdrawn urbanite can afford to disengage from others. In the Berlin of Simmel's time, most of the people on its streets had to be there, transporting and selling things, going in and out of offices, dealing with schools and hospitals; they did not have the option of withdrawing from sensory contact with smelly, jostling humanity.

It might seem that the ancient agora, as we have explored it in Chapter 4, would be a good counter to Simmel's image of Berlin. He theorized that such a space would prove overstimulating, and that people would soon withdraw into themselves, behaving coolly and indifferent to others. In the ancient agora that simply wasn't so. It lasted a thousand years, whereas the Pnyx withered after a few hundred. Sociability of the agora sort mattered more to people than politics of the Pnyx sort. Yet the difficulty with this ancient model was that it was open to the few but closed to the many, open to a male minority of citizens in the city, closed to women, slaves and immigrants.

In modern social thought, there have been two ways of arguing against Simmel, conceiving instead of a vigorous agora open to all, engaging everyone. One of these imagines the agora to be a discursive space, the other conceives the agora as a theatrical space.

Hannah Arendt's Agora

The discursive agora is most notably embodied in the writing of Hannah Arendt in her book *The Human Condition*, published in 1958. She refers to the Athenian agora as a touchstone, but no Athenian man would feel at home in it.

Arendt believed that people in a modern agora should be able to shed their identities, particularly if they were poor, Black or in other ways classified as outsiders. The old German adage *Stadtluft macht frei* translates, as we've seen, as 'City air makes people free'. To Arendt it specifically means that, whatever people's origins, gender, lifestyle or class, these should not mark them as citizens; private circumstances have no place in the public realm.

Arendt was a foe of what now is called 'identity politics'. A sentence that begins 'Speaking as an African American . . .' is no way, to her, to introduce oneself; nor is, 'We workers want . . .' It's not that Arendt was blind to race or class; rather, she thought that identity talk discourages a speaker from engaging openly and fully with others whose identities differ. Identity talk makes the ghetto Black an avatar of rage, the refugee Jew an emblem of suffering, and so on; people are denied their own personhood. The remedy is to create a space where their identities can remain anonymous. She hoped to turn neighbours into citizens.

Her idea should matter to us because it is one way of imagining how people could exit the theatre of defeat which we explored in the previous chapter. There should be a public realm in which ordinary people are relieved of, as it were, performing for their supper, a place in which they can dwell without being judged.

Arendt had lived in that place. The West End Bar and Grill on New York's Upper West Side of New York resembled the German cafés of her student years – a noisy, cramped, stale beer and smoke-smelling spot, not too different from gay Dirty Dick's downtown at night. In the West End Arendt argued, sometimes with students, sometimes with herself. The racket of different things happening at once seemed to stimulate her and to concentrate her energy; in the formal classroom, where all was under her control, she was cooler, less intense, perhaps even a little bored. The West End Bar and Grill was her agora.

Her sense of place sets her apart from the other great philosopher of the public realm, Jürgen Habermas, whose book *The Structural Transformation of the Public Sphere* was published in 1962. It's thanks to Habermas that thinking about public life began to focus on mass media, particularly on newspapers. From the advent of the big-circulation newspapers in the eighteenth century, he argued, their pages incited a wide readership to think about what they read; today, the internet could, in principle, serve the same purpose. About Habermas's newspaper readers in a café, Arendt might have said – I imagine; I never heard her talk about him – that the public life of the café-dwellers begins once they put down their newspapers and start talking to one another.

Arendt's concept of the discursive bears on the coupling of stage and street in two ways. First, because, in her view, any public space can be turned into an agora – a bar, a hospital waiting room or a theatre. She saw theatres used as civic spaces during the social upheavals of her youth, in the 1920s. Second, because hers is a vision of the agora which, like the ancient agora, makes no distinctions between actor and spectator. But unlike in the ancient agora, she believes in equality – and her idea of equality was that people could and should detach themselves from the shell of identity to speak openly and freely with others.

Her agora is a place where words reign. More, it is a place in which people are energized by each other's words. This is her reproach, I think, to George Simmel: in his city, the defensive, inward-drawn urbanite will gradually deflate. People will eventually come, as many residents of Seoul's new neighbourhoods do, to think of their lives as deadly rather than safe. But what if words don't, or can't, do the work of energizing people? Where and how can they otherwise derive positive stimulation in their senses? The answer to this question preoccupied Roland Barthes quite personally.

Roland Barthes' Agora

In 1966, Barthes went to Tokyo to teach, having been asked to unpack for this foreign audience his ideas about semiology, the 'science' of verbal meaning. By that time he had become rather bored with this 'science' of words and, like Arendt, tired of himself as The Professor. Travel to a foreign place seemed at least a chance to recharge his batteries. A year later he returned to Tokyo, this time without teaching. The city aroused his senses: he liked its food, though he could barely digest it; its ancient ceremonies, of which he understood not a word; the TV trash culture, so similar to the fare on Western commercial channels yet with strange interludes; the chatty communal baths, nothing like the gay, sex-serious saunas at home. His book *Empire of Signs* draws on these impressions with such spirit that Japanese readers are themselves entranced by it.

Barthes, perhaps the twentieth-century's greatest literary reader, found Tokyo unreadable. Many of the streets had no names, nor did the numbers on the buildings in a street unroll sequentially. It is hard, he wrote, to know where exactly you are in such 'unclassified' space. The stranger in Tokyo has to walk the streets to know them, 'not by book, by address, but by walking, by sight, by habit, by experience'.[7]

This, I think, was the source of the attraction that Tokyo had for Barthes. Because there were no fixed referents, no verbal substance, the foreigner in the city's spaces has to use his or her senses and imagination. Indeed, Barthes's way of sensitizing himself was often to wander and get intentionally lost in the twisted fabric of Tokyo's streets. Barthes' is a modern-day version of Baudelaire's *flâneur*, who strolls through the city, enticed by a sight or a sound elsewhere, not knowing what they will find.

Indeterminacy stimulated his senses. Once, Roland took me to a Japanese restaurant in Paris, an insider's place where the menu was written in Japanese, with annoying identifications in French like 'tasty fish balls' or 'miso soup with extra ingredients'. These useless descriptions, empty of real reference, gave Barthes great pleasure: 'To know what the dish is,' he said, 'taste it; that's what it is.'

The absence of guiding referents in Tokyo applied to the very centre of the city as well as many of its side streets. The Japanese capital 'offers this precious paradox: it does possess a centre, but this centre is empty. The entire city turns around a site both forbidden and indifferent, a residence concealed beneath foliage, protected by moats, inhabited by an emperor who is never seen.'[8] Whereas the Louvre or Notre Dame are reference points, anchoring the activities around them.

So there was no agora, in the Western sense, as a geographical place. But there still was an agora, as a social space. This agora was constituted by gestures through which people communicate with one another. Barthes thought of these gestures as everyday theatre which brings people together in physical spaces that are otherwise ambiguous or unreadable, indeterminate; theatrical gestures turn empty spaces into living places. For instance, that's what happens when Japanese people bow.

The act is usually accompanied by an exchange of cards. The bower may well not know the status of the bowee. Once the card is exchanged and the person's title is read, the bow is adjusted accordingly. In this, the Japanese bow does resemble the *reverence* performed by Louis XIV. The King's precise angle of bending from the waist and the speed with which he unfolded his arms depended on the status of the person Louis was acknowledging. But the Japanese bow, as Barthes imagined it, is a bonding act; it opens the gates to further communication, it creates a social space.

The word 'social' matters in this version of the bow. 'Social' rather than 'symbolical'. This difference appears if you contrast the

Japanese bow with the gestures made by French wrestlers, a subject he took up in one of his first books, *Mythologies*. The wrestlers put on an obviously fake show, Barthes believed, exaggerating their pain and protesting against the work of the referees for not being fair. They are making a point about injustice by dramatizing how the ring is rigged. Many of the gestures described in *Mythologies* carried a homily of this sort; it is indeed an old tradition in French literature, going back to the storytelling of La Bruyère. Rightly or wrongly, Japan seemed to Barthes a culture without such signifying baggage. A bow is a bow is a bow. The point is to bow properly, to do it with grace; it is the artfulness which gives the bow meaning and creates a social bond.

Barthes's account of making his way in Tokyo connects to his belief in the social bond created by well-performed gestures. The space of the city is indeterminate, one's place in it is created by ritualized gestures. Put in this way, his Tokyo is not such a foreign place. As we've seen in the rituals of the Kaddish, the bodily rituals are doing the same kind of socializing work. The bow differs from the bond of words Arendt theorized; such Japanese rituals are not equalizers – they recognize, indeed ritualize, differences. Above all, the gestures are artful. Here too is something not purely Japanese. Barthes was attuned to fashion, saying once to me, 'How people look matters more than what they say.' By this seemingly Andy Warhol-esque statement he meant that fashion is like bowing; it makes a statement but the statement is not personal. The well-cut suit or dress is a thing in itself; you respond to it, rather than the person wearing it. (He was however a slovenly dresser.) The theatre of the streets is created by the artful body, and this bodily theatre is the way people who don't know one another, who never will know one another, can feel a common bond.

It's not an accident, I suppose, that Tadao Ando's tent theatre shares something of this same ethos: providing an arousing but fleeting experience. In a way, Barthes's idea of bodily encounters is not so different from Baudelaire's evocation of modernity as temporary and partial. All these views of the theatre of the streets share with Arendt's idea of the discursive agora the belief that turning outward is good, turning away from community, from shared, local, intimate understandings towards more impersonal bonds.

In my own view, this turn outwards is what the open city is all about. Openness carries a lot of baggage, as it were. Opening up does not happen simply by clearing away barriers. It doesn't happen easily; you have to work at making a city open. Of all these views, I cleave most closely to Roland Barthes's: that the bonds between strangers are best created by physical experience, by gesture, by gesture which is artful and contrived, rather than natural – gesture which is theatrical. But an immense problem lurks here, as I was to discover in playing music with him.

12.

Bodies Cooperate

The sociable performer

We've rather taken for granted that performers can work together – and rightly so. Despite the supposedly outsized egos of artists, on stage they have to cooperate with people they don't like or there will be no performance. Musicians face a specific problem in that, when travelling, we frequently are working with people we don't know. That's when impersonal gestures serve us: they are ways of communicating expressively to strangers. On the road, we become Japanese.

There is an aspect of cooperation which is closer to the concern in this study with the bodily, non-verbal character of performance, cutting across all forms of performance, from rituals to stage plays, from dancing to music.

Expression comes most naturally to people who are, as the French say, 'at home in their skins'. Every player knows this; to perform well, they have to be at ease physically. If not relaxed, they will not communicate effectively to others; the gestures will be stiff or jerky or distorted. A disconnection appears between what the performer feels inside and what they express to others.

Ability to cooperate with others is grounded in the body. People must be 'at home' with one another. I will try to show this, first of all, by describing Roland Barthes playing the piano. In the previous chapter, my friend appeared as a Diogenes whose lamp illuminated the agora; in making music, his lamp went out.

I. Roland Barthes Plays Passionately and Badly

At the Piano

In Paris, I would occasionally play the piano for Barthes while he read and smoked. He liked to hear the Fauré *Barcarolles*, pieces with a surface prettiness and a more disturbed beauty underneath. A few times we engaged more actively, trying piano four-hands together – some Schubert and transcriptions from Mozart quartets. What struck me was that Roland, so subtle a writer, played both passionately and badly.

Whenever he hit a rough patch – notes he fluffed or simply could not play – he'd suddenly ritard the tempo or play loudly to emphasize the feeling rather than the notes. Many amateur musicians who are physically struggling hype up expression. And like these others, Roland worried too much about making mistakes, which only increased the probability that he would make more of them. He was also squeamish about touching, so he would lean away from me laterally. Tilting his body in this way distorted the trunk's relation to the arms, so that he couldn't use the full weight of forearms in dropping down onto the keys. To compensate, he had then to hammer more forcefully from the wrists, thus dramatizing moments which were not at all passionate in character.

Anxiety crowded out naturalness. In the Schubert F minor Fantasie for piano four-hands, for instance, a little grace note of C to F back to C comes at the beginning of the opening movement to orient the singing right hand, the little flip then reappearing throughout the movement. It feels really good to play this flip, because it stabilizes the hand on the keyboard and releases tension. But Roland was not feeling the pleasure of flipping, as far as I could tell. Rather than making a graceful gesture, he stormed into the melody, hammering the initial C. This distorted the little two-note phrase; the stressed C sounded arbitrary.

As is true more generally, the motions of a tense body are often jerky or out of control because a person gripped by physical anxiety is too wrapped up in him- or herself to gesture freely. The command 'Relax!' is however seldom going to get someone to relax; it will only make them more tense.

A stranger listening to Roland Barthes playing the piano might mistakenly conclude that he didn't understand the music, which was hardly the case; he wrote beautifully about it. The stranger would accurately reckon, though, that at these crisis moments Roland wasn't responsive to others, ignoring the raised eyebrow by which I sought to signal to him that an entrance was coming up, nor would he respond to the ritards I provided which would give him more time to execute a run. He was too wrapped up in his difficulties to be attuned to someone else. Anxiety ridden, 'How much I feel' came at the expense of awareness of others.

Roland knew that something was wrong about how he performed the art he loved. In the essay *Musica Practica* he declared that 'there are two musics . . . the music one listens to, the music one plays. These are totally different arts.' The one comes from 'the desire to make the music' while the other 'relieves the listener of all activity . . . abolishes in the sphere of music the very notion of doing'. The split did not make Roland happy: 'I am,' he remarked to me after one mistake breakdown, 'self-alienating.'[1]

Idealization

Idealization is what got in Barthes's way. Goethe pictured idealization in his novel *The Sorrows of Young Werther*, in 1774. Werther elevates Charlotte to the 'only love', the 'perfect love' – but his love is hopeless, she can never be possessed. Our hero commits suicide. (The book supposedly inspired a wave of suicides among its younger readers.) *The Sorrows of Young Werther* echoes Goethe's own love for Charlotte Buff, who was already engaged to someone else; the more frustrated he became, the more angelic Charlotte seemed to be. Against idealization, Goethe eventually found pleasure in Italy, in walking in a lemon grove, hearing the tolling of bells, wandering the streets early in the morning – I'd say that it is true generally that simple physical loves are better for us than idealized human passion.

Roland was a great self-analyst of the harm idealization can do; it informs some of the saddest pages of his writing. In the essay *Fragments d'un discours amoureaux*, he describes waiting in a café for an absent heart-throb to ring him. The silent telephone prompts a 'scenography of waiting'. There were in fact dozens of young men in love with Roland, but they didn't figure in his experience of desire. The non-caller must be the love of his life – so beautiful, so intelligent, the very ideal of a loved one. 'The being I am waiting for is not real,' he acknowledges, and then quotes the psychologist R. W. Winnicott: '"I create it over and over, starting from my capacity to love, starting from my need for it."' Barthes's description of waiting for the phone to ring in the Odeon café also echoes Schubert's song 'Die Taubenpost'; both evoke *Sehnsucht*, pure longing, the siren voice of Eros. In it, desire and absence are inseparable.

There's a good side in all art to experiencing physical discomfort. Faced with resistance, the artist may get more involved than when things come easily. Moreover, the player is measuring him- or herself against an ideal standard of how the music should sound. As we saw in Chapter 3, believing in a right way which is for the moment his way combats resistance; yes you are struggling, but you are struggling to get it right.

Yet what happens if you don't? As with players like Roland, if you don't feel you can meet the challenge, that you are not measuring up to a performance, you will be driven even more inside yourself. We've visited the experience of not-measuring-up already. It was Herbert Marcuse's critique of the performance principle in everyday labour – the shaming, paralysing gap between the ideal worker you should be and the actual you. On the docks, this gap turned workers inward and led them to drink more heavily and silently as the afternoon unfolded.

The challenge in art, love and work is the same: how to 'de-idealize' what you are doing, but still strive to do it well. This challenge can, I believe, be met in the body.

II. The Body at Ease

I'm going to leave Roland struggling at the piano for a moment, and describe how 'de-idealization' has been dealt with by cellists. The problem surfaces particularly for us in confronting a difficulty built into our instruments.

Vibrato

On a stringed instrument, vibrato is a rocking motion of the left hand on a string which colours a note around its precise pitch; waves of sound spread out in vibrato like ripples from a pool into which one has thrown a stone. Vibrating sound isn't unique to string players; singers vibrate in the larynx, horn players in their quivering lips. In the stringed instruments, the fingertip makes the initial contact, though the energy to rock comes from further back, from the elbow ball-joint, the movement passing through the forearm into the palm of the hand and then to the fingertip.

The difficulty with vibrato on the cello is that the instrument is not entirely user-friendly. It can make a harsh noise when the cellist plays the E and F notes on the G string, a bleating sound like a sheep's call. The defect can be made worse when the cellist vibrates in the danger zone; then it sounds like radio static. User-unfriendliness arises from the sheer size of the cello. High notes on the instrument lie far away on the fingerboard, rather than near to hand. To get there, the left hand has to go into thumb position, which means the thumb has to move from beneath the neck of the cello up on to the strings themselves, a move which triggers a minute resistance in the subclavius, the muscle connecting the armpit to the pectoral mass. Vibrating in thumb position frequently causes the subclavius to tense up.

How can the player connect to an instrument which is not entirely user-friendly? The cellist wants to prevent physical difficulty from deforming expression. I'll briefly describe ways this challenge can be met naturally in the body and more artificially by donning a mask.

Minimum Force

The simplest way to put the body at ease is to deploy minimum force in playing. As an adolescent I once performed the Schubert Cello Quintet with the cellist Madeline Foley, who was fascinated by the famous passages in the slow movement when the second cello can become mired in the danger zone on the G string. She discovered that the ugly noise could be transformed by drawing back the bow towards the neck as the bleat began, while lightening up pressure on the bow. Minimum force can of course aid all sorts of music-making. When Maria Callas entered challenging territory in Bellini's opera *Norma*, she held back her breathing volume rather than force more air through her windpipe.

Working with Ambiguity

Beginners on string instruments are often taught to play notes in tune by the teacher plastering little bands of tape across the fingerboard, so that kids know exactly where to put their fingers. Yet once the seemingly helpful bands of tape are removed, the kids are often chagrined, since the now blank surface offers no hints about exactly where the fingers should go. A better procedure is to leave the board untaped. By having to search from the beginning where the fingers should go, the student in the end makes a more assured, secure and relaxed contact with the fingerboard.

Kyudo

The third way to relax is to stop and do nothing for a moment when you encounter a difficulty, rather than attack it straightaway. There can be a moment of blanking out, of ceasing to feel anxious because you are feeling nothing; then you begin to play, and often you are surprised that you are playing well. A bit of Zen philosophy explains why this happens. In 1948 the philosopher Eugen Herrigel described, in *Zen in the Art of Archery*, how an archer learns to hold the bow in a Zen practice called Kyudo. In a trance, 'the archer ceases to be conscious of himself as the one who is engaged in hitting the bull's-eye which confronts him. This state of unconsciousness is realized only when, completely empty and rid of the self, he becomes one with the perfecting of his technical skill . . .' The essence of Kyudo is to discipline oneself to do nothing: looking away from the target is how you enter in Kyudo; similarly in playing music, looking away from the score or, better, closing it is a ritual which will prepare you to play better.[2]

Barthes's fear of touching can be addressed by Kyudo. Partners at the piano will sit silently, doing nothing, but with their thighs touching each other. This is the Kyudo intervention. Over the course of a few minutes, sexual anxiety or simple squeamishness then may evaporate. When the exercise ends and the players begin to play, they will not lean away from one another, causing their bodies to stress; thigh is comfortable with thigh. I cannot report success with Roland on this score, but have found that it works well when teaching boys and girls to partner in playing piano four-hands.

Artifice Enabling Naturalness

The Barthes problem has altogether another sort of solution, if the performer wears a certain kind of mask.

Nearly a century ago the costume designer Amleto Sartori devised this mask by stretching leather over a wooden mould, then shaping it into a full-face visage, rigid, blank of all expression, usually painted dead-white. Sartori had studied closely the huge variety of half-face commedia dell'arte masks, but rejected the fixed expressions and characterizations they conveyed, since the player had to behave in character with the mask they wore. Sartori wanted to free the actor from playing to type. He was also unhappy with the mime make-up used by Marcel Marceau and other masters of this art. The mime's face did too much expressive work, or so Sartori thought, at the expense of gestures in the rest of the mime's body. (Not true, by the way; a great mime like Marceau uses his whole body expressively.)

Nonetheless, Sartori made an important discovery. Wearing a neutral mask can relax the actor's body. Showing nothing on one's face means that all the energy pours into one's physical movements. Many musicians make a kindred discovery: if you don't grimace, sigh or break out into a rapturous smile when you perform, you play much more naturally, and the listener engages with the music rather than remarking how much you are feeling.

After the Second World War, Sartori worked with Jacques Lecoq, who had trained as a mime. They taught a long line of actors and directors how to use the neutral mask to free the body, their work radiating out to theatre-makers as diverse as Giorgio Strehler and Ariene Mnouchkine. The logic of the Sartori mask would have been obvious to anyone watching dancers downtown in 1963, particularly in Merce Cunningham's New York studio. If a dancer broke into a smile, or betrayed any other facial expression, Mercer's coaches sometimes shouted out 'smiling!' as a reproach. Uptown, the coaches working for the ballet master George Balanchine did much the same thing, which the dancer/teacher Alexandra Danilova called 'clearing the face'. The face was made blank in order that the dancers pour their energies into movement.

The Sartori mask is particularly helpful if you are playing naked. Today naked dancing is a rather ho-hum experience, but fifty years ago it was shocking to the public and deeply uneasy for the performers, as for the Judson dancers. They were playing to voyeuristic sexual fantasies rather than being watched for their art. Wearing Sartori masks helped relieve some of that unease. Their faces covered, they danced more freely because they did so as anonymous bodies.

The blank mask as an artifice enabling naturalness goes back to the debates about gesture taking place in Diderot's time. Imagine Madame Alexis, playing Phèdre, very slowly raising her left arm to the shoulder of her stepson Hippolytus, whom Phèdre craves sexually. Passion does not register on the face of Madame Alexis; her face is a blank. All the expression lies in the gesture of resting her arm on the shoulder of the actor playing Hippolytus – who also does not react facially. This is Sartori's idea of the artifice which frees the body to be expressive, when the face itself become a mask.

In the nineteenth century, and particularly with the advent of Darwinian science, facial gestures were thought important as revealing the animal in human beings. Darwin's *The Expression of Emotions in Animals and Man* advanced the idea that the facial and bodily gestures of all animals are involuntary – as we would say today, genetically programmed. Darwin's human evidence comes in large part from photographs of mental patients, grimacing in pain, or from people in helpless laughter or the throes of anger; it is these images of people in extremis, unable to control themselves, that he compares with the expressions of apes and other higher mammals.[3]

Darwin's book made an erroneous distinction which still rules today. This was and is to divide the natural from the artificial, to suppose that artifices like a Sartori mask are deceptive, hiding what people really feel. In fact, we need artifice to release us naturally, to express ourselves physically. Artifice tames the body in extremis – it creates a broader palette of natural expression than people who are raging or laughing out of control. The important thing about artifice, or bodily techniques like Kyudo, or using minimum force, is that these ways of putting the body at ease allow people to work easily with one another. The relaxed body can become a cooperative body.

III. Wordless Cooperation

In advancing this argument, I have to admit to a prejudice.

When rehearsing, I loathe talky discussions about the composer's intentions, disquisitions on cultural context and the like, instead preferring a raised eyebrow, a grunt or a slight tilt of the torso to communicate with others. These non-verbal signals don't stop the flow of playing together – which is true also in sports, and more generally in a large chunk of labour. Non-verbal expression enables crews of cooks, construction workers or surgeons to communicate effectively and efficiently without stopping to explain what they are doing. On the verbal side, cooperation is too often described as being like a contract, as a goal agreed upon which people then pursue together. That's a superficial view because people have to work together, to see what's possible and what isn't, in order to know then how to relate to each other. Just as cooperation is mistakenly thought to be contractual, so it's imagined that cooperation should run like clockwork, each individual playing a specialized part that supports the activities of others. This image of efficient collaboration the sociologist Émile Durkheim called 'mechanical solidarity'. Deeper collaboration kicks in when there's a difficult or problematic task at hand, so that people working together need to make an effort of mutual understanding rather than simply carry out an assigned, specialized task. As in military operations on the battlefield, unexpected events demand on-the-spot interpretation. A soldier who simply follows the instructions of a military handbook is not going to help the squad or company work well. Rather than a contract, cooperation is a non-verbal process.

Wordless Cooperation in a Hierarchy

The biggest mistake in understanding cooperation is to think of it as a shared process among equals. And it's just here that musical rehearsals prove illuminating. In rehearsing with a conductor, orchestral players are supposedly following the orders of a higher-up telling them what to do. But this is only in theory. In practice, even the most dictatorial conductor cannot give explicit directions for each and every note to thirty players, let alone a hundred. Because the conductor and the players are communicating non-verbally, the conductor has to make a gesture, usually a mere flick of the hand, the raising of an eyebrow, or just a stare, which the player translates into pressing down harder on the bow, blowing a horn more softly or pounding a drum on the rim rather than the centre.

Moreover, there is feedback from the floor to the podium. Most conductors – even dictators like Toscanini – modify the signals they make in response to how orchestra players interpret them. Toscanini's stick work with the La Scala orchestra in Milan was very different from the methods he employed when conducting his own NBC Symphony in New York. Feedback is built into the signals by which a conductor keeps time for the players. He or she has to hear the sound in his or her head a moment before it occurs physically, in order to gesture to the players what is coming up; were the conductor's baton to fall exactly on the beat or at a change of volume, it would be too late – the sound would already have happened. He or she is always ahead, and so can lead. In turn, the players have to judge just when to respond before the conductor's arm reaches the end of its movement. Again, to wait until the full stretch of the arm would be too late. The good conductor – even if leading unfamiliar players – will pick up on this response and adjust the speed and stretch at which the arm moves.

Explanations of conducting often include a chart of hand gestures for different time-signatures. If the time is three beats a measure, the conductor should wave his hands in a triangle; if four beats a measure, make a down, then side to side, then up motion, and so on for each signature. These images are often self-destructing guides. (A favourite tease-torture when I was studying at the conservatory was to give an apprentice conductor the score of Bizet's opera *Carmen*. Following the standard hand-signal approach the conductor would soon tie himself in knots, because the time signatures in many of the arias change so often, and the tempos change so fluidly.) The same thing is true, I think, of the images that Darwin collected for his book on expression. Expressions of manic mental patients in pain tell you that the patient is feeling something, but they give you no way to understand what exactly that pain is and so to respond empathetically.

In sum, the physically relaxed, expressive gestures like those used in conducting mediate between unequals. Cooperation results.

I had the privilege of experiencing wordless cooperation of this sort for one week under the baton of the elderly Pierre Monteux, though the following comments are derived from films rather than my now-feeble memories of sixty years ago. In 1943 he created a conducting school in Hancock, Maine, where among overweight mosquitos and in freezing summer nights he gathered young musicians who served in an orchestra and whom he instructed in the art of conducting. He seemed frail if you looked only at his bent back, or noticed his shuffling gait as he moved to and from the podium. It was otherwise to the musicians he faced. In conducting Beethoven's Eighth Symphony with the Chicago Symphony in 1961, for instance (filmed and still available on YouTube) he draws an amazing sound from the musicians, sometimes lush, sometimes savage, sometimes so rhythmically pulsing that you could dance to it. Aesthetically, the music sounds natural and unforced, a result achieved technically by the conductor making small gestures to the players – sometimes just an elevation of the left wrist to the second violins, or a slight turn of the neck to the right to look at the tympani.[4]

These miniaturized gestures were contained in the so-called 'Monteux box', an imaginary rectangle framed horizontally by the space between his shoulders and vertically by the space between his belly and his neck. In part, miniaturization forced players to concentrate on him visually – there are no big prompts like Leonard Bernstein's whole-body gyrations, which you could follow without focusing on precisely. And just because the Monteux box is largely invisible to the audience, listeners focus on what they hear – rather than, as with Bernstein, watch him dance. Monteux would encourage players to look up from their printed scores at each other as well as at himself, and players indeed did so, imitating the same slight signals of raised eyebrow or forward tilt coming to them from the podium.

The conductor's body needs to be at ease for the 'Monteux box' to work, relaxed in order to make small gestures; a tense body tends to make bigger, often more convulsive ones. And Monteux's conducting exemplified the social side of ambiguous gesturing. This occurred when he gave what became known to us as the 'Monteux shrug'. A slight lifting of the shoulders signalled that all was not well and we'd have to repeat the passage. The shrug did not, however, indicate what had gone wrong. In rehearsals, Monteux often left the solution to the players, rather than putting into words how to fix the problem.

The shrug exemplified one social use of ambiguity. My experience of professional orchestras is that sorting out an ambiguous problem can happen very fast – only one shrug followed by one repetition of a passage and things are set right. It's not all that mysterious; once the bodily movement feels right, the sound will be corrected. The thunderbolts of inspiration, beloved of arts-managers and publicists, seldom strike in the rehearsal room; instead, quieter, bodily, wordless cooperation pushes rehearsals forward.

Among Equals

Wordless cooperation can work in settings where the participants are equals. Again, musical practice provides instructive examples, of which I'll choose rehearsals of the Debussy String Quartet, a piece I rehearsed many times for public performance. Written early in the composer's life, this is a radical piece; in the words of Pierre Boulez, the quartet freed chamber music from 'rigid structure, frozen rhetoric and rigid aesthetics'. That translates into fluid passages in the opening movement when one instrument has to pick up seamlessly from another as though a single instrument is playing. How to accomplish this in rehearsal? If the musicians play their entrances and exits without any expression (neither swelling nor fading away) a seamless connection will begin to take form, like pipes that fit together without any visible join. Kyudo here appears as the momentary suspension of expression to enable ensemble cooperation.

Among equals, bodily cooperation may seem simple, especially if the players have worked together for a while. But still, cooperation is usually open-ended. A raised eyebrow could mean equally we are going too fast or too slow. In the Debussy, tension might cause a player to send a false signal, such as a swell, which the other players might pick up and imitate, just because they are all on an equal footing, no one person in control. If things can be put right, that repair will consist of how the gesture feels. If it releases tension, this will

communicate itself to the others in small details like suddenly leaning forward rather than sitting rigidly backward, a gesture of release
which the other players will pick up. You'll often see this in a performance: leaning forward is a gesture which seems to pass from
player to player. Their bodies are communicating.

Cooperation has become a mantra in the modern office, just
because there's so little of it. Musicians in rehearsal show how cooperation in everyday life might be improved: one obvious suggestion is
that people stop Zooming or emailing, and work face-to-face, physically together, communicating physically. But these rehearsal practices
matter to artists, within a larger framework of art-making.

There is a tension in all creative work between process and product. Endlessly working over a piece of music or a poem – art as pure
process – begins after a certain point to degrade the work. It stales
on the maker, or he or she starts to fuss over details which distract
from the whole. At a certain point the process needs to stop, which
is to say that the artist needs to learn how to surrender. On the
other hand, impulse art, in which an outburst of making is left
untouched and presented as a final product, is usually also bad art;
our first impulses are not usually our best.

The cult of impulse, of spontaneity in art, sometimes takes hold
of artists, by claiming that truth and authenticity are unpremedi-
tated. The performing artist cannot afford to succumb to this cult.
He or she needs to work with others who are not carbon-copies of
him or herself, and so will have different impulses. But even so, the
performer can work naturally, by working non-verbally. This work
requires discipline, or to put it a bit differently, naturalness requires
artifice. The result of this body craft will be that the performer
becomes a sociable artist, responsive to others in an inherently collective art.

13

The Performer Invents

Improvising and cutting

We recall that the ancient Greek word for creation, *poesis*, meant making something which had not existed before. Most performers cannot practise art on these terms. There is a text, a score, a choreography which we are enacting; it can be enacted in different ways, but the score is always a touchstone. Which means, of course, that the performer's freedom is limited. Still, no good cellist would ever proudly announce: 'I play the Bach suites now exactly as I played them twenty years ago.'

The following pages explore how the performer goes about altering a performance. In my biased elderly view, it's only in the later stages of life that performers truly understand how to do this – a gift which ageing makes to art, thought it entails a cruel irony. The elderly musician's handgrip weakens; the arthritic actor can no longer bound around the stage; the dancer's fate, perhaps the most cruel, is that they are deemed old professionally at the onset of middle age. These weaknesses appear just when the performer's understanding of music, script or choreography has deepened and matured. But a performer may not be paralysed by the irony of knowing more while being able to do less. New ways of performing a score, script or choreography can open up: the two most important, in my view, are the capacity to improvise and the knowledge of how radically to cut out things.

In general, ageing felt as a sheer loss does a disservice to oneself and to others; a departed partner would not want the survivor to sink into unending grief. Like the lessons derived from musical rehearsals about cooperation in life, the ways elderly performers renew themselves may thus have a larger reach.

I. Alberta Hunter Improvises

Loss

Renewal by improvising marked the story of an elderly jazz singer, Alberta Hunter, who came out of retirement to transform an iconic work of art. The background to her story concerns the legendary impresario Barney Josephson, who created the Cookery in 1968 – a bar, restaurant and jazz club at 8th Street and University Place in Manhattan. The Cookery would have won no architectural prizes, being just a big, glassed-in room at the bottom of an apartment building. At lunch, it fed mostly professors at New York University. Clean and bland, the place seemed a portent of the gentrification which would erode the bohemia of Washington Square.

From about nine at night, though, the Cookery changed character. In the 1970s the Cookery was one of the few places in the city that showcased high-art jazz, along with the Blue Note a few blocks south. It was also one of the few places outside Harlem that welcomed Blacks in as patrons.

Josephson broke the entertainment mould in perhaps his most famous production, in which the singer Billie Holiday performed 'Strange Fruit', a song about the lynching in 1930 of two Black men, Thomas Shipp and Abram Smith. Written by Abel Meeropol, the lyrics are indirect: it takes a while to feel that the two hanging dead bodies are like fruit on trees. The music is mostly soft, whispered rather than shouted; its *tessitura* – the range of low to high of notes – is compressed. Josephson arranged for 'Strange Fruit' to be presented in a restrained way when Holiday first performed it in 1939. She was spotlit in an otherwise darkened room. No food or drink was served during the song, which ended Holiday's set. People, overcome by the story, usually did not applaud, and there was no encore.

At the Cookery, Josephson asked the elderly Alberta Hunter to sing 'Strange Fruit', recreating the famous work forty years later.

She liked to be called 'Miss Hunter', I discovered, both as a mark of respect and also to make the point that she belonged to no man; for years she had lived with another woman, Lottie Tyler, both in New York and in France. A crisis had occurred in Miss Hunter's middle age when her mother died, and the singer withdrew from singing, working for decades as a hospital nurse.

During this period she performed only very occasionally, so that when she returned to the Cookery she was rusty, breathing in stage-fright gusts. Moreover, the decay of her vocal chords meant that even the limited *tessitura* proved too much for her – 'decay', that is, as measured against the amazing, full-throated recordings she had made in the 1930s.

Improvisation

To deal with these difficulties, Hunter began to scat-sing, a long-established way of performing which she partially reinvented to cope with her disabilities. Scatting involves using syllables or sounds rather than whole words, treating the syllables like the notes on a saxophone, trumpet or bass. Jazz scatting thus incorporates the singer into a group of players, rather than sets them apart. Alberta Hunter performed in the late 1920s with Sidney Bechet, the saxophonist who expanded improvisation based on traditional blues; to work with him, she first began to scat-sing.

Improvisation in early jazz followed the principle of 'blowing', fitting melodic flights into an existing harmonic structure. During the bebop era of the 1940s, improvisation became more harmonically complex, as is reflected in Hunter's recordings of this time in London, for instance 'Down-hearted Blues', a piece she had herself written. The bebop era forged new ways of improvising, crystallized by the horn player Charlie Parker (1920–1955). He organized improvisations around 'targeting', in which the harmonic fundamentals only slowly reveal themselves as the performer plays. Unlike in 'blowing', the course of a line does not follow an established cadence progression. Parker structured the harmonic unfolding by what are technically called '3 to flat 9' relations in a chord. The flat 9 note does not serve as a leading tone, as would a diminished 7th, resolving the harmony; instead, this bigger, dissonant stretch frames further explorations which cut free, in other keys, from this tension.

When challenged technically in the Cookery, Miss Hunter drew on Parker's technique, adapting it to her voice. (I'm drawing on notes I made at the time since musically these performances were so striking.) She sang syllables, but tuned them, in bebop fashion, so that eventually they stretched between 1 and flat 9, which was the furthest she could reach (the notes are a half step more than an octave apart). Once she established the relationship, her pianist partner took over in long improvisations that let her rest her voice.

Improvisation of this sort, which modifies a technique learned in the past, isn't, of course, only musical. It equally served the aged choreographer Merce Cunningham, for instance. He was the presiding father figure for the Judson dancers of my youth, who by the 1990s had to deal with their own ageing bodies. By then, Cunningham's cartilage was largely gone at the shoulder and knee joints, which ached every time he moved. He created some entirely new work to cope with his pain, drawing on digital technology to interact on screen with younger dancers, as in the piece *Hand-drawn Spaces* of 1998. But when he danced himself, he reformatted moves he had designed years before, making greater use of the wrists, and adding a side-shuffling of the legs that did not strain his knee-joints.

These may seem small changes and, like Miss Hunter's scat-singing, not really innovations of a sweeping sort. But they mattered a great deal to the ageing performers. They found a new freedom of expression when they could do less physically. In a way this sense of freedom is not so far off from the freedom musicians of any age might experience in riffing off a printed score.

Improvising on a Score

Monteverdi's *The Coronation of Poppea* is a good example of the parallels between jazz improvising and improvising on a printed, classical music text. The plot of *Poppea* would have driven John of Salisbury to a heart attack, because it is about the triumph of a prostitute who succeeds in having the wife of a king murdered and then has herself crowned as queen. As a celebration of immoral self-fashioning, Pico would equally have hated it. But it is exhilarating to perform because it gives both singers and players a sense of freedom in playing though improvising.

In the late medieval era music wasn't yet printed, and musicians mostly learned by listening to how others sang, blowed, or plucked. Even when there were written scores for vocal music, they usually showed only one fixed line; the other lines were filled in thanks to traditions of rhythm and instrumentation which the player had learned. This situation changed in the time of the Renaissance, as printing pinned down sounds on paper. Printed music would serve the master composer of the Renaissance, Josquin des Prez (*c.* 1450/1455–1521), in part because his music was complex in a new sense. Four or six voice parts were given equal value by Josquin, the voices interacting melodically, the texture of their interaction harmonically ever thicker. Such dense music had to be written out to be performed; thanks largely to printing, the performer became the servant of the composer.

Printed music might thus seem to have limited the musician's freedom of improvisation. Instead, a different kind of freedom arose, as became evident by the time of Monteverdi's *Coronation of Poppea*.

When Poppea is enraged, for instance, the singer can convey this by adding short, sharp repetitions of the same note, called a *trillo*. The singer has to figure out how to make those stuttering bursts sound angry: should they swell step by step in volume or boil over in a sudden explosion which exhausts itself? To decide, the player has to understand what has enraged the character: a sudden, unforeseen disaster, or slow-burning, seething anger which finally spills out? There's no one right way to play the *trillo*; it depends on the singer's interpretation. Similarly, there are places – *passaggi* – where the singer adds notes by walking the base line, as in jazz improv, in order to emphasize the action happening on stage. There are also interjections called *grazie*, which retard the pace of the music, usually stretching out the tempo, as though the music is held in suspension. Finally, the performers assert their presence at moments called *recitar cantando*, which mediate between almost spoken explanations and dramatically acted-out arias. The twists and turns of the plot do require a lot of explanation, so as the explanation stretches out, an accompanist might ginger things up by adding free-form decorations.[1]

In the printed versions of *Poppea*, many of these riffs are written out, but some scholars think that the scores register after the fact what actually happened during rehearsals. Once the musicians have worked out the possibilities, *trillos* and *passaggi* change from night to night in the actual performances. As I say, the freedom of a jazz improviser is something which for centuries had a reflection in classical music. If Alberta Hunter were to have sung *Poppea*, she could have adapted these improvising techniques to her own vocal circumstances and made a convincing job of it.

Late Style

Poppea is a late work for Monteverdi; expression that comes late in a person's life is given, in cultural studies, a special value. The critic Theodor Adorno thought of 'late style' as a refusal of the present, particularly a refusal at the end of an artistic career to engage with the expectations of the public. He sees late style of this transcendent sort appearing in Beethoven's *Missa Solemnis* or in his last string quartets. Late style seems to Adorno to have a socio-economic side wider than classical music. The elderly artist rejects expression that can be exploited by the 'culture industry', the institutional exploitation and cheapening of art, and finally, at the end of life, the artist can cut free. For better or worse, Adorno celebrated the supposed explosion of rare genius in old age.

A more inclusive account of late style comes from the writer Edward Said, who focuses on the 'late' in 'belatedness', as he puts it. The creator feels emotionally centred in an earlier time. Regret for the past, and more largely the feeling that something compelling is ending, marks belatedness. One is not centred in one's own time; one's heart is somewhere else. An example would be Richard Strauss's opera *Der Rosenkavalier*, written on the eve of the First World War, suffused with longing for the aristocratic graces of the vanishing past.

Miss Hunter was dealing with 'belatedness', drawing on what she knew and could do decades earlier – but there is no regret, indeed no attempt to reproduce as faithfully as possible Billie Holiday's version of 'Strange Fruit'. When her memory failed, Miss Hunter also occasionally dropped a line or two entirely, without covering up by scat-singing. Her cuts, I realized after hearing her make them night after night, were cunning. She always cut out parts of the middle stanzas, so that the story remained more obscure; the listener had to engage with and fill in the missing middle. Though I can't prove it, it seems to me that Miss Hunter may have steadied herself by making these cuts – released from the tension of remembering. But it is a dialogue with the past, a dialogue based on the damage age inflicted on her. In that dialogue, she set herself free from being over, from being 'belated'.

II. George Balanchine Makes a Ruthless Cut

The other way an elderly performer can set him- or herself free is by a more ruthless cutting. Rather than rest on one's laurels, one can, as it were, shred them.

The Cut

Like other balletomanes at the New York City Ballet on 1 May 1979, I watched in stunned surprise George Balanchine's revival of *Apollo*.

Balanchine created *Apollo* in 1928 based on Igor Stravinsky's *Apollon Musagète*; it is one of the greatest ballets of the century, and seemed a perfect piece of art. In his *Autobiography*, Stravinsky had declared, 'George Balanchine as ballet master had arranged the dances exactly as I had wished.' Balanchine felt the same about the music; in 1948 he declared that 'In "Apollo" and in all the music that follows, it is impossible to imagine substituting for any single fragment the fragment of any other Stravinsky score. Each piece is unique in itself; nothing is replaceable.' *Apollo* was now, in 1979, radically altered by Balanchine, the beginning and the ending scenes cut, Stravinsky's music cut; at one stroke, nearly a third of the ballet was missing.

Originally, *Apollo* had a clear storyline. Born to Leto, the god discovers his own beauty and power. The Muses of music, poetry and dance perform for him, and he chooses Terpsichore, the goddess of dance, as the one he loves best. At the end, Apollo leads the three Muses to Parnassus, where they live for ever after. Now, Balanchine had taken away Apollo's youth and his apotheosis; there was only the play of dancing in the middle.[2]

When Stravinsky began collaborating with George Balanchine in the 1920s they reasserted the formal values of classicism. In 1936, in the Norton lectures at Harvard, Stravinsky declared, 'in classical dancing, I see the triumph of studied conception over vagueness, of the rule over the arbitrary, of order over the haphazard.' The public expected such balance, and so, on that May evening when Balanchine revealed his new version of *Apollo*, they did not react well. In the *Ballet Review*, Robert Garis called the production a 'depredation'. Balanchine reacted badly to his many critics. To his biographer, Bernard Taper, Balanchine said angrily, 'I don't have to explain why I change things. I can do with my ballets whatever I like.' But he kept on offering explanations. In an interview he declared, 'I took out all the garbage,' as though the cuts were like throwing away things you don't need when you downsize.

Here is 'late style' as Adorno imagined it, the artist set free from the public and from the culture industry which had grown up around Balanchine and the New York City Ballet, an industry full of publicists, fundraisers and tour managers. To a large extent, Balanchine was in fact shielded from their ministrations, thanks to Lincoln Kirstein, the choreographer's professional partner. Rather, he had recovered, I think, an impulse which first appears when children are young, which is suppressed in adulthood, and then freed again in old age.

We are all familiar with the child who takes apart a doll to see what's inside, and how it works; had I given my grandson a dissecting knife, our house would have been littered with cut-open corpses. The destruction of a doll or any toy by the child is more than mere curiosity: it is an aggressive, violent exploration. The intact object seems to have a life of its own which excludes the child; tearing the doll apart is a way of reclaiming it as *your* thing.

Most adult creative work has to repress this sort of violent repossession. We want, on the contrary, to have our creations take on a life of their own, to become something solid and tangible which shows what we can do. But buried in this eminently sensible desire to make something valuable in its own right lies, I think, the impulse to repossess, to start again, to renew – by destroying. And that impulse can be acted on in old age, when the work has stacked up, like a museum full of your past. Which you want to reclaim in order to feel you are not over.

I realize this is armchair psychoanalysing (though why not?). But recovery of this sort has overtly afflicted composers like Brahms, who was an eternal reviser, and performers like Daniel Barenboim, who recorded pieces over and over – not for any profitable motive; he just wanted to make them again. Balanchine took to an extreme this impulse to recover his work – and it seems no accident that he did this with *Apollo*; it was a youthful, perfectly formed classical ballet. He recovered it from its past, and his, by cutting into it.

There are, in the work itself, unstable elements which made this ruthless cut not quite as arbitrary as it might seem. About Terpsichore's solo dance, for instance, the ballet critic Arlene Croce observes, 'We see leaps that do not advance, leaps that go *down*, back–front reversals that seem to maintain the mysterious constancy of a shape even as it changes.' Stravinsky's score similarly runs eighteenth-century harmonies backwards, so that chords move from resolution to irresolution and simple melodies are chopped up, their fragments reassembled in odd patterns as the music moves forward. As Balanchine declared in his Dance Index piece, ' "Apollo" I look back on as the turning point of my life . . . It seemed to tell me that I could dare not to use everything, that I, too, could eliminate.'[3]

Balanchine's ruthless cuts were done in the same spirit as Alberta Hunter's scats and cuts in 'Strange Fruit'. For both, performing an iconic piece involved more than simply repeating it: improvising and severe cutting brought the icon to life.

Even as Stravinsky was beginning to sketch the music that would come to fruition in *Apollo,* he asked himself, in a diary entry of 1917:

Why is it that changes can take place within me from one year to another . . . resulting from man's constant and vital appetite for change – whereas in Art such phenomena are cause for reproach? Constant, unchanging devotion [formalism] is valueless . . . not fruitful.[4]

Stravinsky speaks of the artist's personal 'appetite' for change as somehow at odds with the essential, durable classical forms which he and Balanchine were set on reviving. But it is the inexorable passage of time, taking the artist closer and closer to death, which will challenge the classical idea of perfect finished form.

Many elderly people regret that much of what engaged them when they were young was a superficial waste of time – getting a better job title, looking smart. Balanchine did not regret. Violent reappropriation enabled him to keep creating.

BOOK SIX

Confrontation and Recognition

14.

Confrontation

Visceral, musical, visible

The Romantic poet Percy Bysshe Shelley's declaration, in his essay 'A Defence of Poetry', that 'poets are the unacknowledged legislators of society' is, on the face of it, sheer nonsense. Learning how to rhyme couplets does not enable you to design old-age pensions. Shelley meant instead that language is the vehicle by which we imagine society, and language can be both 'an instrument of intellectual freedom and a vehicle for political and social subjection'. This is true, as we have seen, on the stage. Performers have appeared as the agents of power, from Plato's invisible puppeteers to Donald Trump's virtuoso behaviour at mass meetings. The other side of performing, from Isabella Andreini to Bertolt Brecht, envisions performing as a challenge to power. Both sides of performing, in Shelley's view, are constituted through language.[1] In the following pages, I mean to dispute this. On stage, it is architecture, bodily gestures, costumes and masks that 'legislate' politics – whether to serve or to confront power.

I. No Provocation

Empty Words

Words often have a weak political punch. This was true in the time of the young Louis XIV, who sought to bring clichés such as *'L'état, c'est moi'* to life by how he danced; it was true in the French Revolution, whose leaders used the guillotine to make clear who was an enemy of the state, since the word 'enemy' had become empty of any precise meaning. This is, more generally, a problem of political language. The words themselves in certain circumstances cannot be made to mean anything; they are inherently empty. Empty words were epitomized in my parents' generation in the Spanish Civil War.

To them, the Spanish Civil War of 1936–9 seemed a 'pure' war: the forces of democracy were defending the Spanish Republic against the fascism of General Franco. People from all over Europe and North America, including my father and uncle, flooded into Spain, few of them professional soldiers. Like the Ukrainians fighting Russian fascism today, the international brigades pitted their wits and determination against the mass of planes, arms and manpower which Nazi Germany poured into the country.

But, unlike the resistance in Ukraine, the Spanish Civil War proved a deeply disillusioning event within the Republic's own forces. The left was divided between anarchists and communists, who fought each other viciously, and often the internal war of words descended into assassinations and bombings of the opposition's headquarters. My uncle, as he recounts in his memoirs, was in part saved from being drawn into these internal struggles because he and my father knew very little Spanish. Committed and effective communists in America, they became killers abroad.[2]

Those who did know the language explained the fratricide on the left as a sickness embedded in 'ideologies', whose substance was words: manifestos, speeches, newspaper articles. The words had little relation to action. For instance, when the Soviet Union signed a non-aggression pact with Nazi Germany in 1939, the press offices of the Communist Party went into overdrive to explain this ultimate betrayal of the Spanish Republic as a 'dialectic shift in the on-going struggle'. By 1939, many of the fighters, like my relatives, were sick of words and did not want to hear any more justifications or arguments, any more words.

Octavio Paz, a young Mexican poet at the time, a future diplomat of distinction, was one of those international combatants in Spain who was dismayed by the corruptions of revolutionary language.

The slogans of Soviet Communism had come to seem to him, as to the British writer George Orwell, as empty as those of fascism. Paz sought to renew the left by drawing on non-verbal practices. He first looked for alternatives to verbal provocation in the art of surrealists and in Dada – art that was meant to challenge the existing order through a theatre of the absurd, focused on non-verbal movements and gestures. The same impulse moved his Russian contemporary Vsevolod Meyerhold, who worked with mime as a performance technique in the 1920s, and who inspired Charlie Chaplin and other silent film actors. For Meyerhold, bodily mockery was a more powerful political tool than argument; he created many of the gestures Charlie Chaplin deployed in the film *The Great Dictator*, the Hitler/demagogue deflated by his own crazed gestures which have a Dada-like unreality.

In the 1940s, Paz took yet another turn, embracing 'the political power of ceremonies'. In *The Labyrinth of Solitude* he detailed how certain ancient Mexican rituals provided a way to perform collective resistance without sinking into the verbal mire. The important thing for Paz was that Mexicans came together in separating themselves wordlessly from power. He focused on dances celebrating the cults of death in ancient Mayan times. A bishop from Rome, say, could watch one of these ceremonies of the dead and not realize what was going on. The visiting cleric believed that puppets shaped as skeletons referred to the Miracle of the Resurrection, whereas for the Mexicans the grinning skulls told an older, Mayan story about the inevitable defeat of the powerful by death – a story aimed at the visiting white Roman bishop.[3]

The Carnivalesque

In spirit, these Mexican rituals exemplified what the Russian critic Mikhail Bakhtin, writing in the 1930s, called the 'carnivalesque'. This term described a particular performance that took place in many medieval towns and cities once a year, in which for a day peasants dressed up and acted as their masters, and nobles played peasants and household servants, obeying those who usually obeyed them. Bakhtin invested a great deal of hope into carnival role reversals. The masters might gain some sense of what it feels like to be treated as an inferior – but, more importantly, Bakhtin hoped that the peasants and servants would get a taste of what it feels like to be free, and the taste would linger. In the shadow of Stalin's Russian tyranny, Bakhtin imagined that the carnivalesque could prove an energizing practice, even provoking his own countrymen to revolt. In 1939, Stalin, perhaps sensing danger, made Bakhtin a 'non-person', silenced, invisible.

Bakhtin had misread the medieval carnivals. They worked like opening a steam valve to release pressure. Carnival over, things returned to normal. The release consisted of appropriating the costumes and gestures of the masters, even more than mimicking their speech. The return was similarly marked by resuming old clothes and shows of deference. Role reversals in carnival have worked like this since ancient times. Athenian women, for instance, celebrated a festival called the Adonia, when one night a year they climbed up ladders to gather on the roofs of houses within which they were largely confined during the day. The women threw pots of herbs down into the street, as a warning to men to keep away, while the roof-dwellers drank and sang to celebrate female solidarity. But when daybreak came, the celebrants climbed down from the roofs, cleaned up the mess they had made in the streets, and re-entered their houses, becoming once again silent servants.

The celebration of politically liberating ritual by Paz and Bakhtin has a larger frame in the fundamentally uneasy relations between performance and ritual, as explored in Chapter 1. Something is needed other than ritual, with its fixities and norms. It's not that there is something 'wrong' about the carnivalesque, but that ritual is not a creative event. A different kind of performance, more original, has to do the work of challenging and undermining the master.

II. In Place of Words

Just this happens, for instance and notably, in Mozart's opera *The Marriage of Figaro*, when it is staged in a certain way. It might seem that the politics of the opera lie in the words of its libretto. *Figaro* was based on a play by Beaumarchais portraying a servant smarter than his master who outwits the master's sexual predations. The play is taken today to be political, since it allies class and privilege with injustice. At the time, though, in the 1780s, it was played as and taken to be mere comedy, much enjoyed by the queen Marie Antoinette and by many of the aristocrats it skewered. A century earlier, as we saw in Chapter 8, Louis XIV sought to overcome stale verbal declarations of kingly supremacy by staging dancing in which he was the star. In *Figaro*, the process reverses; its music, the blocking of characters on stage and their gestures can be contrived to give confrontational politics more punch.

Figaro's arias are full of phrases which seem at first decorous, but then, when he repeats them, alter melodically or harmonically so that the initial impression is reversed; we hear Figaro sneering at himself being gracious. Throughout the opera, performers can emphasize this scored sneering through making ritards, accelerandos and other disturbances of pulse which mock the polished declarations of the Count. Even when *The Marriage of Figaro* is performed on the bare concert stage, without costumes or sets, audiences get what's going on just by listening. The sounds they hear dispose them to take the side of the servants.

Aural politics has existed from the very beginnings of opera, from Monteverdi's *Coronation of Poppea* down to modern works such as Britten's *Billy Budd*. You don't need to know the language or the libretto to get it. And it's why, as long as the music is faithfully observed, an opera like *Figaro* can be transposed from an elegant drawing room to a Louis Vuitton luggage store (as the director Peter Sellars once proposed to do) without the opera losing its bite. The bite is in the music.

The performer playing Figaro can, as it were, strengthen that bite. We recall from Chapter 3 – I am in a gathering-together mood – the red gun used in a staging of *La forza del destino* to make an otherwise absurd murder work on stage. At the very beginning of *Figaro*, in Act I, Scene 1, gun-play can be made to serve a more political effect. At the end of this scene, set in the workroom in which Figaro and Susanna live, Figaro seizes a musket from a closet and prances around the bed, table and chairs as though he is on a commando mission to shoot the Count, who is threatening Susanna's honour. In measure 121, when he hits a high F, he is meant to pull the trigger and pretend to wince at the recoil. All good fun. But this scene can be made politically telling if the gun is loaded with a stage blank bullet. An explosion actually occurs on the high F, and then Figaro should push the gun away and stare at it. The opening scene is fast moving, but at this point he should keep perfectly still, to convey first his disbelief, then his dawning awareness that he could actually kill the aristocrat. No longer good fun.

Proper blocking can equally sharpen the political edge of this opera. Act III, Scene 1 is set in the Count's study, the room from which he rules his little empire. He is alone with Susanna, who has contrived a plot with the Countess to expose the man's infidelities. At the beginning of this scene he sits at the desk writing, while she stands waiting for his orders, one way spatially to show the difference in power. As he becomes aroused by her, he springs away from the desk and makes her sit with him on a sofa. To seduce her, he then goes on his knees to plead with her; now the power positions are reversed. But at this point he sings one of Mozart's most beautiful, heartfelt arias ('Mi sento dal contento pieno di gioia il cor') and is revealed as deeply lonely, in need of love more than of sex. She tells him she will have a tryst with him later in a garden, and over the Count's kneeling body, his head in her lap, she forces out words of false love – she must frown to the audience even as she lies. And then she bolts from the sofa.

The blocking of their two bodies makes this scene work as a power game: standing, sitting alone, sitting together, kneeling, rising and running. The blocking defines their inequality. But this is not a simple difference, because the Count is not a simple person, and Susanna, after his great declaration, is filled with shame at her own deception as well as with loathing of him. If the performance is to work well, the players' postures must convey their isolation; if Susanna stands ramrod straight, the sobbing Count never looks at her.

If the blocking and postures are done right, this scene will dramatize inequality of a complex, mutually uncomprehending sort, rather than crude domination. The words alone don't do so; they are inconsequential or half-thoughts or elemental. The performers need to act against the words, and in this way deepen our sense of the gap between master and servant. It's sometimes said that these embodiments are 'added' to the meaning; quite the contrary, they make the meaning. Embodiment is particularly needed if the language of confrontation has become stale.

The same is true in the street. Techniques like these in *The Marriage of Figaro* can be deployed in political protest.

III. A March on Washington

On 28 August 1963, the 'March on Washington for Jobs and Freedom', took place. It had been organized by Bayard Rustin, a leader of the Black civil-rights movement, who aimed to mobilize national support, in the nation's capital, for the struggle over racial injustice that was taking place in the racially segregated American South. Today, the event is remembered for Martin Luther King's 'I have a dream' speech at the end. But this speech was the culmination of a carefully designed, grippingly theatrical event.

The authorities had mobilized attack dogs, water cannon and mounted policemen to combat the violence they expected, evidently believing that any large gathering would inevitably become a violent mob, as described by Gustave Le Bon in Chapter 3. But Rustin had organized a political ceremony which threw off balance the authorities' expectation of a bloody confrontation, such as had been happening throughout the South.

Non-violence was a creed for Martin Luther King, who had been much influenced by Mahatma Gandhi's civil-disobedience movement in India. The creed is not, as commonly thought, one of passive resistance; Gandhi sought out places and activities to which the authorities were likely to respond violently. For instance, he campaigned for the masses to make salt, since salt production was a monopoly trade controlled by the British overlords in India; he knew that ordinary people drying and packaging salt would be treated as criminals by the British. Gandhi's belief was that in responding violently to innocent activities, the British would expose the sheer hollowness of their right to rule.

In America, non-violence took on a different character. Rather than focus on a single activity, King understood that he had to challenge discrimination across the board. The struggles in the South to desegregate schools, restaurants and public transport were inseparably linked; a racially integrated school implied a racially integrated bus, which implied a racially integrated restaurant. However, systematic linkage increased the likelihood of violent reaction by the dominant powers, who would seek to evade responsibility by claiming that the protesters had provoked them into using state violence.

This overreaction was the dynamic Rustin had to defeat. On the whole he succeeded. Though there were a few minor scuffles on the march, nothing happened to justify state violence. Which left the police, the National Guard and the FBI perplexed; they looked at these huge, orderly crowds and didn't seem to know what to do. They were irrelevant.

Rustin took some elementary precautions by planting the national and international press into the crowd itself, rather than standing or filming from the sidelines, so that anything untoward could be exposed from within. But as an organizer, his creative work went far beyond this. For instance, 'kettling' is a frequently used technique of crowd control – compressing people together, keeping the protesters inside the boundaries of the official route. Kettling also makes it hard for spectators to join protesters, since they are separated by police barriers. Rustin and his team subverted the authorities' efforts to kettle simply by wearing them out with details street by street – where exactly were the points where spectators were allowed to join in? Where should portable toilets be located? What licence should each street-food vendor apply for (there were different licences at that time for American and 'foreign' street-food)? The police were not used to protesters who choreographed protest so carefully. The authorities were particularly surprised, I think, because of American racism's assumption that Blacks are spontaneous, out-of-control, ill-disciplined creatures, the assumption of unruliness that the plantation overseer had made in the centuries of slavery to justify his whip.

Rustin's own experiences as a performer helped him shape the march. As a young man, he had been a skilled actor and singer. In his high school, he gave performances of Donizetti's 'Una furtiva lagrima' from Donizetti's *L'elisir d'amore* (which is no mean feat for an adolescent). He chose a university, Wilberforce University, in large part for its music programme, becoming 'more deeply entrenched', as he later recalled, in composers such as Palestrina and Bach. As an adult, he still sang; and his path crossed Alberta Hunter's when both performed at Barney Josephson's jazz club, Café Society. Most importantly for him, he got to know Paul Robeson, the greatest Black actor and singer of his time, when they performed together in 1939 in the play *John Henry*. If not the usual background for a political organizer, it was useful in thinking through alternatives to the usual political theatre of confrontation.[4]

Rustin and his team applied something like the logic of porosity to the streets which, as we have seen, architects have used in theatre buildings. From the train station and bus parking-lots which brought visitors in, there were many entrances and exits protesters could use to walk to the Washington Mall, their ultimate destination. In aerial photographs, the crowd in the Mall looks tightly packed, but on the ground the marshals made sure pathways were kept open so that people could easily enter or leave. The planners thus made it easy for spectators to join the protest, if so moved, and for the marchers to leave the march, if nature called. The porosity was inefficient, since the crowd gathered more slowly than if along one route, but more dramatic. It conveyed the message that the people were everywhere in the city, and that today, in this city, they were free to move as they pleased.

Rustin modelled the relation of streets to the Mall in terms of wings (the streets) leading to and off the stage (the Mall). The streets, to be sure, were full of sign-carrying protesters, but Rustin wanted to keep them moving towards the Mall, filling it up, so that the sheer size of the crowd would become a striking phenomenon in itself. In organizing the march, he decided that crowds should fill the stage as in Act II of the opera *La Bóhème*: the stage should fill slowly from the wings, rather than the curtain rise on a scene already populated.

The designers of the Half Moon had to deal with the problem of distracted attention, and so did Rustin, once the Mall was full. Most of the speeches on the Mall stage couldn't rivet the attention of the mass of protesters, who were far away; the danger was, as at all demonstrations, that people would just drift off. Rustin solved this problem with mini-events on the ground, like the bands from different parts of the country playing local music, and speeches programmed with only small-scale amplification throughout the crowd. The denouement, Martin Luther King's momentous speech, worked, in terms of crowd choreography, because all the small events were suddenly stopped and the microphones were linked together, thus focusing the mass of people on a figure few could see.

At the time, Rustin's choreography met with some criticism, because there were few raised stands along the routes and in the Mall enabling people to see. Rustin responded that he wanted to underline equality and commonality by putting everyone on the same horizontal plane. It's a consequent response, because, as we saw in Chapter 4 on the city's three stages, from its very beginning in ancient amphitheatres an elevated seat coupled with the distinction between actor and spectator. To see better in an amphitheatre, you literally rose above and got further away from the action.

The choreography of equality on the same horizontal plane comes with a cost, as appeared in Chapter 11 about the stage rejoining the street. On an equal plane, only the people immediately near a performer are going to see and hear what they are doing. An equal plane inevitably shrinks the size of a performance. Rustin faced a seemingly unsolvable problem owing to number of participants, estimated at around 800,000, and the equal mass of non-marching spectators. There are ways to get around the nexus between ground plane / small size in a performance, as in the Occupy Wall Street protests a decade ago: the people at the front of Occupy's crowds would speak or hand-signal to those behind to let them know what was happening in front – the 'Occupy megaphone', as it was called. The procedure is cumbersome, and depends on a dedicated audience putting up with the slow messaging. Usually, the staging of a ground-plane protest means that one's immediate neighbours matter more, because the intimate physical connection determines if people stay in or gradually drift away. Just here, Rustin had a personal problem.

The Masked Crowd

There was more to this march than met the colour-orientated eye, owing to Rustin's life as a gay man. In his time, Harlem was much less tolerant of homosexuality than bohemian Greenwich Village. Prejudices against gays of colour were not simple in communities of colour, as poor parents struggling to maintain their families intact viewed homosexuality as yet one more destabilizing force. Which meant that Black gay men were doubly marginalized. There was no question for Rustin, however, of living a closeted life. He had made no secret of his sexuality from the time, in the 1930s, when he had joined the Communist Party. He had been arrested for 'offending public decency' in 1953 and served a brief time in prison.

Just as he had lived openly as a gay communist, so now in

organizing the March on Washington he meant it to be inclusive of anyone, Black or white, straight or gay – and, more consequently, of any class. He knew that, for the project of racial affirmative action to succeed, he needed to make events like this feel open to white working-class people. If they felt excluded, the unions to which they belonged could not give institutional help, nor could the Democratic Party participate fully. In this event, it mattered that the mass of people were not separated by their identities.

To achieve this inclusiveness, Rustin made use of the neutrality of unprovocative words, printing for instance generic posters 'against racism' or 'for the people', which anyone could carry. He sought to organize the flow of the crowd so that members of different local organizations marched together rather than stood with their own people. As far as I know, Rustin had no theory about 'cooperative bodies', but he certainly knew as a performer how important it is to be physically at ease on stage. At the march he did everything he could, in the face of hostile authorities, to create a relaxed, informal atmosphere among those who in their private lives might well have been at odds. In this, the inclusive march differed from right-wing political events, which almost always dramatized a sharp, demonizing distinction between Us and Them.

The march addressed the question of who 'we' are in an Arendtian way. 'We' lost its exclusive semiological referent pinned to race; it thus made visible the values of 'integration' and 'equality'. Rustin's choreography shows how masking can serve a political purpose; by hiding identity, masking promotes solidarity.

IV. Unsettling Recognitions

In Chapter 2, we canvassed the moral ambiguity of Judas the betrayer of Christ. The consequences of playing the false friend moved the betrayer to tears; he was unsettled by what he was doing. In one of *Hamlet*'s great scenes, Shakespeare probes this upset, exploring how it might be turned against the powerful.

Hamlet's Play within a Play

The overall story turns on the young Prince's mother and uncle, conspirators and lovers, who have murdered his father then covered up the crime, and now act as though legitimate rulers of the realm. Hamlet's discovery of the murder comes early on, shocking him because outwardly Claudius, his uncle, acts as benevolent and kind: '. . . one may smile, and smile, and be a villain!' (1.5.107–8). When his mother, Gertrude, tries to comfort him for the loss of his father, the young man reverts again to the malign power of acting: comfort and benevolence 'are actions that a man might play, / . . . these but the trappings and the suits of woe' (1.2.76–86).

Hamlet will use a theatrical device to challenge 'the trappings of woe', a device that works on the emotions of the murderers themselves. 'I have heard,' Hamlet says,

> That guilty creatures sitting at a play
> Have by the very cunning of the scene
> Been strook so to the soul, that presently
> They have proclaim'd their malefactions.
> (2.2.588–92)

He arranges for his uncle and his mother to watch a play which he pretends will innocently amuse them. The show has two parts, first a silent acting out by mimes of his father's poisoning (the poison is poured into the sleeping king's ear), during which the Queen pets the poisoner. Then the same action is repeated with a rhyming dialogue. At this point, Claudius can stand it no more and abruptly stops the production: 'Give o'er the play . . . Lights! lights! lights!' (3.2.268–70).

Hamlet's play within a play is like a mirror which people avoid because they can't stand to see their reflection. On stage, this sort of unsettling has to be carefully prepared. The spectators in the audience, as well as the spectators on stage, have to be taken in unawares.

In *Hamlet*, the mime-show draws both sets of spectators in, since no characters are identified; at first, the spectators on stage don't imagine that the mummery has any relation to themselves, just as, in Mexico, the archbishop watching the ritual of the dead rising up had no idea, at first, that the performance was meant to be about rising up against him. When the unsettling recognition comes, the archbishop does not flee, like the guilty spectators on stage, but he has the celebrants put in jail. Thereafter they become a *cause célèbre*, turning the devout Mexican community against him.

The mummers have to pull off this kind of provocation following the principle of 'Show, don't tell'. In good productions of *Hamlet*'s play within a play, they should mime gestures that are hard to recognize as violent. Pouring the poison in the sleeping king's ear, for instance, should be done, rather than with a dropper, with a jug or, in modernized productions, a bottle of San Pellegrino water. It shouldn't be obvious that there is poison inside. Similarly, at this point a good actress miming Gertrude will smile lovingly at the sleeping King while her lover kills him – the silent act should invite us to ask, 'What's going on?' Then the rhyming couplets will become more arresting, more menacing, provoking the disturbing recognition.

The play within a play, exposing the crime of uncle and mother, differs from the unmasking of the characters' true behaviour. The unmasking of a person's real character is a standard stage trope. It's brought to a musical height in *The Marriage of Figaro* when the Count discovers that the woman he was about to make love to is not the servant Susanna but his wife in disguise. In *Così fan tutte* Mozart stages the same disguise followed by sudden recognition, now deploying two pairs of lovers: the men, disguised as Albanians, make love to each other's partner, and the women fall in love with the false lovers. Then comes the unmasking revelation.

Instead, the play within the play involves a larger but more perplexing phenomenon, a purely theatrical way of 'speaking truth to power'.

Mis-en-abyme

In literary terms, this truth-telling involves a *mis-en-abyme*. Roland Barthes defined the term as the 'negative reflection' of an appearance, like switching black and white when photoshopping an image. The American psychoanalyst Roy Schafer deployed the *mis-en-abyme* as a 'mirroring therapy' whereby the analyst repeats back something a patient says so that the patient can examine it critically. The term also has a political dimension.

A straightforward declaration that someone or something is false can be met, as Americans today know all too well, by a flurry of 'alternative facts', so that the difference between truth and falsehood becomes merely a difference of opinion. The *mis-en-abyme* is a device for undoing this evasion of truth by mimicking what the powerful say in such a way that it becomes discredited.

The *mis-en-abyme* destroys the actor's self-confidence. In everyday life there's nothing more disturbing than to see yourself mimicked, the stupid or negative aspects of what you do acted out for you. Brecht's idea of political theatre, in his early collaborations with Erwin Piscator on plays such as *The Good Soldier Schweik*, deployed mimicry rather than direct denunciation, so that spectators could identify with and then become alienated from the characters on stage. Something very similar is going on with Figaro's arias; it's his recapitulations of florid and pompous themes that deflates them.

We hardly expect a dictator to renounce power because of the *mis-en-abyme*, but his authority can be undermined by a theatrical technique like this. He will be laughed at, whereas simple denunciation will not get under his skin. *Mis-en-abyme* works differently from the mockings in the carnivalesque, when the powerful know things will return to normal, people are just letting off steam. *Hamlet*'s play within a play carries no such assurance – the false king flees because the display might go on and on. The carnivalesque provides a catharsis, the *mis-en-abyme* withholds it. In that withholding lies its strength.

The *mis-en-abyme* is confrontational – but what does challenging power do for the challenger? In Shakespeare's play, Hamlet remains deeply unhappy; in the street, confrontation is a cathartic event for protesters and resisters. Should it be?

V. The Liberating Performance

Hegelian Detachment

Every parent has to deal with the following scenes: your child smashes a toy in order to grab your attention, or your adolescent drops out of university to make you 'take him seriously'. The point of transgression is to elicit recognition; the angrier or more upset you become, the tighter the bond. Such juvenile behaviour is 'disobedient dependence', as I've named it elsewhere in a study of authority in the workplace. In adult life it can have profoundly negative consequences for the employee bidding for attention. The boss sets the terms of recognition; the employee loses sight of their own needs, apart from the boss's regard.[5]

Disobedient dependence is not an idea original to me. It can be traced back to the philosopher G. W. F. Hegel in the early nineteenth century, specifically to a passage in *The Phenomenology of Spirit* on 'Lordship and Bondage'.

As a general proposition, Hegel declares that human beings are fulfilled 'only in being acknowledged' by others; 'a process of mutual recognition' is necessary for each person to feel complete. That general truth discolours the relations between masters and servants. The 'bondsman', as Hegel calls him, 'wants recognition from the lords – the servant cries out "I hurt!" or "You are hurting me!"' The master who doesn't respond, who doesn't even notice, is the lord whom people are most likely to fight against; indifference is insupportable. This is for Hegel the crux of authority. It doesn't matter when an authority figure is right, just or reasonable; instead, he is the point of reference. As in dependent disobedience, the bondsmen are fighting for recognition *from* him. The master sets the terms for the struggle for recognition.

A list of servants today might range far beyond the workplaces I studied forty years ago. It could include women, gays, immigrants, ethnic minorities. What Hegel knew is that, even if the sexes or religions have equal rights under the law, the struggle for recognition will go on in civil society. See me! Acknowledge my presence! Do not treat me, like the protagonist of Ralph Ellison's novel, as an 'invisible man'! If the servant wants freedom – rather than recognition – then he or she has to step outside of the master's frame of reference.

For Hegel, the personal passage out to freedom occurs in four steps. The servant is first stoic about their own suffering, then becomes sceptical about the lord's right to impose pain. A period of detachment ensues, in which the servant feels both free of the master but also unsure and unhappy about what they should do. Reason will ultimately figure out how this unhappiness can be resolved.

For Hegel, performing art plays a role in this process, just at stage two. Comedy helps the servant cast doubt on the master's right to rule – as in *The Marriage of Figaro*. Hegel's understanding of comedy goes back, I think, to the archaic Greek idea of *mitis*, that the ancient gods like Prometheus were shapeshifters and tricksters and so were never pinned down to one form. Comedy of the Mozartian or commedia dell'arte sort also has a trickster power – mocking, ironizing, unsettling things as they are.

Brecht called Hegelian detachment by another name, *Verfremdungseffekt*, in which the spectator gradually ceases to identify with the characters and actions on stage, steps back and begins to think independently about the production. It's in essence a Hegelian idea – but the stepping back has to be carefully staged. Usually, people will believe what they see, or at least will identify with characters and events. Brecht understood that silence can have this distancing power. No more arguing. The end of dialogue. No more 'meaningful communication'. According to an Ethiopian proverb, 'when the great lord passes the wise peasant bows deeply and silently farts'. The great problem is that silence is still oriented to the presence of a 'great lord'. Rather than keeping silent in general, the *Verfremdungseffekt* emerges from silent resistance to a specific master.

So too, Hegel is imagining performing art as political when it frees the spectator from identifying with a specific master enacted on stage. A play is not, of course, like a seminar in which the structural characteristics of domination might get a thorough airing. Still, there's a trap in this kind of political theatre when it's applied to the street: free yourself from the toils of dependent disobedience, reject a particular master and you might think you've solved the problem. Which you haven't, because another person will take their place. You need a more impersonal release from identification, one that makes you a truly independent being.

This might seem far from what art can do, but it was the point of a modern piece of performance art, *The Artist is Present*, on show in a New York museum in 2010. The artist is Marina Abramović, who sits silently on a chair for a total of 736 hours and 30 minutes. Members of the public are invited to sit at a table opposite her for as long as they wish, from five minutes to a whole day. She maintains steady eye-contact with them as long as they stay. Seemingly, her stare is commanding, mesmerizing. The gobbledegook issued by the museum's press department claimed that, under Abramović's steady gaze, the sitters had flashes of illumination, suddenly feeling in touch with themselves, and so forth. After the event, however, many reported figuring out household bills or contemplating lunch. This isn't the kind of detachment Hegel had in mind.

A more consequent form of detachment is embodied in the work of another performance artist – more consequent because withdrawal from engaging with the powerful is the prelude to reconnecting with other people.

Tania Bruguera Shifts her Art

In 2008 I attended a performance staged by Tania Bruguera outside Tate Modern in London. She had arranged for two actors to impersonate mounted policemen in the museum's cavernous Turbine Hall. They guarded entrances to the galleries, sometimes forcing visitors away, sometimes herding them into tight little spaces from which they were not allowed to move. Bruguera, a Cuban artist whose work has often been repressed by the Cuban authorities, wanted to show Tate viewers what crowd repression felt like.

The most interesting thing about *Tatlin's Whisper #5*, as her piece was called (a title which I still don't get), lay in the reaction of one slice of the visitors to the exhibition. Everyone knew this was a staged event, and mostly the public cooperated, doing what the mounted policemen told them to do – save for a few visitors attending some days after the show opened. These were rather elderly people dressed in tweeds and sensible shoes and clearly familiar with horses. The resisters spoke to the beasts authoritatively, and the horses obeyed and moved back from the entrances. With the entrances cleared, the public walked in. The actors on horseback were nonplussed – their steeds, not knowing about performance art, had broken the spell.

When I told Bruguera about this scene later, she looked, surprisingly, quite pleased. The staging of the piece prompted political action; the elderly persons resisted being oppressed by her. Tania wasn't being clever. Her own work as a performance artist was becoming less about making a display of confrontation and more about involving the public.

This shift appeared in 2018 when the Tate asked her back. Now she devised a piece named *10,148,451*, which refers to the number of people who in the year before migrated from their homes to other places across the globe. Bruguera wanted to use Tate Modern as a place where refugees could come together. One magnet drawing the public in was a rather complicated piece of machinery on which people lay down on a giant, motion-sensitive screen and then wig-gled their legs and arms, whereupon the motion revealed the image of a well-known refugee on the screen beneath them. This stage lure, originally attracting children but later adults as well, was cou-pled to a longer-term project of bringing to the Tate the large number of refugees living in its vicinity.[6]

The Tate advertised Tania's 10,148,451 as transgressive – which exactly missed the point. Tania did not want, in 10,148,451, to make a show of 'radical will', as Susan Sontag once called it; she wanted instead to create a community.

Her piece puts me in mind of the dilemma which the Judson dan-cers felt. In retrospect, it seems that they may have been mistaken in fearing that their artistic innovations had alienated the community of elderly Poles and Italians whom Trisha Brown sought to engage 'democratically'. The elderly people in Washington Square were not, indeed, alienated by Brown's wall-climbing dancers; they took a continuing interest in what the young people were doing and stayed in the church community. In the same way, the refugees gathered together by Tania's piece were not put off by the fact that they knew nothing about the technology that activated the screen on the floor.

It might seem forced to weave together these varied threads of political theatre – but there's one simple way in which they do form a single strand. They all practise politics without words. This prac-tice seems to me more compelling than political debate. When I was Hannah Arendt's pupil, her belief in the word was one reason I could not become her follower. Thinking back to my formative years in New York, when the Julliard Conservatory seemed so iso-lated from those engaged with the politics of racial justice, when the Judson Dance Theater struggled with issues of social class, it now seems that these mattered more than the manifestos of the New Left and its quarrels with the Old Left. Visceral theatre fills the absence left by empty words.

15

Recognition

Performing that dignifies life

As I draw together the threads of this essay, memory leads me back to the Algonquin Hotel in New York in the late 1970s, to a lunch with Norbert Elias. He was a young academic in Frankfurt who fled when the Nazis came to power in 1933, first to Paris and then to Britain. With an intermission in Africa, after the war Elias settled into an émigré's existence at the University of Leicester in England. His could have been the story of anyone of my parents' generation, save for one thing. In the mid 1930s he had written a great book on culture, *The Civilizing Process*, which had then been forgotten for decades. He had come to New York, forty years later, to try to resurrect the book in an English translation. My German was too primitive really to help him. He took my failures as a translator with Jewish stoicism: of course things do not work out. At the end of the lunch, Elias remarked something like, 'Europe is dying inside you,' about my assimilation into America. Perhaps so.

I. *Kultur* and *Zivilisation*

Many cultures draw a line between what the German language calls *Kultur* and *Zivilisation*. On the one hand there are the behaviours, values and rituals which shape everyday life. These are unself-conscious performances; people just do them. This is the realm of *Kultur*. On the other hand, there are behaviours which have to be learned: manners and courtesies which allow us to get along with one another non-violently, as well as pretendings and ruses of the Machiavellian sort in politics and business. These lie in the realm of

Zivilisation. *Kultur* is often construed as a kind of innocent expression coming from the heart, whereas *Zivilisation* seems more artificial and theatrical.

In *The Civilizing Process*, Elias sought to get beyond this black and white contrast of heartfelt and calculating. *Zivilisation*, both the good and the malign sort, arises from self-control. He traced the history of how, as the modern era unspooled, people slowly developed codes of self-control, so that in time they no longer had to think about these behaviours; self-restraints lodged within them. The good, non-violent kind of *Zivilisation* was, he knew, fragile; Elias had witnessed it break down on the streets of Germany in the 1930s; it could happen again, he said, any time.

Elias chose to tell the full story of self-control by focusing on the human body and on material culture. His work detailed how men and women gradually masked bodily functions like farting; began using forks instead of their hands to eat; curbed swearing when speaking. He had in mind something more sweeping than manners of an elegant sort. Schools, for instance, became in the seventeenth century regulators of children's behaviour, rather than just inculcators of knowledge. Dutch teaching manuals laid out how children should be taught not to fidget, to speak rather than shout. By the time the little ruffians left school, there would be no need to tell them what to do; bodily self-discipline would be so deeply engrained in them as to come naturally.

The work of civilizing oneself is not, as it were, a one-way street. Self-control comes and goes. The wild creature in the child is first tamed under parental discipline and at school. The adolescent then rebels, casting off restraints in the name of being their own person. The young adult is chastened by the jostling of other egos, confusions of personal desire, and limits on personal ability. The adult ultimately accepts these limits and makes a life within the constraints of normality.

The civilizing process seems thus to resonate with Pico della Mirandola's Renaissance ideal of a person as their own maker, but there is a big difference. Rather than expanding experience, as Pico held, the civilizing process contracts it. Freud, a generation older than Elias, subscribed to something of the same view, as in *Civilization and its Discontents,* written a decade before *The Civilizing Process.* The date matters. Though written before the horrors of Nazism, Freud opposes civilization to barbarism, an opposition located inside the human breast, then radiating out into social relations. The beast within needs to be tamed within, rather than caged. To leave off raging and violent impulses, people must change within themselves. The rigid imposition of social control imagined by Thomas Hobbes cannot transform the beast within. For Freud, civilization kicks in with the experience of renunciation, bred of reining in one's physical and emotional impulses for the sake of living with others.

Freud was a realist in two ways. First, he knew how fragile and how exceptional the process of civilizing oneself is: barbarism is the norm. Second, he understood that renunciation cannot give people pleasure. This is the discontent of civilization; you act in a civilized rather than barbaric way because morality, religion or experiences of compassion and empathy call to you.

There is a social side to *Zivilisation* as self-control and renunciation that figures in Elias's writings but not in Freud's: *Zivilisation*'s relation to class. Self-control appeared as a crude measure of social inequality in books of manners written around 1630, when adult low-status servants and peasants became marked out as unable to control themselves in farting, as in speech. The social inferior blurts things out, speaks in a loud voice, whereas the more civilized person suggests, hints, holds back. Of course, this is palpably wrong, which never stopped more privileged people from believing it – as a submerged prejudice. 'Gross' became allied with 'low class'. By Victorian times, this prejudice had morphed into the idea of propriety – that crude, bourgeois version of good manners. Elias added a bodily dimension to Marxist critiques of inequality: the repression the bourgeoisie practised economically on workers, it practised bodily on itself.

By the nineteenth century, art played an unhappy role in this class-based construction of *Zivilisation*. The Victorian essayist Matthew Arnold declared, in *Culture and Anarchy*, that civilization consists of high art inaccessible to 'common people'. The prejudice has hardly disappeared. Television watchers of a certain age will recall the plummy, aristocratic voice of the art historian Kenneth Clark discoursing on the arts as the heights of civilized achievement. Clark was a 'popularizer', which is perhaps the most condescending stance the man of culture can take towards the masses – explaining and 'enlightening', that most condescending word of all.

The relation of art to *Zivilisation* becomes less snobbish if we focus on performing art in particular. Chapter 3 traced the ways in which stage art can divorce people's experience of violence on stage from the reality of pain. The willing suspension of disbelief can indeed induce crowds to practise violence together on the streets. For Gustave Le Bon the violent street is a space of theatre, as in the worst days of the first French Revolution. Le Bon's sobered-up individual is the sort of self-restrained person Elias imagined as civilized in the good, non-violent way.

The realm of performing thus appears antithetical to *Zivilisation*. Or rather, I imagine, if Elias, Freud and Le Bon could weigh up the virtues of the open stage, as appeared in Book Five, these would seem to be lighter, less consequent in substance, than the malign powers of the stage. Malign performing is not just about violence; it is also a way to demean experience, as for the dockworkers in New York, or to paralyse action, as for the young climate deniers in Washington.

II. Art as Experience

A more positive view of the role of performance in culture comes from the great American pragmatist thinker John Dewey. His book on art and society, *Art as Experience*, appeared in 1934, only five years before Elias's *Civilizing Process*, and was very different in spirit. Dewey was seventy-five. He had an intuition that his lifelong preoccupations with education, racial justice and democratic socialism might somehow connect to artistic expression. Dewey confirmed this intuition while a resident at the Albert Barnes Foundation, a Philadelphia institution which housed works by Matisse and other modern painters. However, Dewey also looked beyond Europe. He studied Pueblo Indian pottery, Bushmen rock-painting, Scythian ornament, African sculpture and Chinese calligraphy. Within America, he took African-American painting seriously at a moment when 'Black art' featured in American mass culture mostly as entertaining, sexy music.

Dewey gave a shape to these various ways of incorporating art-making into life by distinguishing 'an experience' from the more flowing, amorphous term 'experience'. *An* experience coheres when its behaviours and sentiments synergize; the whole is more than the sum of its parts. Say, in wandering down a street, a person is stopped by a stranger of another race asking for directions. At first withdrawn, then realizing the stranger wants only to know where to go, the stroller becomes aware that racial stereotyping has wrongly prompted fear of the other. The person will thus have had *an* experience; an event which has a shape in time, rather than just a flow of sensations. More, the experience is socially expansive, because the next time a stranger of another race is encountered, the person will not immediately shrink back.

Dewey was not naive. He knew that most experience lacks this shape and so is less illuminating. Most experience consists of un-differentiated flow, the 'stream of consciousness', as William James described it. James's contemporary Henri Bergson thought this flow to be life-enhancing, like losing oneself walking along a crowded, ever-changing street. Though respectful of Bergson, Dewey did not accept this view. Consciousness can be stimulating only if shaped around material things.

Dewey was not a popularizer, in the condescending mould of Kenneth Clark. Rather, he was democratic in spirit, because he believed that the maker and the consumer share the same experiences of class, gender, race, ethnicity, the same inner confusions, the same searches for meaning. Dewey rejects any deification of art and the artist; we are all stuck in the same mud. The artist is special only in that he or she has command over the materials and the craft which could prove illuminating to other people, who enter into the experience – ideally – as interrogators, not fearing to criticize and judge. His view empowers the spectator.

The spectator's relation to the stage has followed two trajectories. In one, embodied in the Comédie Française of Montesquieu's time, the spectators largely ignored the stage; they were absorbed in one another's appearances and doings. An older trajectory came from the Greeks, in which spectators submitted to the stage. Dewey broke with both versions – he rejected the very idea of being a spectator. Instead, he wanted participation, imagining performance, as did the creators of ancient Greeks' celebrated rituals, as an inherently collective experience bringing people together.

The pragmatist philosophers who came after Dewey were unhappy about the belief in art as a shared, unified experience. This is how Richard Rorty thought about changes in the sciences. Rather than 'standing on the shoulders of giants', as the old cliché has it about scientific knowledge, Rorty thought new work tends to kick the giants in the groin. For Arthur Danto, a philosopher preoccupied with visual art, the work of making art involved creating gaps, discontinuities, transgressions which cannot be healed. They were pragmatists who focused on culture's stresses and unresolvable resistances.

And yet there is something essentially inspiring about Dewey as a philosopher of art. He picked up on a dimension of civilization which Norbert Elias does not much credit: how art can expand experience in ways that make people more open to others. Let's say, using the word at last in a positive sense, how art can 'civilize'.

III. Performing Civility

'Civility' is the cousin of the word 'civilization', but they are not sibling words. Civility is about behaviour that respects others. Even more, civility does not belong in the same family as culture. Today, instead, *Kultur* in its traditional sense has become the enemy of civility. *Kultur* is driven by resentment against those others who are different. *Kultur* focuses inwardly, on identity.

In the Algonquin, Elias and I began to discuss the opposition between civilization and culture, all important to him as it was to my forebears. *Kultur* had, in Nazi times, derailed his life, but Norbert – as he became to me over lunch – seemed free of self-pity. He proved to have even more of a taste for abstraction than I have, but lunch ended without Theory providing a solution to how one might become civilized in the good sense. Had we looked out the window of the restaurant, though, we might have seen an example of civility, performed on the street.

The Algonquin Hotel lies on the eastern edge of Times Square in New York's theatre district, in those days hardly civilized in Elias's sense. The side streets of Times Square teemed with drug dealers and addicts, and were sometimes carpeted with overdosed bodies, while prostitutes loitered in the doorways or solicited for business at the roadside.

The street-level raunchiness somewhat obscured the presence of a huge number of small offices and workshops in buildings whose interiors resembled rabbit warrens. Many of the workshops serviced the theatres, as costume and scenery shops; others serviced the music trade, making and repairing instruments. The *New York Times* had its own huge labour force in Times Square, since sections of the newspaper were actually printed in 43rd Street in those days. Added to the masses of workers were the theatregoers, about 80,000 each night when the theatres were full.

After the theatre, in restaurants which were for some reason mostly Greek, playgoers mixed with workers coming off their shifts at the *New York Times*. During the day these same restaurants fed the office and craft workers, plus the taxi-drivers who congregated there at lunchtime for cheap 'cab-driver' specials. The busy scene here contrasted with the area around Dirty Dick's Foc'sle Bar downtown in the afternoon, which was quintessentially an interior, with a single group withdrawn into itself.

Outside the restaurants there was an equally mixed crowd, day and night, especially during theatre intermissions, when people came out to the street to smoke and were prey to pickpockets as well as to addicts out of control. There was not much of a police presence in Times Square then, so the playgoers had to fend for themselves, managing chit-chat with each other, as well as navigating the addicts and the prostitutes.

They did so by performing civility. Threats from addicts and prostitutes were dealt with by not noticing on purpose. People had those sorts of conversations, slightly forced, slightly artificial, as though no intruder loomed. More positively, in the restaurants the mixed crowd sorted itself out so that the printers at the newspaper kept tables to themselves, on which the theatregoers at night and the cab-drivers during the day did not intrude, although these Greek restaurants were usually crowded and empty seats were scarce.

These are seemingly trivial civilities. Do they count as artful? I would say these courtesies do, even though they had no choreographer like Bayard Rustin. The forced conversations on the pavements when intruders loomed contrasted, for instance, with the avoidances of the crowd streaming around my wounded friend Jamal; in Times Square, people play-acted rather than turned away.

After we left the Algonquin, we went in search of the 7th Avenue subway a few blocks away. Elias wore a hat – I think it was a Homburg – which made him stand out in a crowd where most men were already hatless. As we entered the subway, he asked for directions from the ticket-taker to somewhere in upper Manhattan. She furnished them in detail, in Haitian-inflected English, so it wasn't clear how much he understood, but he raised his Homburg as a courteous gesture, and she inclined her head to acknowledge him. He had performed civility.

Notes

Introduction

1 *Free Jazz*, Rhino Records, CD re-issue, 1998
2 Josiah Fiske (ed.), *Composers on Music: Eight Centuries of Writings: A New and Expanded Revision of Morgenstern's Classic Anthology* (Boston: Northeastern University Press, 1997), p. 271

1. Acting and Ritual Stand Side by Side, Uneasily

1 Victor Turner, 'Symbols in African Ritual', *Science*, 16 March 1973, vol. 179, pp. 1100–105
2 Hillel Halkin, *After One-Hundred-and-Twenty: Reflecting on Death, Mourning, and the Afterlife in the Jewish Tradition* (New Jersey: Princeton University Press, 2016); Leon Wieseltier, *Kaddish* (London: Vintage, 1998). I would particularly recommend Leon Wieseltier's insightful book.
3 Walter Benjamin, *Illuminations*, 'The Storyteller', trans. H. Zohn (New York: Shocken Books, 1969)
4 Cicero, *De Oratore*, trans. G. L. Hendrickson and H. M. Hubbell, Loeb Classical Library (Cambridge MA: Harvard University Press, 1939)
5 Allen Ginsberg, *Kaddish and Other Poems, 1958–1960* (San Francisco: City Lights Books, 1967)
6 'Kaddish' by Allen Ginsberg, *Programme*, director Robert Kalfin, Chelsea Theater Center, New York, 1972
7 Ibid.
8 Richard Schechner, *Environmental Theater* (New York: Hawthorn Books, 1973), *passim*

9 Leonard Bernstein, Symphony No. 3 'Kaddish', Boosey & Hawkes, 1963, rev. 1977

10 Gibson Kente, *The Call*, Pretoria State Theatre, South Africa, 2003

2. The Moral Ambiguity of Performing

1 J. Piaget, *The Construction of Reality in the Child* (New York: Basic Books, 1954)

2 D. W. Winnicott, *Playing and Reality* (London: Penguin, 1971), p. 120

3 J. L. Austin, *How to Do Things with Words* (Cambridge, MA: Harvard University Press, 1962); Roland Barthes, 'The Death of the Author', in *Image Music Text*, trans. Stephen Heath (London: Fontana, 1977)

4 *Machiavelli and his Friends: Their Personal Correspondence*, trans. J. B. Atkinson and David Sices (DeKalb, IL: Northern Illinois University Press, 1996), pp. 262–5

5 My thanks to the conductor Michael Tilson Thomas for introducing me to the world of New York Yiddish theatre. For its history, see Nahma Sandrow, *Vagabond Stars: A World History of Yiddish Theater* (New York: Harper & Row, 1977)

6 Denis Diderot, *Rameau's Nephew*, trans. Richard Howard (New York: Hill and Wang, 1971), p. 32.

3. The Most Troubling Performance

1 Aristotle, *Poetics*, Book XXIV, trans. S. Halliwell, W. H. Fyfe, D. A. Russell, D. Innes and P. Demetrius, Loeb Classical Library (Cambridge, MA: Harvard University Press, 1995), p. 63

2 Quoted in T. H. Huxley, *The Major Prose of Thomas Henry Huxley*, ed. A. P. Barr (Athens, GA: University of Georgia Press, 1997), p. 357

3 M. Weber, *Sociology of Religion* (Boston, MA: Beacon Press, 1963), p. 271; M. Weber and S. Kalberg, *The Protestant Ethic and the Spirit of Capitalism* (London: Routledge, 2013)

4 S. T. Coleridge and J. Shawcross, *Biographia Literaria*, vol. XIV (Oxford: Clarendon Press, 1907)

5 Quoted in J. Bate, *Radical Wordsworth: The Poet Who Changed the World* (New Haven, CT: Yale University Press, 2020), p. 99

6 T. W. Adorno, 'Freudian Theory and the Pattern of Fascist Propaganda', in G. Roheim (ed.), *Psychoanalysis and the Social Sciences*, Vol. III (New York: International Universities Press, 1951), pp. 408–33

7 A. Artaud, 'The Theatre of Cruelty', in E. Bentley (ed.), *The Theory of the Modern Stage: An Introduction to Modern Theatre and Drama* (London: Penguin, 2008)

4. The City's Three Stages

1 Richard Sennett, *Flesh and Stone: The Body and the City in Western Civilization* (London: Faber & Faber, 1994), pp. 61–6

2 Plato, *The Republic*, Book VII (New York: Books Inc., 1943), 514a,2–520a,7

5. The Stage Withdraws from the Street

1 I. Jones, quoted in J. Laver, *Drama – Its Costume and Décor* (London: The Studio Publications, 1951), p. 76

2 S. Serlio, *Regole generali di architettura*, Book 2, Chapter 3, trans. in A. M. Nagler, *A Source Book in Theatrical History* (New York: Dover Publications, 1959), pp. 73–81

3 Ibid.

4 Ibid.

5 Montesquieu, *Persian Letters*, Letter 26, trans. Margaret Mauldon (Oxford: Oxford University Press, 2008)

6 Richard Sennett, *The Fall of Public Man* (New York: Knopf, 1977), pp. 141–9

7 Charles Baudelaire, 'Le Cygne', in *Les Fleurs du mal*, ed. John Tidball (London: Bishopston, 2016), p. 283

8 Wolfgang Amadeus Mozart, Prussian Quartets, nos. 21–23 (K575, K589, K590)

6. Making a Life On Stage

1 S. Greenblatt, *Renaissance Self-fashioning: From More to Shakespeare* (Chicago, IL: University of Chicago Press, 2005). An illuminating study to which I am greatly indebted, though I follow his theme in a different way.

2 Aristotle, *Problems*, Vol. II, Books 20–38, *Rhetoric to Alexander* (Problemata XXXI), ed. and trans. R. Mayhew and D. C. Mirhady, Loeb Classical Library (Cambridge, MA: Harvard University Press, 2011). Cf. Richard Burton, *The Anatomy of Melancholy* (London: Penguin, 2023).

3 G. Pico della Mirandola, *Oration on the Dignity of Man*, trans. A. R. Caponigri (Wahington D.C.: Gateway, 2015), p. 7

4 Ovid, *Metamorphoses*, Book IV (Dallas, TX: Spring Publications, 1989)

5 Jacob Burckhardt, *The Civilisation of the Renaissance in Italy*, trans. S. G. C. Middlemore (London: Phaidon, 1950), p. 122

6 William Shakespeare, *King Lear*, Act I, Scene 2 (Oxford: Clarendon Press, 1877)

7 Goldoni, quoted in P. L. Duchartre, *The Italian Comedy* (London: Dover Publications, 1996), p. 262

8 P. Jordan, *The Venetian Origins of the Commedia dell'arte* (London: Routledge, 2014), p. 71

9 Ibid.

10 On the Elizabethan stage, see J. Orrell, *The Quest for Shakespeare's Globe* (Cambridge: Cambridge University Press, 1983)

7. A Change of Clothes

1 Richard Sennett, *Flesh and Stone: The Body and the City in Western Civilization* (London: Faber & Faber, 1994), pp. 225–6

2 M. Douglas, *Purity and Danger: An Analysis of Concepts of Pollution and Taboo* (London: Routledge and Kegan Paul, 2002)

3 P. Aries, *The Hour of Our Death*, trans. H. Weaver (New York: Knopf, 1981)

4 A. D. Napier, *Masks, Transformation and Paradox* (Berkeley, CA: University of California Press, 1986), p. 9

5 A. Sofer, *The Stage Life of Props* (Ann Arbor, MI: University of Michigan Press, 2003), pp. 32, 42–9

6 M. Weber, *The Sociology of Religion* (Boston, MA: Beacon Press, 1963)

8. The Art of Charisma

1 P. Beaussant, *Le Roi-Soleil se leve aussi* (Paris: Gallimard, 2000), p. 151

2 *Memoirs of the Duc de Saint Simon, a Shortened Version 1691–1709* (New York: 1500 Books LLC, 2007), p. 103

3 J. Homans, *Apollo's Angels: A History of Ballet* (New York: Random House, 2010)

4 Heinrich von Kleist, 'On the Marionette Theatre'. I use the excellent English translation by Idris Parry, https://southerncrossreview.org/9/kleist.htm

5 'Uber das Marionettentheater von Heinrich von Kleist', trans. Kevin J. M. Keane, https://de.wikisource.org/wiki/%C3%9Cber_das_Marionettentheater

6 Quoted in J. Kavanagh, *Secret Muses: The Life of Frederick Ashton* (London, Faber, 2004)

9. A Theatre of the Defeated

1 https://www.youtube.com.watch?=DgG177q2XTk&feature=youtube

2 Herbert Marcuse, *One-Dimensional Man: Studies in the Ideology of Advanced Industrial Society* (London: Routledge and Kegan Paul, 1964)

3 H. James, *The Ambassadors*, Book V, Chapter. 2 (New York: Harper, 1903)

4 Richard Sennett and J. Cobb, *Hidden Injuries of Class* (London: W. W. Norton & Company, 1993)

5 Aristotle, *Poetics*, trans. S. Halliwell, W. H. Fyfe, D. A. Russell, D. Innes and P. Demetrius, Loeb Classical Library (Cambridge, MA: Harvard University Press, 1995)

6 T. J. Scheff, 'Catharsis and Other Heresies: A Theory of Emotion', *Journal of Social, Evolutionary and Cultural Psychology*, vol. 1, no. 3, 2007, pp. 106ff. See also T. J. Scheff, *Catharsis in Healing, Ritual and Drama* (Berkeley, CA: University of California Press, 1979)

10. A Theatre of Fear

1 A video taking the large view of this occasion was made with António Guterres, Secretary-General of the United Nations, Rowan Williams, former Archbishop of Canterbury, myself and two student activists, https://www.youtube.com.watch?v=MV5y8rMAwyU

2 E. Conway and N. Oreskes, *Merchants of Doubt: How a Handful of Scientists Obscured the Truth on Issues from Tobacco Smoke to Global Warming* (New York: Bloomsbury USA, 2010)

3 J. Mizen, 'Anchoring Europe's Civilizing Identity: Habits, Capabilities and Ontological Security', *Journal of European Public Policy*, vol. 13, no. 2, pp. 270–85

4 E. R. Dodds, 'On Misunderstanding the "Oedipus Rex"', *JSTOR*, Greece and Rome, 2nd series, vol. 13, no. 1, 1966, pp. 37–49

5 Cicero, *The Nature of the Gods*, Book 2, Part 2, section C, trans. P. G. Walsh (Oxford: Oxford University Press, 2008)

11. The Stage Rejoins the Street

1 Richard Sennett, *The Craftsman* (New Haven, CT: Yale University Press, 2009)

2 L. Beranek, *Concert Halls and Opera Houses: Music, Acoustics and Architecture* (New York: Springer, 2004)

3 https://www.lse.ac.uk/sociology/assets/documents/Cities-News-2012-2.pdf, https://lsecitiesstudio5.wordpress.com/

4 Alexander Pope, *An Epistle to the Right Honourable Richard Earl of Burlington, Epistle IV* (London: printed for L. Gilliver, 1731)

5 Tadao Ando, conversations with R.S.

6 G. Simmel, 'Die Grossstadt und das Geistesleben' (The Metropolis and Mental Life), in Richard Sennett (ed. and trans.), *Classic Essays on the Culture of Cities* (New Jersey: Prentice-Hall, 1969), p. 36

7 Roland Barthes, *Empire of Signs* (London: Anchor Books, 1983)

8 Roland Barthes, *Empire of Signs*, trans. Richard Howard (New York: Hill and Wang, 1982), p. 36

12. *Bodies Cooperate*

1 Roland Barthes, 'Musica Practica', in *Image Music Text*, trans. Stephen Heath (London: Fontana Press, 1977), pp. 149–54

2 E. Herrigel, *Zen in the Art of Archery* (London: Pantheon Books, 1953)

3 A. Trumble, *A Brief History of the Smile* (New York: Basic Books, 2nd edn, 2005), pp. 50–55

4 https://www.youtube.com/watch?v=jMj-EVi5T-k

13. *The Performer Invents*

1 If you want to know more about these riffs, you might consult, as we did in our production, the excellent work by Richard Wistreich, 'Monteverdi in Production', in John Wenham and Richard Wistreich (eds.), *The Cambridge Companion to Monteverdi* (Cambridge: Cambridge University Press, 2007), pp. 251–79

2 Igor Stravinsky, *An Autobiography* (New York: W. W. Norton & Company, reissued 1998), p. 134

3 See the excellent piece by Eva Resnikova, 'The Mystery of Terpsichore, Balanchine, Stravinsky and "Apollo" ', *New Criterion*, September 1983, p. 24

4 Cited in Igor and Vera Stravinsky, *A Photograph Album: 1921 to 1971* (New York: Thames and Hudson, 1982), pp. 13–14

14. *Confrontation*

1 J. B. Halsted, 'Percy Bisshe Shelley: "A Defence of Poetry"', in J. B. Halsted (ed.), *Romanticism* (London: Palgrave Macmillan, 1969)

2 W. Sennett, 'Communist Party Official, Communist Functionary and Corporate Executive, Individual Memoirs in Government and Politics', typescript of an oral history conducted in 1980–97, Catalogue II, Regional History Office, The Bancroft Library (Berkeley, CA: University of California Press, 1984), iv, p. 401

3 Octavio Paz, *The Labyrinth of Solitude: Life and Thought in Mexico* (New York: Grove Press, 1961), pp. 18–23

4 John d'Emilio, *Lost Prophet: The Life and Times of Bayard Rustin* (New York: Free Press, 2003)

5 Richard Sennett, *Authority* (New York: Knopf, 1980)

6 Tania Bruguera, *10.148.451*, Tate Modern Exhibition, https://www.tate.org.uk/whats-on/tate-modern/hyundai-commission-tania-bruguera